GOOD AND EVIL SPIRITS

AND THEIR INFLUENCE ON HUMANITY

GOOD AND EVIL SPIRITS

AND THEIR INFLUENCE ON HUMANITY

Thirteen lectures held in Berlin between 6 January and 11 June 1908

ENGLISH BY A.R. MEUSS

INTRODUCTION BY MARGARET JONAS

RUDOLF STEINER

RUDOLF STEINER PRESS

CW 102

The publishers gratefully acknowledge the generous funding of this publication by the estate of Dr Eva Frommer MD (1927–2004) and the Anthroposophical Society in Great Britain

Rudolf Steiner Press
Hillside House, The Square
Forest Row, RH18 5ES

www.rudolfsteinerpress.com

Published by Rudolf Steiner Press 2014

Originally published in German under the title *Das Hereinwirken geistiger Wesenheiten in den Menschen* (volume 102 in the *Rudolf Steiner Gesamtausgabe* or Collected works) by Rudolf Steiner Verlag, Dornach. Edited by R. Friedenthal, H. Knobel and F. Weidmann. Drawings in the text by Hedwig Frey are based on sketches in the shorthand records. This authorised translation is based on the 4th edition of 2001, which was reviewed by A. M. Balastèr and U. Trapp

Published by permission of the Rudolf Steiner Nachlassverwaltung in Dornach

A catalogue record for this book is available from the British Library

ISBN 978 1 85584 397 4

Cover by Mary Giddens
Typeset by DP Photosetting, Neath, West Glamorgan
Printed and bound in Great Britain by Gutenberg Press Ltd., Malta

CONTENTS

LECTURE 1

BERLIN, 6 JANUARY 1908

How spiritual entities influence our existence. Spirits of the astral plane and Devachan. The group souls of animals, plants and minerals. Good-natured and ill-natured Moon, Mars and Venus spirits. Inventive and wild Saturn spirits. Different ways in which these elemental spirits act on the earth and on human beings. Chyle, lymph and blood as the bodies of spirits from other planets. Influence of Saturn spirits through sense organs (odours, scents). Opposition of lung and liver. The Prometheus legend.

pages 1–14

LECTURE 2

BERLIN, 27 JANUARY 1908

Planetary existence, Sun existence and zodiacal existence as stages in cosmic evolution. 'Time' and 'eternity'. Saturn as dawn of our planetary state. Its origin as 'sacrifice' made by the zodiac. Ascending and descending powers of the zodiac. The seven aspects of the human being and of higher spirits. Man is receptive, sublime spirits are creative. The significance of the constellation Scales for evolution of the human I. The Christ as the 'Mystic Lamb' and humanity. Their relationship in the zodiac.

pages 15–26

LECTURE 3

LECTURE 4

LECTURE 5

future theosophical life. Art in the design of profane buildings such as railway stations. The catacombs. Christians an example for the spiritual striving in our time.

pages 167–180

EDITOR'S PREFACE

The lectures in this volume were given by Rudolf Steiner in the Besant Branch of the Theosophical Society in Berlin during the first six months of 1908. They were part of ongoing work on the basics of spiritual science with anthroposophical orientation, and continued the lectures given in October and November 1907 (German collected works GA 101, not translated into English). This means that the audience had been familiar with anthroposophy for some time. Rudolf Steiner also gave lectures on the subject of this volume in various other cities at that time, published in the German collected works GA 98 (again, not presently translated).

Following directions given by Rudolf Steiner, the term 'theosophy' was in earlier editions replaced with the terms 'spiritual science' or 'anthroposophy', as appropriate. Rudolf Steiner wanted to avoid confusion with the Theosophical Society, the Anthroposophical Society having separated from it in a serious conflict in 1912. These changes have also been applied in the present edition. (See also Translator's Notes, p. xiii.)

TRANSLATOR'S NOTES

Origins of the text

Translation serves to build bridges of various kinds, one of which is between the origins and the destination of a text. All but one of the lectures in this volume were taken down and written up by Walter Vegelahn (1880–1950). It is important for the way one handles a translation to know how reliable the sources are. My researches yielded the following information.

> Walter Vegelahn was born in Berlin. His father was a coachman to the crown prince, his mother a seamstress. Trained against his will as a bank clerk he used all his spare time to educate himself further, also at the worker's college where Rudolf Steiner taught. He loved the theatre. Joined the Giordano Bruno Association. When the bank he was working at ceased to trade in 1902 Vegelahn became an actor. He joined the Theosophical Society the same year, mainly because he was interested in Rudolf Steiner himself and above all the public lectures. Having learned stenography as part of his commercial training he started to take shorthand notes of lectures and then wrote them out so that they would be available to members. He had a remarkably good memory which gave those papers the quality of almost word-by-word records. In 1908 Rudolf Steiner and Marie von Sivers appointed official stenographers and he was one of them. Constant practice meant that he was by then able to take down lectures in full. He died of a stroke in 1959. [Based on information provided by Ulla Trapp-Geromont in *Anthroposophie im 20. Jahrhundert*, Verlag am Goetheanum, Dornach 2003]

Acknowledgement

On the other side of this particular 'bridge', where the focus is on the destination of the texts, I am much indebted to Peter Heathfield who has patiently checked my translation for typing or other errors that had eluded my own checks.

Theosophy or anthroposophy?

One thing which has puzzled me is the statement made in the 'Editor's Preface' [from the original German edition]:

> Following directions given by Rudolf Steiner, the term 'theosophy' was in earlier editions replaced with the terms 'spiritual science' or 'anthroposophy', as appropriate.

The terms 'theosophy', 'theosophist' and 'Theosophical Society' are nevertheless quite widely used in the text, and I have followed the original exactly. Perhaps we may take it as an indication of the state of flux which existed at the time. It must have been very difficult for the people involved in those days. Flux, or even uncertainty, does have the positive aspect of challenging us to give more serious consideration to an issue and to use our own judgement.

Anna R. Meuss
Stroud, October 2013

INTRODUCTION

There are parts of the world, perhaps surprisingly Iceland and Ireland in the West, where the presence of invisible beings in the landscape is still taken seriously, and the destruction of certain natural features is sometimes avoided, even by local councils when building work is carried out. However, by 1908, when these lectures were given, the existence of such entities would have been treated dismissively by most educated people—although not by folk in more remote rural areas, who had long believed in gnomes, fairies, elves, pixies, trolls and so on, and even miners, who might still be paying some attention to the tradition of strange beings under the earth (which they called 'kobolds' on the Continent or 'knockers' in Cornwall).

Within the Theosophical Society, in which Rudolf Steiner was still lecturing at the time, there would have been acceptance and discussion of the likelihood of invisible entities, and interest in spiritualistic phenomena was generally rife at this period, with the practice of holding seances in which souls of the dead were said to manifest. This mixture of naïve belief and enthusiasm for 'proof'—especially photographic—of the normally invisible realm on the one hand, and the ever-growing grip of scientific materialism and refutation of a 'spiritual' world on the other, was the background to these lectures in Berlin. They were originally published as *The Influence of Spiritual Beings upon Man*, and this new translation contains two additional lectures.

The course contains the idea that there are in fact many different kinds of spiritual entity, ranging from the higher hierarchies of angels down to hindering demons. The notion of animals, plants and minerals having group souls is introduced—even the inert stone having a spiritual counterpart in the invisible world. Different beings are connected with the planets. How some of them have come into existence, and the planets' influence for good or ill, especially on the human organs, is discussed. Some remarks here will surprise people familiar with traditional astrology. The planetary beings and their connections with those higher beings referred to as the spiritual hierarchies are introduced in connection with the evolution of earth, and the previous stages of its existence are discussed in considerable detail, elaborating the relevant chapters in *An Outline of Occult Science.* We come to learn that the present earth is a planet on which love must be developed, rather than wisdom, which was the task during its previous incarnation as 'Moon'. Steiner's examples from mythology and the nature of the pagan gods, which were how the people at those times understood some of these beings, are further aids to our understanding.

Spiritual beings belong to the zodiac also, and we are told that it is not a static band of fixed stars, but is still evolving in that certain constellations must develop 'through the power of the developing human being'. Here, Rudolf Steiner gives us a remarkable picture of how the Christ relates to the zodiacal constellations and to our own higher aspects. This unusual picture, of 'ascending and descending constellations', is not treated elsewhere to my knowledge.

From these cosmic considerations Steiner leads on to the actual spirits of the kingdoms of nature—the elemental beings—and we learn about the four classes in connection with the four elements: gnomes, undines, sylphs and salamanders or earth, water, air and fire spirits. (In later lectures, notably *Harmony of the Creative Word*, Steiner would develop these insights in much greater detail.) But there are not only nature spirits. Elementals are created by human activities—lying leads to 'phantoms', bad social systems to 'spectres', and coercion of the views of others to 'demons'. People engaged in magical practices have long known of them, folk tales of malicious spirits are not without foundation, and we have a possible clue to certain ghostly and poltergeist phenomena. Much later in 1924, in Torquay, Steiner would elaborate on how these sorts of beings come about and manifest (in the lectures published as *True and False Paths in Spiritual Investigation*).

Spirits are also formed in the association of humans and their animals—not just when keeping pets, but in a working relationship. And other spiritual entities connect us with the arts. Music, sculpture, architecture, painting and poetry all involve us with certain kinds of beings (who may not be harmonious if the art form in question is disharmonious). Whether we pursue the arts as creators or art lovers, we are interacting with these entities. Our different 'bodies' and higher sheaths also connect with the arts in a certain way. Here, Rudolf Steiner begins to discuss the importance of developing and appreciating the arts for the future of humanity, a theme which he would unfold in greater detail, not only in later lectures but in actual creative activity as he gave indications to interested artists.

The mention of Richard Wagner may cause some concern today. It should be remembered that Steiner was speaking about Wagner's *music*, which he saw as carrying a true spiritual inspiration, and not about any opinions which Wagner may have held—which were also the regrettable opinions of many contemporaries. The 'bad' elemental beings connecting to such distorted views evidently could not interfere with the spiritual power of his music.

Rudolf Steiner's intention was to awaken his hearers to the existence of these beings and to how they interact with all aspects of our lives. His own remarkable clairvoyant faculties enabled him to carry out the necessary research. Without developing clairvoyance ourselves, we cannot see these beings, except perhaps in rare moments when we are experiencing shock or illness. However, by learning about a framework of their activities to build upon, we can allow our imaginative capacity to come to life as we think through what is relayed to us. In more recent times, accounts of conversations have been published between people—perhaps with newly developed faculties—and some of these beings. It is all too easy to scoff that such individuals are 'away with the fairies'. We have a better chance today of realizing some of these possibilities, as our understanding of the 'etheric' and 'energy fields' is also a growing area of enquiry. The first conditions for training our faculties to become aware of another world are open-mindedness, a calm acceptance and reverence towards such possibilities. Rudolf Steiner hoped that spiritual insight could then truly become spiritual *research*.

Margaret Jonas, May 2014

LECTURE 1

BERLIN, 6 JANUARY 1908

Today we'll need to discuss some facts and entities in higher worlds and how these relate to human beings, doing so from the spiritual-scientific point of view. From the beginning it will be necessary, though it may seem that there's no need for this in a theosophical branch meeting such as this, to say that the lecture will be one that is given for theosophists who are considered to have reached an advanced stage. There has to be occasion also for such things in a theosophical branch meeting. Anyone who has perhaps only been attending these Monday lectures for a relatively short time may still feel taken aback by some of the things discussed today; but we would not be able to progress if we were not also prepared to talk about things at the higher level of theosophy. Anyone who may be completely new to it all and is perhaps still waiting to be convinced of the spiritual-scientific truths may feel that some of the things said today are a kind of utter lunacy; but such areas must also be considered on occasion.

The lectures given here most recently[1] have shown that when we clairvoyantly ascend to the higher worlds from the physical plane we meet spirits there which do not belong to our physical world, yet as spirits of the higher worlds they are so complete in themselves that we can refer to them as persons, for those worlds, just as we refer to human beings here on the physical plane as persons. You have seen that in the animal world whole groups that are the same or similar belong together in a group soul or a group I, and that we meet the lion soul, the tiger soul and other group Is of animals on the astral plane that are like complete persons there. We may meet them when—to use a commonplace term—we go for a walk on the astral plane, just as here on earth we meet the human individuals of the physical world. In yet higher regions, on the Devachan plane, we find the Is of whole plant groups, and in the highest parts of Devachan we find the Is of minerals as persons complete in themselves, just as human beings are here on the physical plane. We see from this that we meet spirits in these higher worlds that may be said to extend their organs, their individual limbs, down into the physical world. If someone were to show his fingers by pushing them through holes in a curtain or a paper screen, we would only see that person's ten fingers; he himself would be behind the screen. That is how it is with the group Is of animals. Here, with our physical eyes, we see something extended down like limbs by higher spirits on the astral plane, and the actual I is behind the screen that separates the physical from the astral world. And it is correspondingly the same with the other group Is, those of plants or of the mineral world. Moving up to higher worlds from this starting point in the physical world we meet there not only the spirits I have just been mentioning, spirits extending their limbs down to the physical world, but also a whole number of other spirits which we may equally call persons complete in themselves in those worlds. Their physical limbs are, however, not so immediately apparent and demonstrable as those of the group Is of animals, plants and minerals.

The astral plane and the Devachan plane are highly populated worlds. We find there all kinds of spirits the revelations of which are not so evident here, yet their influence, their activities, come to expression here on the physical plane. They do have a great deal to do with the physical plane, with the whole of our human life today. We won't understand human life unless we know that spirits living in higher worlds up above are active in human life. Much goes on in the human body which is not under human control and does not reflect the human I. It is the doing, action, the revelation of spirits in the higher worlds. These are the things we want to speak of today.

Turning our attention to the astral plane we meet there certain spirits—just one of many kinds—that do not appear to have a reflection, a revelation, among the entities on the physical plane which we are taking note of at first, yet they do have a connection with our physical plane. We meet them there on the astral plane as astral spirits with a distinct will, distinct intentions. Their existence within our own immediate world is such that, as I said, we can find them on the astral plane; but they are related, of the same kind, as spirits that inhabit our present Moon, actually in a kind of physical existence on our present Moon. Someone who is able to come closer to these things through clairvoyance will know that these are spirits which in a way are human-type spirits there, in the Moon arena, except that compared to human beings they are like dwarfs, for they barely reach the height of a child of six or seven. There, on the Moon, they have a singular opportunity to be active. Physical conditions are very different there; the atmosphere is very different, for instance, and the consequence of this is that these spirits when they withdraw to their home world, as it were, gain the ability to roar prodigiously, producing tremendously powerful, terrible sounds. These dwarfish entities are able to be present in our world as astral spirits.

You will have to think of conditions in the higher world as much more complex than one usually does. As soon as we speak of the higher worlds, there is a definite connection between the individual planets, and so there is a connection between Moon and Earth similar to the way you telephone from Berlin to Hamburg, for example, and the spirits living on the Moon are thus able to have an influence on Earth with the help of astral powers. These spirits, we might say, are merely the bad aspects of others which we also find in the astral world—kindly disposed spirits which compared with present-day human nature, even the gentlest, are still much, much more gentle, very gentle also with regard to speech. The speech of those spirits does not have the brittleness of human speech, where we have to give a lot of thought first before expressing ourselves, if we are to put our thoughts and ideas into words. We might say that thoughts flow from the lips of these spirits, not just the expression of thoughts in words but the thoughts themselves are flowing from their lips in gentle speech. These spirits are also to be found in our astral world; their true arena is on yet another planet. Whereas the spirits mentioned first have their home on the Moon, these second ones live on Mars; they inhabit it, and are in fact the main population there, just as certain human races are the main population on our Earth.

If we then ascend further towards the Devachan plane we find spirits which are also gentle and peaceful by nature and in a certain respect are extraordinarily intelligent. Where others are at home on Moon and Mars, those particular spirits found on the Devachan plane have their real home on the planet Venus. On Venus we also find a second kind of spirits who—unlike the gentle, lovely ones—are a wild, raging variety, their main occupation being to wage war against and rob one another.

Then on the higher parts of the Devachan plane we find two kinds of spirits that are most difficult to describe. We can only do so by analogy, saying that they are infinitely inventive, discovering something at every moment in life, for it would be wrong to say that they think it up. This gift of invention they have is as if one were to look at something and at the same moment—even as one looks at them—the idea would come as to how it may be configured differently. The invention is there immediately. These spirits, whose home is on Saturn, are the opposites of others who are like the other side of the coin to them—wild, gruesome, having all the wild, sensual greed and desire that might be found in man, but to a much greater, terrible degree.

These spirits which I've just mentioned are in no way unrelated to our life; they do certainly extend their actions, influence and revelations into our life, and for people gifted with clairvoyance their influence makes itself felt particularly when certain conditions pertain on Earth. The spirits that have their home on the Moon, for example, are present on Earth under all kinds of conditions—as astral spirits, of course—for instance when someone is subject to delusions, when there are lunatics somewhere. Such spirits particularly like to be around madhouses as astral spirits. They are also almost always to be found close to mediums and sleepwalkers, some of whom have masses of these spirits whirling around them, and a great many of the influences on these people are due to the presence of such creatures. Where there is love and kindness, however, where people are humanitarian, you will find the gentle, mild Mars spirits as astral creatures, and these spirits are active in the powers developed there. This is their nourishment, the atmosphere in which they can live and from which they in turn influence human beings.

In places where human inventions are made, where engineers are busy in industrial workshops, the atmosphere is right for those inventive Saturn spirits I described. And in places where acts evolve that have something to do with presence of mind, one has spirits from Venus.

You see, therefore, how human beings all the time have elemental spirits, as they are also called, flitting around them. People are truly never alone, for whatever they do or undertake also provides occasion for a number of spirits to unfold. The lesser and greater things people do, their most idealistic and thoughtful actions and their worst actions, provide occasion and cause for creatures to be present that intervene in human powers and are active in them. We have to know them if we truly want to understand life. People who do not see such things for what they are go blindly through life. It is not just theory or a theoretical requirement we have there but it is a matter of all these things needing to be really practical. Only then will people gradually learn in further Earth evolution how to behave and deal with things in the right way when they come to see more and more which creatures are called in by which kind of action or situation. Everything people do is like a call going out to unknown spirits. The Moon spirits may dare to approach not only lunatics or mediums but for instance also young children if these have been so senselessly over-fed that greediness develops; the spirits can then approach them and ruin their development. You see, therefore, how necessary it is to know what people call to life in the world around them with the whole way in which they act and behave.

In other ways, too, these spirits are not unconnected with people. They do have a profound relationship to our immediate human build. Only one thing in the human body really belongs to the human being or can belong to him more and more, and that is the blood. Human blood is the direct expression of the human I. But when people fail more and more to see to it that they inwardly strengthen, firm, their I with a strong, robust will, with a strong and robust soul, if the I is lost to them, as it were, other spirits can also anchor in their blood, and that is then very serious and bad for them. On the other hand many other spirits are still anchored in other parts of the human organism today, are contained in it. Let us look and see everything that extends its feelers into this human body, is anchored in the human body. We'll have to give some thought to this human physical body.

You know that the blood flowing in our veins, spreading through the human body, reflects the human I, and that it comes to give greater and greater expression to the I when the I itself finds its centre, its inner energy core, more and more strongly and robustly in itself. It will gain mastery of other parts, other inclusions in the organism, only in a more distant time in the future. Today these ingredients of the human body hold many other spirits in them. Let us take a closer look at the three levels of juices—chyle, lymph and blood—to help us with our study.

Perhaps you know already what significance these three kinds of juices have for human beings. You know that when people take food it first passes to the stomach through the organs that prepare it, is mixed and prepared with the appropriate juices that are secreted from the glands, so that it can be processed in the intestines. The food is taken to a fluid state, the pulpy fluid taken forward by the intestines. Any part of it that can be nourishment for the human being is taken into the body through small organs called villi, to serve as nourishing juices for the body, building it up anew over and over again. This is one of the kinds of substances we have in the living body. We call it chyle.

And perhaps you also know that apart from this chyle, which comes into existence because food enters into the living human body from outside, there are vessels going wholly in the same direction in the human body which contain a kind of juice which in a way is similar to the white substance in our blood. This juice also flows through the whole human organism in particular vessels, and the vessels often run side by side with the blood vessels we call veins because the blood they contain is bluish red. These vessels actually also take in the chyle. The fluid they contain is lymph. That is a juice which, we might say, is spiritualized compared to the actual food juice, the chyle. These lymph vessels filled with lymph run through the whole human body; they even pass through the bone marrow, in a way, and the fluid in them also takes in the food pulp, the chyle. Everything in the left half of the body and the lower extremities, from the left side of the head, the left side of the trunk to the left hand and both legs, all the lymph spread out and flowing apart there comes together and flows into the left subclavian vein, terminating in the blood circulation there. Only the content of the lymph vessels in the right side of the hand and the trunk comes together and takes the lymph into the subclavian vein on the right side. In this way the lymph vessels reflect an important fact.

You see how this divides the human being into two, not symmetrically but in such a way that one part includes all the lower parts of the body and the left side of the trunk and the head, and the other part consists of the right side of the trunk and the head. This, then, is a second juice which pulses through the human being, a juice which is much closer to the soul sphere than is the case with the chyle, the gastric and intestinal juice of the food pulp, though states of soul do also have a profound influence on the digestion and the whole circulation of the food juice. States of soul are, however, much more deeply connected with the lymph juices. In someone who is very active, lymph flows much more actively than in someone who is indolent and lazy, doing nothing. And so we can mention many states of soul that are connected with the movement of lymph in the human body.

The third juice is the blood, and we have spoken of this on a number of occasions. It divides up into a red, life-giving blood rich in oxygen that flows in the arteries, and a bluish red blood rich in carbon that flows in the veins. Just as our blood is revelation, reflection of our I, so lymph is in a way the reflection, the revelation, of the human astral body. Such things come to expression there in not just one direction. In another way the nervous system is a reflection of the astral body. In the way we want to look at it today, lymph actually reflects, reveals the astral body. Just as someone may have two occupations, so it is with the human astral body. On the one hand it builds up the nervous system, on the other it creates lymph. The human ether body also builds up and develops the whole glandular system, and in another way it is also the developer and regulator of the movement of chyle, the food pulp. This gives you a first picture of these juices moving through the human body and the elements of human nature as such.

Now we must clearly understand that the I is definitely not the only master in the human astral body, the human ether body. In the course of their evolution human beings are progressively gaining mastery of their astral and their ether body by transforming the astral body into

Spirit Self or Manas, and transforming the ether body so that the I gains mastery of the Life Spirit or Buddhi. But for as long as man does not have mastery of these parts of himself, other spirits will be connected with these aspects of human nature.

Other spirits are embedded in the human astral body like maggots in cheese (please forgive this unappetizing analogy). Astral spirits are incorporated in the astral body, have something to do with it, which as I told you have their true home on Moon or Mars, depending on whether they are benign or evil by nature. They anchor in the astral body. And the lymph, that whitish juice flowing in human beings, belongs to the body of the spirits that live in our astral world. They are not as tangible as the animal groups, those spirits that we find on the astral plane, though their real home is on the Moon or on Mars. But they are of such a kind of astral nature that in a certain other direction we may say: Just as in the animals, for instance in a pride of lions, we have a kind of revelation of the spirit which we meet as a whole person on the astral plane, as the lion I, so we have—though not as tangibly—the lymph which flows through the human body as the revelation, the extended limbs, of these astral spirits.

Do these astral spirits therefore have a kind of physical existence—you may ask—just like the animal group soul has its manifestation here on the physical plane? The answer to this question would have to be: Yes, they do. In the case of the animals, we saw that the astral group I extends its individual extremities into the individual lions; these astral spirits also extend their physical nature in here. But they cannot extend them into the physical plane from outside in the same way. They need entities on the physical plane in which they live as parasites, taking hold and boring into them. They are parasites on human beings here. If there were no human beings here they would soon depart from this earth, being unable to find dwelling places; they would not like it here. But there are entities—people and higher animals—who have lymph, and it is there, in this lymph, that these spirits come to physical manifestation. It is therefore not just matter that pulses in our bodies but in every circulation of this kind those spirits also move, hordes of them, spirits that rotate through human beings, move through them and have their body in the lymph, whilst actual human beings, governed by an I, initially have their bodies merely in the blood. The lymph is given its character depending on whether it is more Moon spirits of this kind or more Mars spirits of this kind that circulate in the human body. If more Moon spirits circulate in the body, the individual tends to be more wicked, angry, wrathful; if there are more Mars spirits, the individual tends to be gentler, kinder, more lenient. You see, therefore, that not only juices flow in us but also spirits, and we can only understand human nature if we know that human beings have not only juices in them but also spirits.

If you use clairvoyance to study chyle, initially the outward reflection of the human ether body, you find similar spirits anchored and integrated there as well. Initially they are the spirits we have been characterizing earlier as good Venus spirits on the one hand and bad Venus spirits on the other. Their home is on Venus and they are present in our devachanic world. For someone with clairvoyance they are persons there, and their reflection, their manifestation here in physical life comes in the human chyle, strange though this may seem. In the chyle, which is present throughout the human body, we find these spirits whose real home is on the devachanic plane, and—in so far they assume a physical body—on Venus. Venus forces are in a way connected with the whole of vegetation here on earth and everything else that lives on our Earth. You will thus see the connection which exists between human food and what this food makes of human beings. This is anything but irrelevant. The influences of the Venus spirits live in all plants, and of course also in the animals. These are either good, gentle and lenient or the wild Venus spirits described to you, rapacious and fighting one another. Depending on which of them influence our animals or plants, the meat or plants are such that when they turn into chyle they build virtues or vices into human bodies.

You now see from a standpoint that is higher than it has been possible to show you in previous lectures[2] how important it is to know human food from a spiritual-scientific point of view, to know the influence under which one plant or another is, and which animal is subject to one influence or another. You can learn from this that someone who knows, for instance, that one or another kind of plant and animal thrive in a country and are under a particular heavenly influence will understand how the particular character of that nation must develop, because in everything people there take in by way of food coming from the surrounding area they eat not only the things known to be contained in the food through chemistry but also certain spirits, and it is these which pass through the mouth into the stomach, spreading out in people's essential nature. Here the prospect opens up for us of seeing how the deeper geographical nature of a country reveals the character of a nation.

Do not forget a remark which you may find in the published lecture on the Lord's Prayer.[3] There such a fact was presented from a completely different point of view, and it was said that people relate to the spirit of their nation through their ether bodies and are connected with their more immediate environment through their astral body.

Here you see light thrown from an even more profound point of view on the way the character of a nation develops out of the spirits taken in with the food. It is one of the means used by the great spiritual guidance of earth to distribute the different national characters over the earth by distributing the foods which have different effects in such a way that one or another national character shows itself in the food harvested. This does not take us in a roundabout way to materialism, but spiritual science shows that all things material are a revelation of the spirit, and that spiritual influences spread out also in human beings in a way of which people are not aware.

It is more difficult to understand the way in which the Saturn spirits influence human beings. These are spirits which will have an invention the moment they look at something. On the other hand they develop dreadfully nasty passions of a sensual kind. Anything human beings may develop in this respect is but a trifle. These Saturn spirits insinuate themselves into the human body in an even more mysterious way, doing so through sensory experiences. An idea arises in you when you turn your eye to something beautiful, pure and noble; a different idea comes if you turn your eye to something dirty, ignoble. At the same time as external impressions evoke an idea in the soul, the Saturn spirits insinuate themselves, good ones and bad ones. With everything you have through mere sympathy or antipathy with your surroundings in what you see and hear and smell you expose yourself to the insinuation of Saturn spirits of the one kind or the other. They enter through eyes and ears and through the whole of the skin as you are sentient of things. It is truly horrendous when occult observations are made to note what nasty spirits creep into human noses with some of the scents that are most favourably regarded in society when we are in such an environment, quite apart from what is getting into the noses of those who are actually wearing those scents.

You see how subtle and intimate observations made from the spiritual point of view of even the most ordinary things must be if we want to be clear about life. Much could be said about people who know, more or less consciously or unconsciously, how to command such spirits which influence people above all through smells, insinuating themselves into people with those smells. If you had deeper and more intimate knowledge of the history of a particular age, especially French history in the days of Louis XIII, XIV and XV, with all the arts developed in those days, when aromas did indeed play an important role in games of intrigue, you would have an idea of what people are capable of doing who, consciously or unconsciously, know how to command the spirits that insinuate themselves into human sensory perceptions in scents and aromas. I could refer to quite an attractive book that has recently been written by the minister at a minor court.[4] He wrote it, of course, having no knowledge of these facts, but he understood the effects. A most interesting book about a minor court where an important catastrophe occurred in recent years. In the book the minister and dignitary, writing his memoirs, described the effects of a person who in a way knew how to command the aromas and their spirits. And he did so with a degree of satisfaction, being armed against this and not deceived. You see, things are not without significance and do have an effect in practical life. If we take life not blindly, like a materialist, but as someone with eyes to see, we can sense the spiritual influences everywhere, and if you know the influences you also understand life.

You see how we have to think of man as a highly complex entity, member of all kinds of different worlds and comrade to all kinds of spirits. Those who advance progressively along the road of occult development to higher insights get to know the particular nature of these spirits and this makes them free of them, giving them a clear overview of them. To take in the truth about the higher worlds is to be really free, really mature, for with this we get to know our way about the influences and impulses that pulse and flow through our life. Getting to know one's way about is also to grow free and independent.

And just as we may refer to certain juices pulsing through the human being, so we may also point to individual human organs in which spirits of the higher worlds also come to expression, to revelation. The spirits earlier described as the Saturn spirits do, for instance, come to expression in a way in the human liver. You have to understand, of course, that if you truly want to get to know it spiritual science is a highly complex field.

When we spoke of human evolution in Saturn development it was made clear that Saturn powers brought about the first beginnings of the senses. And Saturn still influences people today, and the liver is the human organ, the internal organ, on which the Saturn powers have a powerful, intense influence. Because of this, human beings, being in the process of developing more and more beyond all things of Saturn, must grow more and more beyond the powers anchored in their liver. It is indeed in the liver that the powers are anchored in man that we must grow beyond more and more. They were, of course, necessary before, so that human beings achieved their present form and configuration. The liver contains the powers which we must most of all overcome. You can, in a way, check this out by considering an external revelation, an outer reflection. You can convince yourself, for instance, that during the time when human beings are above all developing their bodies, that is, in the time before birth and immediately after birth, the liver is biggest in relation to the rest of the body. It then grows relatively smaller and smaller. If you were to give the size of the liver relative to the rest of the body at birth you would be able to say that it is like 1 to 18. Later the relative size of the liver is reduced so that it is like 1 to 36 relative to the rest of the body. It is reduced by about half, and human beings overcome the powers anchored in the liver simply in the course of their natural development.

Human beings can expect to develop higher and higher spirituality on Earth. External physical evidence of this is that they have gained the ability to overcome the powers in the liver. In a way the lung is the opposite of the liver. It is the organ which does not stuff all things egotistical into the human being—which is what the liver does—but opens human beings up freely to the outside where they are in constant communication with the outside world by taking in air and letting it go again. Combustion takes place in the lung. The reddish-blue blood rich in carbon enters into the lung where it is combined with oxygen to turn it into red blood fit for life. Matter combines with oxygen in a burning flame, and combustion also occurs in the lung. Breathing is a process of combustion, in a way, and this breathing and combustion gives human beings the expectation of ever higher and higher development. The powers that come to their final conclusion in the liver have built up the human being. The powers which we receive like fire from the air are going to take away those powers that tie us to the Earth. The fire which we receive from the air, which comes to expression in our breathing, is the principle that will take us into higher and higher spheres.

Myth and legend will again and again prove more profound, more full of wisdom, than modern science, however advanced this may seem. The aspect of human life we have just been mentioning is magnificently portrayed in the myth of Prometheus. The story that Prometheus brought fire down from heaven for humanity says that Prometheus is involved in the process that is reflected in our breathing, a process that takes us higher and higher. At the same time, however, it tells in a truly marvellous way that Prometheus must pay the price for having risen above the powers that tie human beings to Earth, opposing the power of Earth, and for being the first to have made it possible for human beings to have this power of fire. His suffering is marvellously told as the fact that lies behind the myth—an eagle feeds on the liver of Prometheus who is bound. Is there any better and wiser way of showing that the powers that enter into us with our breathing gnaw on the liver, and that someone who anticipates something which humanity will be doing in a distant future will be like one who is crucified as the principle which comes from the air feeds on the liver.

In so far as they come from initiates, myths therefore present the great wisdom of existence. There is not a single myth originating in the mysteries that does not reflect profound wisdom, and we are able to substantiate this. Equipped with the facts of occult science we then approach these myths with reverence, myths which, as we rightly say, have been revealed to humanity by spirits from the higher worlds so that people may first learn from images the things of which they should later develop a clear idea. This will emerge more and more—the myths are full of wisdom and if one wants to find the most profound wisdom in some particular sphere of life one must go to the myth. This was understood by those who created their works from the very depths of art. Profound truth is the basis, for instance, of the whole way in which Richard Wagner[5] relates to mythology, though he gave expression to it in works of art. Our age will rise again from merely physical ordinariness to a stream that is wholly spiritual. If you thus look into the things that pulse in our time, you will more and more deeply understand the mission of spiritual science.

We started by considering higher worlds and this has led us to see the actual mission of spiritual science. It is to provide people with an opportunity to get to know life and in the things they do in life introduce them more and more into something that is mysteriously involved when they move a hand, when they are active in spirit, soul and body. They have companions around them, and by gaining insight in the spirit they will become more and more aware of these spirits, living and working in harmony with them. Spiritual science will thus show them the full reality and enable them to bring insight and wisdom into their lives.

LECTURE 2

Today we'll make a somewhat greater excursion into cosmic space, and this should show us the inner process of world evolution on the large scale and also the close connection of this with human evolution on Earth. Nothing is unconnected in the world. To follow these complex interrelationships in the universe will, of course, need a great deal of time, and we will only gradually come to the more detailed aspects of what goes on in the world.

You will have seen from earlier lectures[6] that certain spirits inhabiting other cosmic bodies have a relationship to our own life, an influence on the lymph, as we call it, on the chyle, as we call it, and indeed often on sensory perception coming in and going out through the senses. You were able to see from this that the spirit acts far and wide through the universe.

Today we'll look at the matter from another point of view, first of all remembering something which has been stressed on a number of occasions.[7] It is that, like man, our Earth has itself gone through a number of different incarnations and will also do so in future.

We generally look back on three incarnations of the Earth: one immediately before the present one, we call it the old—not our—'Moon'; another which came before that, which we refer to as 'Sun'; and one that was even earlier, which we refer to as 'Saturn'. Looking ahead we foresee that our Earth will change into a 'Jupiter', a 'Venus' and a 'Vulcan'.

These are the consecutive embodiments of life for our planet Earth. If you think a little about these stages in the evolution of our own Earth, you can see from this a 'Sun', as it is called in occult science, with a number of planets moving around it. If we then also speak of a planetary 'Sun' state and say that our Earth itself was 'Sun' at an earlier stage of its evolution, we are in some respect saying that this Sun which is the centre of our planetary system today, has not always been Sun. It may be said to have advanced to Sun status, Sun rank, in the universe. There was a time when it was united with the substances and forces that were in our Earth, skimmed off the cream for itself, as it were, something which even today has the highest potential for development, and separated from the Earth, leaving us behind and a number of forces that depend on a slower rate of development. Higher spirits were taken along, and the Sun placed itself and these higher spirits at the centre of our system. So two stages earlier the Sun as it is today had only planetary existence; it has advanced from the planetary to the fixed star state. You see, therefore, that all things can change, are in evolution, in the universe. A Sun is not a Sun from the beginning. A fixed star has not simply become such but first had to go through the lower level of planetary existence.

Now you may well ask me what will happen after this, as such a fixed star continues to develop. Just as the fixed star or Sun state has evolved from a state of planetary existence, so will its evolution continue in the cosmos. However, we'll get a better understanding of this further development if we take a brief look at the further evolution of our Earth.

It is true, our Earth has separated from the Sun for part of its evolution. The Sun is, as it were, moving ahead on a fast route with its spirits. The Earth and its spirits are at present taking a different course. But one day these spirits and the whole Earth will be with the Sun again, having been given opportunity in their current separate existence to complete their present development; for our Earth will unite with the Sun again. It will go together with the Sun again even in our present Earth stage, just as it separated from the Sun in the course of Earth evolution. But it will have to separate once more during the Jupiter stage. The spirits dwelling on Earth will have to go through the Jupiter stage separately. Then Earth and Sun will unite again, and at the Venus stage our Earth will be permanently united with the Sun, taken up into the Sun for good. At the Vulcan stage our Earth will itself have become Sun within the Sun, having added something to Sun evolution, a bit of existence which the spirits that have always remained in the Sun could not have achieved at all in spite of being higher spirits. Earth existence had to be such that human beings could develop the way they have, with that everyday conscious awareness which alternates between waking and sleeping. For that has to do with the separation from the Sun. Spirits that are always living with the Sun do not know night and day. The awareness in the senses which we call clear daytime consciousness, a state that will develop to higher levels in future, will take things learned about outer physical space with it into Sun evolution. And so we will also give something to the essential nature of the Sun, making it richer. And the gain made on Earth, with the gains made on Sun, will give rise to Vulcan existence. This Vulcan stage is a higher one than our present Sun stage. Thus the Earth and the Sun will continue to develop until they are able to unite in Vulcan evolution.

Now you may also ask: Once a planet has developed into Sun, what will be the further development of this Sun in cosmic evolution? We may say that our Earth itself will be Sun when it has reached its Venus stage, and on Venus all spirits are Sun spirits, and indeed even more so than are the spirits on the present Sun. So what will the whole of such a planetary evolution lead to?

You see, what we are going to discuss now will seem quite grotesque and warped to everyone who has gained definite ideas in modern astronomy, as it is called. But it is true; it is the reality of cosmic evolution. When a planet such as our Earth has risen to Sun existence, when it has gradually united with its Sun and the whole then ascends beyond Sun existence, this gives rise to a yet higher stage of evolution, something which in some respect you may also see in the heavens. Something arises which we call a 'zodiac' today; that is the stage above fixed star development. So once the spirits are no longer limited to just one fixed star but expand their own evolution enormously, going beyond fixed stars, so that the fixed stars are like bodies embedded in them, this higher stage of evolution will be zodiacal evolution. The fact is that the powers influencing a planetary system from a zodiac have themselves evolved in a planetary system earlier on and progressed to a zodiacal stage.

Now I would ask you to recall the evolution on old Saturn, the first embodiment of our Earth. This Saturn did, as it were, shine out once in cosmic space as the first, early dawn of our planetary existence. You also know that on old Saturn the first beginnings of our physical body began to develop. Even in its most solid state this Saturn was in no way as solid, physically solid, as our Earth is now. It existed in a thin, subtle form. Its material was the heat present in all existence today, known as 'fire' in occultism. And we can now envisage the reality to have been that the constellations of the zodiac surrounded this first dawn state of our planetary existence, though not, of course, as they are today. Those signs of the zodiac surrounded old Saturn in such a way then that it was hardly possible to distinguish individual stars. They were not very bright, more or less like streaks of light spreading out from Saturn. You'll find it easiest to get an idea of this if you think of this old Saturn surrounded by streaks of light just as our Earth is surrounded by a zodiac. And in the course of Earth evolution itself, the masses of light condensed into the star masses of today's zodiac. To put it in an abstract way we might say that the zodiac has differentiated out of the original massed streaks of flame. And what gave rise to those massed streaks of flame?

It has come from the old planetary system which preceded our own. Saturn was preceded by planetary evolutions at a time which, speaking in real astronomical and occult terms, we cannot really call 'time' in the present-day sense, for it was somewhat different from our 'time'. We can say that for present-day ideas and present-day human concepts it is legendary, a concept that cannot be expressed in any term we have. We can use analogy, however, and say that the powers which preceded our planetary system in an earlier planetary existence had dissolved into those streaks, and then this first early dawn stage of our Earth, old Saturn, gradually gathered itself together from just a small part of that material, with the powers that were in the zodiac shining down from the universe.

A particular characteristic emerges if we compare planetary existence with zodiacal existence. Occultists use two words for the difference between the two. They say that everything that has come together in the zodiac is in the sign of 'permanence', and everything come together in planetary existence is in the sign of 'time'. You may get an idea of what this means if you remember that for concepts that are far-reaching indeed the zodiac remains unchanged. Every one of the individual planets may go through long periods of evolution that differ greatly from one another, changing a great deal; but relative to this the principle that is active in the zodiac up above stays quite permanent, firm. These terms must, however, be seen as relative. If we then extend our concepts even further, the difference in these changes is only one of speed. Changes come slowly in the zodiac; changes in the planetary world and also in fixed-star existence are quite rapid compared to developments in the zodiac. The difference is merely relative after all. For all human ways of thinking, we might almost say that planetary existence is the sphere of finiteness, and zodiacal existence the sphere of infinity. As I said, this is relative, but sufficient for human thinking for the time being.

We may say one thing, therefore, and I would ask you to take note of this. Something that has been in a planetary existence, has become Sun, ascends to heavenly existence, zodiacal existence. And what does it do when it has reached this zodiacal existence? It sacrifices itself. Please take note of this term. In a mysterious way old Saturn, the first dawn state of Earth, came into being through a sacrifice made by the zodiac. The powers that gathered together the first, subtle Saturn mass were those that stream down from the zodiac, bringing about the first germinal beginnings of the physical human being on Saturn. And the process continued. You should not think of this happening only once. Essentially it happens all the time. Within a planetary system, as we call it, powers that have developed to the higher level are sacrificed once they have gone through a planetary system themselves. We may almost put it like this: Something which is at first in a planetary system develops to Sun existence, then zodiacal existence, and then gains the power of being creative itself, sacrificing itself in its planetary existence. And the powers from the zodiac are 'raining' down onto planetary existence all the time, and rising up again all the time. For the part of us that is to be zodiac one day must gradually rise up again. So we may say that the distribution of powers in our Earth is such that on the one hand powers descend from and on the other they ascend to the zodiac. This is the mysterious way in which the zodiac works with our Earth. Powers descend, powers ascend. These are the steps on the mysterious 'stairway to heaven' where powers descend and ascend. Reference is made to this in various ways in religious writings. You also find it in Goethe's *Faust*:

> Angelic powers ascend and redescend
> And each to each their golden vessels lend.[8]

As far as we are concerned, for our human powers of comprehension, these powers began to descend during the Saturn existence of Earth. And when the Earth was at its midpoint, the step had been taken where the powers would gradually ascend again. Now we have reached a point beyond the middle of our evolution, as it were. At the midpoint of our evolution we were in the middle of the Atlantean age; and the things humanity has gone through since Atlantis are really something that goes some distance beyond the middle of our evolution. We may say, therefore, that in a way more powers are ascending now than are descending from the zodiac.

Thinking of the zodiac as a whole you have to envisage a part of its powers descending, another part ascending. The powers that are in the process of ascending development today we take together under the constellations Ram, Bull, Twins, Crab, Lion, Virgin, Scales. About five constellations relate to the descending powers—Scorpion, Archer, Goat, Water Carrier and Fishes. So there you see powers raining down from the zodiac and rising up again—seven constellations for the ascending, five for the descending powers. The ascending powers correspond to the higher aspects of human nature, the higher, more noble qualities. The descending powers must first go through the human being, must first gain the level in man that will enable them to be ascending.

In this way you will understand how everything in cosmic space can influence everything else, how everything in cosmic space must be in context and relate. But we do have to remember that this activity is always going on, is always there. At any moment in our evolution we are therefore always able to say to ourselves: Yes, certain powers are now moving out of human beings and in again, powers that descend and those that ascend. For every one of those powers the moment comes when they change from descending into ascending powers. All powers that become ascending have previously been descending. They descend as far as the human being, as it were. And in the human being they gain the power to ascend.

When our Earth was at the midpoint of its evolution, having gone through three planetary stages—Saturn, Sun and Moon—and had arrived at its fourth planetary state, with Jupiter, Venus and Vulcan still lying ahead (as 'Earth' therefore in the middle part of its existence) it had to go through three 'states of life', also called 'rounds'. Three are behind it, and it is now in the fourth. Then it had to go through three 'form states'—arupic, rupic and astral—before achieving physical existence. It is therefore also in the middle part where its form states are concerned. As physical Earth, in the fourth form state of the fourth life state in its fourth planetary existence, it had to go through three races— the first was Polar, the second Hyperborean and the third Lemurian. The Atlantean race is the fourth. In that race humanity had just reached the midpoint of the developments of which we are speaking. Following the middle part of Atlantean evolution humanity has gone beyond, and following the middle of the Atlantean race the time has come when altogether conditions have begun for humanity in which ascent is greater than descent. If we were to determine the ratio of powers descending and ascending to the zodiac before the middle part of the Atlantean age, we would have to say that they were in balance. We would have put things differently then, counting Ram, Bull, Twins, Crab, Lion and Virgin as ascending powers. The Scales would have to be counted among the others, those that are descending.

There is, however, something else involved in all this. You have to understand that in speaking of such cosmic events we are not speaking of physical or etheric bodies but of spirits that dwell on the heavenly bodies to which we are referring. When we speak of man in spiritual-scientific terms we say that the complete human being whom we are contemplating is a sevenfold entity consisting of physical body, ether body, astral body, I, Spirit Self, Life Spirit and Spirit Man. He is not yet complete but will be so when his sevenfold nature has fully developed. However, in the vast universe there are not only entities such as human beings in their process of development. There are others, for instance some where we cannot say that they have a physical body as their lowest part. We have to count differently with other entities. We can write down the levels of existence of human beings like this:

7) Spirit Man
6) Life Spirit
5) Spirit Self
4) I
3) astral body
2) ether body
1) physical body

Some entities have the ether body as their lowest level. They are also sevenfold, having an eighth level above that of Spirit Man. With them, it begins with ether body, astral body, and so on, and they come to an end in a level that is above our Atman, or Spirit Man. Other entities have the astral body for their lowest level; they then have an eighth and a ninth level above Spirit Man level. Entities exist where the lowest level is the I, which means that they do not have a physical body, ether body and astral body in the sense we know them, but show themselves to be such that the I urges outward, without the three enveloping principles. These are spirits which send out Is in all directions. They have an eighth, ninth and tenth level to them; in the Book of Revelation they are said to be 'full of eyes within'.[9] Others have the level of the Spirit Self, Manas, as their lowest level. They then have an eleventh level. And finally there are spirits that begin with the Life Spirit; they have a twelfth level. So there are spirits which have the Buddhi as their lowest level, just as man has a physical body as the lowest level, and the highest level of existence for them is one to which we best give the number twelve. Those are sublime spirits that go far beyond anything human beings are able to envisage. How is it altogether possible to give an idea of those marvellous, sublime spirits?

If we want to characterize human nature in one particular aspect we see someone who with regard to the universe is a recipient. Things, entities, are spread out around you. You perceive them and form ideas of them. Imagine a world around you that is empty or pitch-dark. You would be unable to perceive anything through the senses, nothing would give you ideas. You depend on receiving your inner content from outside. It is characteristic of human beings that they are recipients. The content of the human soul, the inner life, is initially received from outside; things must exist out there if the soul is to gain content. The human ether body is configured in such a way that we could not know anything of life if we were not indebted for everything that presents itself in us to the whole universal world surrounding us. The spirits which I have just been characterizing as having the Life Spirit as their lowest level of existence are in a completely different situation. The life of these spirits does not depend on receiving things from outside; they are power centres, giving out, creative. As you know from the way I have always spoken of the way in which the I also works into the ether body, the Buddhi is nothing but a reconfigured ether body, so that in substance the Life Spirit is also an ether body. Yes, the twelfth level is also ether body for these most sublime spirits, but an ether body that sends out life, its influence on the world being such that it does not receive life but gives it out, is continually able to make it an offering.

We now ask ourselves: Can we form an idea of a spirit which is somehow connected with us and is letting life flow out in such a way in our universe? This outflowing life is all the time giving new life into the world. Can we form an idea of this?

Let us go back for a moment to the beginning of today's lecture. We said that ascending and descending powers exist, ascending to the zodiac, descending from the zodiac. What has altogether put man in a position where something can rise up from him himself? What has happened so that something can stream out and upwards from his essential nature? He got into this position because his I was first prepared for a long time and then progressed more and more. This I was in preparation for a long, long time. For essentially all existence on the Saturn state of Earth, on the Sun state and on the Moon state, when the enveloping forms were created that would take in the I, was preparation for the I. Other spirits did there create the dwelling place for the I. Now, on Earth, the dwelling place has been created to the point where the I has been able to occupy the human being, and from there the I in man began to work on those outer enveloping forms from inside. The fact that the I was able to work from inside did at the same time mean that the excess, the imbalance, arose between ascending and descending powers. For as long as the I was not yet able to work in the human being, the ascending powers developed, up to the midpoint. And when the I struck in, the powers had gone so far that ascending and descending ones were in balance. The impact of the I in man meant that ascending and descending powers were in balance, and it was up to man to get that balance to move in the right direction. Because of this occultists called the constellation reached at the moment when it began to approach the I the Scales. Up to the end of the Virgin the activities of the I were being prepared for in our planetary evolution, but this did not go as far as the I. With the Scales the I had begun to take up its role, and with this the I brought about an important element in its development.

Just consider what it means that the I then reached this stage of development. The I was from then on able to take part in the powers that belong to the zodiac, it was able to have an influence on the zodiac. It is absolutely true—the more the I endeavours to reach the highest point in its development the more does it work into the zodiac. Nothing happens in the inmost I which does not have consequences reaching as far as the zodiac. That is absolutely true. And since man with his I really has the potential to develop as far as his Atman or Spirit Man, he is more and more developing the powers that will enable him to influence those Scales in the zodiac. He will gain full control of the Scales in the zodiac when he has pushed his I through[10] to Atman or Spiritual Man. Then man will be an entity that lets something flow out, moving from the stage of time to the stage of permanence, of eternity.

As humanity thus follows its course, there are also other entities for whom the element which for man is the greatest influence he can exert is but the lowest influence they have. Let us now look for these entities, where the lowest element is the kind of influence which the Scales are for man. If we write down the human being in the zodiac, we have him go as far as the Scales. The entity which in its essential nature belongs wholly to the zodiac, its powers belonging wholly to the zodiac, an entity which in planetary life only comes to expression in that lowest element we call Scales—whereas in man the lowest element is indicated by the Fishes—is the one which, as you can see, spreads life over the whole of our universe:

	♈ Ram	12th level	
	♉ Bull	11th level	
	♊ Twins	10th level	
	♋ Crab	9th level	Mystic
	♌ Lion	8th level	Lamb
7) Spirit Man	♍ Virgin	7th level	
6) Life Spirit	♎ Scales	6th level	
5) Spirit Self	♏ Scorpion		
4) I	♐ Archer		
3) astral body	♑ Goat		
2) ether body	♒ Water Carrier		
1) physical body	♓ Fishes		

Human beings take in life; this entity lets life shine out over the whole of our universe. This spirit is capable of making great sacrifices. It is inscribed in the zodiac as the spirit that sacrifices itself for our world. As human beings strive upwards into the zodiac, so this spirit sends its sacrificial gift to us from the Ram, which belongs to it as the Scales do to man. And as man directs his I upwards to the Scales, so does this spirit let its essence flow over our sphere in sacrifice. It is therefore known as the 'Mystic Lamb' offering itself,[11] Lamb being the same as Ram. Hence the sign of the self-sacrificing Lamb or Ram for the Christ. The Christ is here characterized for you as belonging to the whole cosmos. His I strives up to the Ram; and as the I streams as far as the Ram it becomes the Great Sacrifice itself, relating to the whole of humanity, and in a way these spirits and powers existing on Earth are his creation. He is in the Sun in the whole of his essential nature, and is connected with the Moon and the Earth in his creations. His power is located in the sign of the Lamb. The powers enabling him to be the creator of these spirits therefore is in the constellation of the Ram or Lamb.

This is one of the aspects, one of the views we arrive at when from our closely confined existence we look up into the heavens, seeing how the powers of heaven and the spirits influence one another in cosmic space. And with this the powers that go from one heavenly body to another gradually are for us like the powers that go from one human soul to another as love and hatred. We see powers of soul move from star to star and come to see that everything those powers bring about and do in cosmic space is written in the heavens for us.

LECTURE 3

BERLIN, 15 FEBRUARY 1908

THE aim of these Monday lectures is to take advanced theosophists, that is, people who have been steeping themselves in theosophy and, above all (and this is much more important), taken the theosophical way of thinking and theosophical attitudes to higher and higher levels. This means that if we truly pursue this aim, people who join later will find it more and more difficult to follow. They may perhaps still be able to follow with the rational mind, but it will be more and more difficult to see the sense and soundness of elements from the higher levels of theosophy when they are presented. It will therefore need quite a bit of good will, especially on the part of those who have only been attending for a short time, to follow these lectures in the Branch with feeling and sentience. It has to be stressed again and again that we would not progress unless we had opportunity also to cast light on the higher levels of spiritual existence in one place or another. This is to be done in these lectures.

In the last lecture I spoke of the evolution of our whole planetary system. Before that we looked at this planetary system itself, in so far as individual planets are inhabited by all kinds of spirits which on their part have an influence on our living human body. Today we will continue with this. We are going to broaden our view of the planetary system and in the process get to know something of the secrets of the state of our world, doing so from a spiritual point of view.

If you consider any of the usual theories on the origin of our planetary system, of which there are so many today, you are first of all taken back to a kind of original nebula, a misty, absolutely vast form from which our Sun and the planets orbiting around it have clumped together, as it were, and only physical forces are as a rule considered to have been the driving force in the process. You know that this is called the Kant-Laplace theory,[12] and you also know that people whose understanding just goes far enough to see the individual planets gradually separating out from the nebula and reaching the state they have today are most proud of this insight, and will stress again and again that it is really very little in accord with the tremendous advances that have been made to speak of spiritual powers and entities with regard to this process. You know there are popular books where saying such a thing is said to be the most outdated and superstitious view there can be.

Now the understanding of a theosophist would also be enough to get the right idea of everything presented on the subject. It does go a bit further, however. He'll know that physical forces of attraction and repulsion are not enough, that all kinds of other things are involved as well. Today, theosophists still have to accept that scientists call them extremely stupid and highly superstitious. But we are living in an age which in a strange way offers hope—we may reasonably say—for our theosophist. We might say that the theories, views and insights gained from the facts of science itself in the usual way today are like small, out-of-breath, dwarflike creatures huffing and puffing a long way behind the facts. For the facts of modern science are really far ahead of the 'belief' held in it. Their nature is such that new confirmation of theosophical truths keeps coming up over and over again. But this is of course not recognized as such. I would merely point out that we have often spoken here of the astral body's influence during the night, of how physical body and ether body are worn down during the day, and during the night it is the astral body which repairs and builds up, getting rid of the products of fatigue. To put it into these words would simply not be acceptable in modern science. But the facts speak clearly. When we read in an American paper,[13] for instance, that a scientist has established the theory that sleeping activity in man is involving and constructive, whilst activity in waking hours is destructive, this is again a scientific fact where the theories in natural science huff and puff behind like little dwarfs that can't catch up. Taking the spiritual-scientific view, you have great vistas filled with light that have been gathered from a spiritual view of the world.

Contemplating the genesis of our present solar system from the spiritual-scientific point of view we need not in any way, just as little as in other areas, directly contradict the things said in physical science. For in theosophy there is no objection to the things physical science only and alone seeks to establish—the things eyes would have been able to see in the course of evolution. If someone had put a chair out into cosmic space at the time of the nebula and sat down on it, if that person had lived long enough and now watched how the individual spheres separated out, his physical eyes would not have seen anything other than the things said in physical science. But that would be just as if you had two people before you, with one slapping the other's face, and an observer came along and said: 'One was passionately angry with the other and that made his hand move so that the other got his face slapped'. The other person would say: 'Sheer phantasy; I did not see any anger or passion, I just saw a hand move and make an impact; that is how the other individual got his face slapped.' That is the outward, materialistic description, the method used in modern science. It does not contradict the spiritual investigation of the facts. Anyone who thinks, however, that the materialistic description of the fact is the only one will, of course, feel very superior in his scientific grandeur to anything spiritual science may yield. So the modified Kant-Laplace theory may certainly be valid but spiritual powers and entities were active within this whole process of separation, of crystallizing out.

Experimenters show us very nicely today how everything may proceed according to this Kant-Laplace theory. All you have to do is take a droplet of oil, not too large, floating in water. You can very easily introduce a small cardboard disc into the equatorial plane, putting a needle through the centre. If you make the needle rotate really fast, small drops of oil split off, and it is easy to imagine a cosmic system in miniature and so show how a cosmic system separated off in space. The experimenters have, however, forgotten one thing and that is that they were there themselves to make the necessary preparations, that they then spun the needle, and that things which do not happen of their own accord in miniature also cannot happen of their own accord in the cosmos at large. It is supposed to happen of its own accord out there! It really is not that difficult to understand these things; but the correct physical principles are so worn out that people who don't want to see them really don't need to see them. Spiritual powers and spiritual entities were active in this whole process of planetary development, and we will now learn a bit more about them.

Let me remind you of the frequently stated fact that before our Earth became 'Earth', it went through earlier embodiments, different planetary states—the Saturn state, the Sun state and the Moon state— and having gone through these then reached its present Earth state. Now think of Saturn, let it come alive before your mind's eye, floating in space in the far distant past. It was the first embodiment of our Earth. Its essential nature was such that there was really nothing there of the plants, minerals and animals we see around us today. In the beginning this Saturn consisted only of the very earliest beginning of man. We can only speak of this old Saturn as perhaps a conglomerate of human beings. At that time the human being, too, existed only as the very first beginnings of a physical body. The whole of old Saturn was made up of many individual physical human bodies, more or less the way a mulberry or blackberry is made up of individual small berries. And this old Saturn was surrounded by an atmosphere just as our Earth today is surrounded by air. But compared to 'atmosphere' as we know it today it was spiritual. It was entirely spiritual, and human beings were at their earliest stage of evolution on Saturn. Then came a time when Saturn entered into a situation similar to that of a human being who is in a kind of devachanic state between death and rebirth. This state entered into by a cosmic body is called pralaya. Saturn thus went through a kind of devachanic state from which it emerged again in a kind of outwardly perceptible existence, the second planetary state of our Earth, as Sun. This Sun state took man further forward. Certain spirits which had remained behind now made themselves felt as a second realm, apart from the human realm, on the Sun, so that we would now have two realms. There followed a further devachanic state, now of the Sun, a pralaya, after which the whole planet changed into the Moon state; it then went through a further pralaya, after which the Moon became Earth.

When our Earth emerged from the purely spiritual, devachanic state, when it was for the first time given a form of outwardly perceptible existence, it was not the way it is today but such that seen from outside it might indeed have been taken for some vast nebula, just as it is described in physical science. But we have to think of it as vast, far greater than the present Earth, going far beyond the outermost planets which are part of our solar system today, far beyond Uranus. In spiritual-scientific terms we envisage it as emerging from a state of being spirit and not merely a kind of physical nebula. Someone speaking of it as a kind of physical nebula and nothing else is about as wise as someone who has seen another person and on being asked what he has seen says he has seen muscles attached to bones and blood. He would merely be describing the physical part. For the nebula contains a superabundance of spiritual powers and spiritual entities. They are part of it, and the things that happen in the nebula are a consequence of the activities of spirits. Everything physicists describe is as if they had put a chair out into cosmic space and were looking at the whole business. They truly describe it like that observer who denies the anger and the passion that led to the slap and sees only the moving hand. In reality the things which happen there, with cosmic bodies and spheres emerging, is the work of spiritual entities; we thus see the nebula as the garment, the outward manifestation of a superabundance of spiritual entities.

The spiritual entities are at different levels of development. They do not arise from nothing but have a past; they have Saturn, Sun and Moon pasts behind them. They have all gone through them and are now ready to apply what they have gone through in actions, to do what they have learned on Saturn, Sun and Moon. And they are at many different levels of development. Some had gone as far on old Saturn as human beings have on Earth today. They had their human stage on old Saturn, and at the beginning of Earth evolution were therefore at a considerably higher level than man; they were and are far beyond human beings. Others have gone through their human stage on the Sun, others again on the Moon. Human beings are waiting to go through their human stage on Earth. Looking at just this fourfold hierarchy we already have a large number of different spirits at different stages of development.

We call the spirits that went through their human stage on the Sun 'fire spirits'. You should not think, however, that these fire spirits, which were human on the old Sun planet, looked then the way human beings do today. They went through their human stage in a different outward form. The old Sun planet had an extraordinarily fine, light form of matter, much lighter than matter is today. There were no solids or fluids then, only gaseous matter, and the bodies of the fire spirits were merely gaseous in spite of having gained the human stage. One can go through the human stage in all kinds of different forms in cosmic evolution. Only human beings on earth go through it in the flesh. The spirits ranking as human on the old Moon were in a kind of watery state, being above human beings even on the Moon.

These spirits and an abundance of other spirits were connected with that nebula at the starting point of our solar system. You may easily imagine, for instance, that the process which for humanity began on Saturn started in some different way for other spirits on the Sun. Just as the first beginnings of the physical body started on Saturn, so did other spirits follow on the Sun, just as there are always new infants starting school. They have only got so far today that now, in a physical body, they exist in today's animals. On the Moon the spirits came in that exist in today's plants, and the minerals we have today have only been added on Earth. So they are the youngest members of our evolution, and I have told you of their pleasure and pain in an earlier lecture.[14] So there were not only advanced spirits in the nebula but also spirits that had not yet reached the human level.

In addition to those I have listed so far there were the spirits of which we said that they remained behind at certain stages of cosmic evolution. Let us take the fire spirits. They had completed their human stage on the Sun. Now, on Earth, they are truly sublime spirits, two levels beyond man. The level they have reached is one which humanity will only reach once they have gone through Jupiter and Venus existence and reached Vulcan existence. Then they will have matured to be as the sublime Sun spirits were when Earth began its evolution. Other spirits have remained behind, however. They could have gone as far as the fire spirits on the Sun but—there are reasons why they remained behind— were not able to evolve to the full height achieved by the fire spirits when Earth was at the beginning of its evolution.

All of you will remember that at a certain stage of its evolution, at the very beginning—and this is something you can easily reconcile with the nebula theory—the Earth was still united in one body with the Sun and the Moon. So if you were to mix the three heavenly bodies Earth, Sun and Moon together in a huge cosmic pot you'd have a body which did once exist. Then came the time when the Sun departed, leaving Earth and Moon behind, and after this a time when the Moon also withdrew and our Earth came to be the way it is today, with the Sun to one side of it and the Moon on the other.

So now we ask ourselves: Why was it that three bodies developed from one body? You will easily see why it happened if you consider that there were such highly developed spirits in the nebula, connected with its external existence. They were two levels above the human stage. They would not have found anything to do directly on a cosmic body such as our present Earth; they needed a dwelling place that had very different qualities. On the other hand, human beings would have had to be consumed, as it were, if they had stayed connected with the Sun. They needed a less powerful, milder form of existence. And so the fire spirits had to take action and lift the Sun out of the Earth, making it their sphere of activity. This was not just a physical event. We have to see it as an action taken by the fire spirits themselves. They took their dwelling place and everything they needed by way of substances out of the Earth and made the Sun their sphere of activity. Their nature was such that they were able to cope with that tremendous rapidity in evolution. If humanity were to have been exposed to this tremendous rapidity in evolution individuals would hardly have been young before finding themselves to be old again. All evolution would have been at the double. An existence like that on the Sun could only be borne by spirits that were two levels higher than man. They went away with the Sun, leaving Earth and Moon behind.

We are now also able to say why the Moon had to separate from the Earth. If the Moon had stayed connected with the Earth, man would again not have been able to achieve his existence on Earth. The Moon had to be ejected, for it would have mummified the whole of human evolution. Human beings would not have had such a rapid evolution as they would if the Sun had stayed. They would not have grown old so rapidly, but they would have grown into woody, dried-up mummies, with their development so slow that they would have been mummified. To get exactly the degree of development that would serve man, it was necessary to take out the Moon with its powers and its subordinate spirits. This is also why the spirits connected with the Moon are the ones I described as spirits that for the whole of their life stay at a level which a child of about seven reaches on Earth today. Since their existence was limited to seven years of human life, with only the physical body developing, they needed an arena such as the Moon. If you also consider the fact that not only these various spirits were connected with the nebula but also a whole number of spirits at all kinds of different levels of evolution, you will understand that not only such cosmic bodies as Earth, Sun and Moon separated out but also the other cosmic bodies; all of them separated out because arenas had to be created for the relevant stages of evolution of all those different spirits. There were spirits which initially, when the evolution of our Earth began, were hardly able to follow the further evolution, still being so young in the whole of their evolution that any further step would have meant perdition for them. They needed somewhere, as it were, where they could preserve their complete youthfulness. All the other places exist to provide dwelling places for spirits that are more advanced. A place had to be created for the spirits that had arisen last of all during Moon existence and had therefore remained at a very early stage of development. Because of this that place has very little connection with our earthly existence. The body we call Uranus separated out. It became the arena for spirits that had to remain at a very backward stage.

Evolution then continued. Everything in our system, apart from Uranus, was then contained in a primordial pulpy mass. In Greek mythology all that existed before Uranus separated out was called 'chaos'. So Uranus had then emerged, all else was still chaos. Spirits were also connected with this which at that time had reached the stage at which we human beings were when our Earth had gone through its Saturn stage. And Saturn was created as a special arena for those who, being at this level where they had only just begun their existence, were not able to go along with all that followed. A second cosmic body thus separated off, the Saturn which you still see in the heavens today. It came into existence because there were spirits which were at the level at which humanity had been during the Earth's Saturn state. This Saturn thus arose as a separate cosmic body and, apart from it, everything else was there that belongs to our present-day planetary system. Earth with all that exists on it was also in this primordial pulpy mass. Only Uranus and Saturn were outside it at the time.

The next thing to happen was that yet another planet separated off that was to be the arena for a particular stage of development. This was Jupiter, the third planet to split off from the nebular mass which for us really would be the Earth. Whilst Jupiter and the other planets we have mentioned were outside, Sun and Moon were still united with the Earth. Those planets had indeed split off from the chaos when Earth still held within it the substance which today is in our Sun, when our Earth was still completely at one with the Sun and the Moon. At the time when Jupiter split off, the precursors of today's humanity gradually developed, that is, today's human beings emerged again, just as a new plant grows from seed. Those human seeds had developed gradually during the old Saturn state, the old Sun state and the old Moon state. Now—when the Sun was still united with the Earth—these human seeds emerged again.

Human beings could not have continued to develop like that; they could not tolerate the tempo when the Earth was still together with the Sun. And then something happened which we understand well if we realize that the spirits we referred to as fire spirits removed their arena from the Earth. The Sun pushed its way out of the Earth and we now have Sun and then Earth and Moon together. In some way or other, which we won't go into in detail now, because it would go too far, Mars in its turn remained as an arena for particular spirits. It did then actually pass through Earth and Moon in its further course, and in doing so left iron, as we know it today, behind in the Earth cum Moon. Mars is therefore also responsible for everything deposited in living creatures as iron, namely in the blood. Someone might however say: Iron is present everywhere, also in the Sun and so on. That should not surprise us, for just as there were other bodies in the nebula, so Mars was in it everywhere with its iron, which it then left behind. It is also present in all other planets. Once again we have a situation where scientists are establishing marvellous proof today that this is just as we are presenting it here on the basis of spiritual science. You will no doubt remember that I once spoke of how symbolically we move from the green sap of plants, chlorophyll, to human blood. Plants as such developed before Mars made this passage and they have kept their natural quality. Then the iron which is present in red blood was deposited in life forms that are today organized to a level higher than plants. It was wholly in accord with these spiritual-scientific facts when it was recently discovered in a laboratory in Bern that blood cannot be compared with chlorophyll.[15] This is because it was deposited later. We should not think that blood depends in any way on the substantiality of the chemical element iron.[16] I am saying this particularly because someone might come and say that one cannot speak at all of a connection between chlorophyll and blood. Today, scientists find that blood has to be seen in connection with the element iron, whereas chlorophyll does not contain any iron. It is nevertheless fully in accord with the view presented in spiritual science; it is merely that one has to see things in the right light.

For reasons we have mentioned before, the Moon then separated off—so that we have the Earth on its own and the present-day Moon as its satellite. All spirits which essentially are of a higher kind than man— we have called them fire spirits—moved to the Sun. But there were others that had not advanced far enough to be able to cope with Sun existence. You must realize what kind of spirits these were. They were far beyond man yet had not reached the point where they could live on the Sun, like the fire spirits. Other places had to be created for these spirits. None of the other places would have served them, they were for spirits of a different kind which absolutely had not reached the great age of the spirits that must be counted among the fire spirits but nevertheless have not completely taken the cosmic route. These were mainly two genera of spirits that had remained behind; two special arenas were thus created for them in that two other planets split off from the Sun— Mercury and Venus. These two planets split off from the Sun as arenas for the fire spirits that were far above human existence but would not be able to cope with Sun existence. And so you have Mercury near the Sun as arena for the spirits that could not have lived with the fire spirits on the Sun, and Venus as arena for spirits that in a certain sense had remained behind the Mercury spirits but were still far above man.

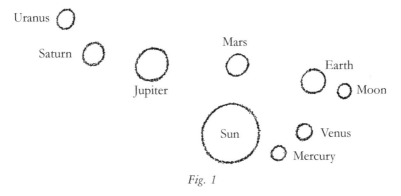

Fig. 1

So you have seen these different cosmic bodies develop from the nebula for inner reasons, brought about by spirits. You will have been able to see that if one stays wholly with the physical, it does go the way we are told in modern science; but we need to gain real insight into the spiritual background, why it has gone that way. Those spirits created their own dwelling places, where they were able to live, within the original nebula. They may be said to have existed side by side in harmony for as long as everything had not yet split off, and they have not lost the connection but are certainly acting on and through one another. The actions of Mercury and Venus spirits on the Earth are of very special interest. Think yourself in the time when the Sun was just splitting off from the Earth, the Moon split off, and humanity began to exist in its present form. Man achieved this existence in the present-day form in that one of the Sun spirits condescended—if I may put it like this—not to have its further existence on the Sun but to connect with the Moon. This created a sublime regent acting from the Moon. Apart from this, less sublime spirits dwelt on the Moon, but one of the Sun spirits allied itself with Moon existence. As a divine spirit the Sun spirit which united with the Moon—this really made it a spirit that had been transferred in the universe—was Yahweh or Jehovah, regent of the Moon. We shall see why this happened if we consider the following.

We have seen that if the Sun had stayed with the Earth humanity would have consumed itself in the rapid course of evolution. If only the Moon were to bring its powers into play, human beings would have been mummified. It was exactly with powers of Sun and Moon working together that the equilibrium arose which sustains humanity in its present-day rate of development. When the Earth had come across from the old Moon man had a physical body, from Saturn, an ether body from the Sun, and an astral body from the Moon. Having three bodies now, with the seed germinating with three bodies, man now had a different form. You'd be surprised if I were to tell you, for the form human beings have today has evolved very slowly and gradually from the time when the Moon separated. The bad, inferior powers on the Moon could not have given them their present form. They could have given form, but only an inferior one. You see from this that the powers that give form must come from the Moon. The powers coming from the Sun are constantly changing the form. For man to be given his present form it was necessary for a creator of form to act from the Moon. There was no other way. This is how the development of the I human being began at that time. The fourth element in essential human nature began, and Yahweh was giving man the seed for a form that would enable human beings to have an I.

At this point human beings were not yet capable of doing the work of which I was speaking. I told you that human beings must work from the I to transform first their astral body, then their ether body, and then their physical body. This is something they would only be able to undertake gradually. Just as children still need teachers today, so human beings needed encouragement on our Earth to take them forward once they had been made ready. There were two kinds of encouragement. Considering the whole of cosmic evolution you can imagine where they came from.

The spirits closest to man were the Venus and Mercury spirits. It would not be until the end of the Atlantean age that human beings would be able to make the first feeble attempts to let their I influence the three bodies independently. Until then they needed 'teachers' whose influence was to continue well beyond this Atlantean age. And those teachers were the spirits that were active on Venus and Mercury. You should not think of them being like the teachers of today; you have to imagine that it was the Venus spirits which gave man intellectuality. Outwardly human beings had no idea that these Venus spirits were influencing them, just as they did not know that certain spirits acting from the Moon were influencing their outward form. I showed you how the different juices influence human beings. The powers of these spirits influenced human beings in the same way until they were able to work on their own bodies. The intelligence we find in human beings today was mediated to them by the spirits that had remained behind on Venus as fire spirits of a lesser kind. The first clairvoyant human beings would consciously perceive others to be their teachers—the teachers in the great mystery centres of ancient times. In the ages that came before that, the Venus spirits had that extensive influence more or less on the whole of humanity, and there were also mystery centres where the most advanced people of that time were given spiritual instruction by higher spirits, by the fire spirits. The sublime fire spirits of Mercury were the actual teachers in the mysteries. They would first appear, if we may put it like this, in a spiritual embodiment, teaching the first of the initiates. Just as the first initiates came to be the teachers of humanity at large, so did the Mercury spirits act as teachers for the first initiates. So you see at the same time how spirits from other heavenly bodies influenced humanity in a quite perceptible way; but those influences were of a highly complex kind. You can see this from the following.

You will remember that in my *Theosophy* it was just a rough differentiation to say that human beings consist of physical body, ether body, astral body, I, Spirit Self, Life Spirit and Spirit Man. You know that the more correct differentiation is physical body, ether body, astral body and then, differentiating the principles transformed by the I—sentient soul, rational soul and spiritual soul. It is only in these that we have the Spirit Self or Manas, then the Life Spirit or Buddhi, and finally the Spirit Man or Atman. The human soul principle thus presents as intercalated as sentient soul, rational soul and spiritual soul. Studying human evolution on Earth, we may also say: First the sentient soul developed in addition to the three principles that have been brought across from the Moon, then the rational soul, and the spiritual soul essentially only developed towards the end of the Atlantean age, when human beings first learned to say I to themselves. It was only then that they could learn to work consciously, from inside, on the principles that made up their essential nature. Speaking of human beings of body, soul and spirit, we have to differentiate the soul itself into sentient, rational and spiritual soul. These only developed gradually. The spiritual soul is not yet able to have an influence, for it was the last to arise. These principles therefore must also be given encouragement from outside. Spirits are involved in this from outside, the situation being that Mars with its spirits influences the sentient soul. When the rational soul was due to develop, Mercury had already split off and with its spirits influenced the development of the rational soul. Jupiter, having existed for a long time already, influenced the development of the spiritual soul.

In the human soul element you thus have the activity of three cosmic bodies—the work of Mars in the sentient soul, of Mercury in the rational soul, and Jupiter in the spiritual soul. And Venus with its spirits is active when the Spirit Self is forced into the spiritual soul. Mercury was also active for the first initiates. This means that the Mercury spirits have a dual function—initially one of which human beings were quite unconscious, developing the rational soul. Then they were the first teachers of the initiates, working in a very conscious way. The Mercury spirits therefore always have a dual function, something like the way teachers in rural areas have to teach the children and also look after their fields. The Mercury spirits had to develop the rational soul and also be the great school teachers of the great initiates. You can also understand all this is a perfectly logical way.

Now you may ask why it is Jupiter which acts on the spiritual soul, seeing that it is such a backward planet. But these things are not explored using logical reasons but by investigating the facts of the spiritual worlds. Then you would indeed see that the spiritual soul is encouraged by the Jupiter spirits, with backward Venus spirits supporting them on the other hand. The way things work in the cosmos is such that you must not take things in an outward, schematic way but have to understand that when a planet has achieved a mission its spirits can later also take up another mission. At the humanity stage of the second human race the Jupiter spirits were involved in developing the ether body; they then followed their own development for a bit, and when humanity had reached the point where the spiritual soul could develop they had to intervene again and help to develop the human spiritual soul. All things active in the cosmos are interacting in many different ways, and you simply cannot schematically move from one to the other.

So you see how a physicist looking out into cosmic space sees only the purely external bodies of spiritual organisms, and how spiritual science then takes us into the spiritual background, the principles that bring about whatever a physicist sees. I would say that we should not be under the delusion to which someone is subject who takes the droplet of oil, forgetting that he is rotating it himself. We have been looking at the spirits which make the separated-out parts into what they are. We have not given ourselves up to the delusion that the whole continues to rotate when we are not there; we have been looking for the one who makes it rotate, the actual spirit behind it, so that we can see more and more how the things said in spiritual science are in full accord with the things discovered in natural science. But you'll never be able to derive the things said in spiritual science from the facts of external science. This will at best let you arrive at an analogy. On the other hand when occult means let you arrive at spiritual facts, you will always be in accord with whatever a physicist is able to say, though there are things which external science will need to discover first. A theosophist will therefore always be able to stand up to a physicist. He knows very well that anything which happens in the physical world may well be the way a physicist would describe it. But there is always also the spiritual event. This will not prevent some scientists who consider themselves greatly superior from calling the theosophist a fool or worse. But the theosophers may keep their calm. It will all be completely different in a mere 50 years; for a continuance of purely materialistic science would be very bad indeed for the weal and health of humanity—if things were truly to remain as they are today—unless spiritual science were to counteract it.

LECTURE 4

TODAY we are going to consider a subject which is connected with the great, all-encompassing look into cosmic space we took on the last occasion. We will go more closely into spiritual development within the more spatial and material development than we did last time. Then we saw how spirits direct and guide the tremendous process of evolution of which external, physical science speaks inaccurately, theosophy or spiritual science accurately.

The last time we saw how the individual planets, the individual bodies in our cosmic system arose from a common original substance, and we accepted in general terms that spirits of many different kinds are actively involved in this evolution. In other lectures we also said that in spiritual science we see not merely physical, material things in the individual bodies in our system but physical and material principles connected with superior and inferior spirits, with spirits of the most sublime kind that elevate evolution for the weal of the whole system, and also with inferior spirits that intervene to inhibit and destroy. We have to be clear, of course, that something which seems to be inhibition and destruction in some place will, when all is said and done, be after all part of the wisdom that governs the whole system. So we might say that when something seemingly destructive, inhibiting and evil exists in some place, evolution is so wisely guided in the way the whole proceeds that it is changed for the good, the best. The sentience we want to gain in our minds today is of the existence of spirits of a sublime kind, spirits that are creative. Human beings will have to work at evolution for a long time yet before they gain the rank of creative spirit. We want to concentrate especially on a class of spirits who had a part in developing our cosmic system when the Earth began its evolution in our world as Saturn.

Our Earth began its evolution as Saturn, progressing through Sun and Moon evolution to its present configuration. At that time, when our Earth was Saturn, everything was, however, utterly different on this Saturn body than it is on our earthly planet today. No solid masses of rock, no mineral world as we know it, nor water in the present sense, not even air. The only one of today's elements present then may be said to be comparable to heat, to 'fire', as occultists call it. You also would not have the right idea if you were to think that the fire on Saturn looked like a candle flame today, or a gas flame. You gain the right idea if you consider what is pulsing up and down in your own body, and consider the fundamental difference in this respect between a lower animal that has retained certain stages of evolution and a human being. A lower animal has the temperature of its surroundings. An amphibian has no real inner warmth but depends for warmth on its environment. Human beings have their own, regular internal temperature as something they must have. Their organism must ensure, if the outside world is cold, that it can maintain its temperature at a certain level. As you know, if this temperature is out of order, with a fever and so on, the health of the physical body is also compromised. You know that human beings inwardly have the measure of their temperature, and they have to think of something like a power behind this which generates that temperature. This power is not water, nor earth, nor air but a separate element, and this was the only element present on old Saturn, the first embodiment of our Earth.

If you'd gone for a walk in the universe at that time—imaginary, of course, but it is good to imagine how it might have been—you would not have seen Saturn; it did not shed any light at all at its earliest stage. Cosmic bodies need to turn into a Sun first, or relate to the Sun, before they grow luminous. If you had come closer to the old Saturn you would have noticed as you came closer: I feel heat here! You would have noticed that it got warm at some point, and you would think that there was a space where it was hot; it would be like walking into an oven. The existence of old Saturn made itself known by this power of heat only. That was a subtle state of matter, and people today can hardly imagine it, especially if they are learned physicists. But it existed, a state more subtle than a gas, finer than air, and all there was of man at that time, the very first beginnings of a physical body, consisted of this. If you were able to remove everything from yourself except the blood temperature you would have those earliest beginnings of the human being again. But this would not be possible, for we cannot live like this. With our mineral world, water world and so on today, it is not possible to live the way humanity did on old Saturn. At the time it was possible. So you have to think of everything removed from you which you have as juices, for instance, tissues, solid parts. You also have to leave aside the oxygen you take from the air. You have to imagine that only the temperature you have in the blood remains, though of course in a totally different form— a physical human being consisting of heat only. A horrific idea for a modern naturalist, but all the more correct and real for all that.

That was the beginning of the human being, of his physical body. None of the animals, plants or minerals we have on Earth existed on old Saturn. At that time Saturn consisted of nothing but potential human beings, and they were brought together there just as the small berries in a blackberry make up a bigger one. In just that way the Saturn mass was a large berry made up of lots of small berries that were human beings. Old Saturn was a sphere like that. If we were to examine the surroundings of that Saturn, the way we examine the surroundings of our Earth, finding it to be surrounded by a mantle of air in which things like mists, clouds and so on occur, we would not find material things around Saturn. Instead we would find spiritual substances, spiritual entities in the mantle around Saturn, and these were all of them of a higher kind than man was on Saturn when he was in his first beginnings at that time.

Let us now turn to a particular kind of spirits that were connected with Saturn existence. We find there the spirits of will, then the spirits of wisdom, spirits of movement, of form, of individual nature, the spirits of the sons of fire, and the spirits of the sons of twilight. Today we'll give special consideration to the spirits of form, for, as we shall see, they played an important role at the beginning of our present Earth evolution. So we'll pay special attention to spirits among the many present in the atmosphere and surroundings of Saturn, the spirits of form, knowing full well that by today these spirits of form have also gone through an evolution, just as all spirits go through evolution. Human beings received the ether body on Sun, the astral body on Moon, the I on Earth and so grew more and more complete. In the same way the spirits of form have gone through their evolution.

These spirits of form did not have a physical body on Saturn. The lowest part of them was an ether body which we may compare with the human ether body. The physical body we would have to think absent, with the ether body the lowest part of the spirits of form. They then had an astral body, an I, Spirit Self or Manas, Life Spirit or Buddhi, Spirit Man or Atman, and an eighth principle which was one level higher than the level human beings will be able to reach as they evolve through the Earth's embodiments. So these spirits of form acted in an outward direction on Saturn through their ether body, just as human beings on Earth influence the world around them through their physical bodies. They did not have hands with which to work on Saturn, nor feet to walk with, and so on; those things are all part of the physical body. But their ether body came to expression in that they were all the time letting fructifying vital juices in a very fine state of matter radiate in from the Saturn mantle. We can imagine Saturn the way we described it, and fructifying vital juices from the ether bodies of the spirits of form radiating on to Saturn from the surroundings, continually and from all sides, like rain. The nature of Saturn itself was such that it did not retain these fructifying vital juices but acted like a mirror, reflecting them back all the time. This created—I am now giving a more detailed description than in earlier lectures[17]—the mirror images of Saturn of which I spoke. You can imagine the heat substance of Saturn all the time receiving the rays from the ether bodies of the spirits of form and reflecting them back again. We can get a rough picture of it by thinking of rain dripping down to earth from the clouds, collecting on earth and then rising again as vapour. We must not think of there being a period of time in between but a process with no time in between—lavish abundance of vital juices streaming in and being reflected, with the first beginnings of human physical bodies on Saturn looking like mirror images. They actually consist of mirror images. A good picture for the physical beginnings of man on Saturn is to think of someone standing in front of you, with you looking into that person's eyes. You are sending your light into the eye of the other, and your image shines back to you from his eyes. That is how it was with the spirits of form in the surroundings of old Saturn. They sent their live-giving juices down into the heat mass of Saturn, and their own form, their image, was reflected in this heat mass. These mirror images were the first beginnings of the human physical body. Even on old Saturn, man was literally in the image of his god.

If we now move on to the Sun, which developed from old Saturn, further evolution came because the spirits of form no longer needed an ether or life body; they gave up the ether body. They were then no longer radiating down the fructifying vital juices but gave away the ether body, and as a result the initial physical beginnings of man were imbued with the ether body. The ether body given to human beings on the Sun had first developed from the ether body of the spirits of form, was a piece of their ether body. The heavenly spirits had been mirrored in hot Saturn by making sacrifices to it and creating images; they gradually grew more independent, able to do the greater thing and put off their ether body, sacrificing it. They could now fill the image initially created with life, with their own vital energy. If you were able to give life to the mirror image that you see in the eye of another, making it independent, so that it would have a life of its own and be able to step out of that eye, that would be a deed like the one done by the spirits of form at the transition from old Saturn to the Sun. It marked a significant step forward in our cosmic evolution.

You know of course—I'm just mentioning it—that all legends and myths have wide-ranging significance, and when we have the true facts of world evolution in the mind's eye the myths show themselves to be surprisingly true. Let us consider the step forward from Saturn to Sun. On old Saturn the life-giving powers radiated in, were reflected and received again by the mantle, the Saturn atmosphere. In ancient Greek mythology the hot Saturn sphere was called Gaia and the atmosphere

Chronos. This is the myth. The life-giving powers of Chronos were continually shining down onto Gaia, onto Saturn, and went back again, were absorbed. This was Chronos continually devouring his own children. One has to feel the truth of such a myth. If you don't you do not have the right attitude to it.

Just consider what it means that in ancient Greece we find a myth which gives us such a wonderful picture of this truth. There is only one way of explaining this, and it is this. The most advanced human individuals who were guiding humanity's further development in the mysteries knew exactly the things from world evolution which we make known in theosophy today. Just as we are here talking about these things, so they spoke in the ancient mysteries in Greece. These truths were clothed in images for the masses, and those images are today known to us as myths. In the light of such insight it is strange to see people who believe that the truth of humanity was only discovered in the last 40 years and that everything known in earlier times had just been ideas of childlike imagination. We really have to speak of a childlike idea when people say again and again how much wiser we are today.[18] That is indeed a childlike notion.

So we move from Saturn to Sun and consider the further evolution of the spirits of form. They have given up their ether body, 'squirting it out' and conferring it on the body of the Earth, where the human bodies imbued themselves with the ether body of the spirits of form. They now have the astral body as their lowest part, and this higher development means that they have not just one principle that is a level above the Spirit Man or Atman but also another one, so that we must now say they consist of astral body, I, Spirit Self, Life Spirit, Spirit Man, and an eighth and a ninth level which are above anything human beings can for the time being achieve in their complete sevenfold evolution.

What kind of 'outer aspect' do the spirits of form present? Those around Saturn let the 'life rain' drip down on to the planet. On the Sun the spirits of form come to expression in the drives, desires and passions radiating in towards the Sun, in everything that is anchored in the astral body. Someone who might have sat on the Sun and looked out into cosmic space would not have seen lightning flashes or heard the roll of thunder, but in the astral light around them they would have perceived the passions of spiritual entities—passions all around—and you'd have to think not only of low passions. These passions, affects, all around continued to work on the planet from outside. If we consider how the myth continues we literally see the Titans, the active passions, bringing their influence to bear from outside in the course of Earth evolution, active passions coming from outside, from the spiritual air circling the Sun when it was a planet.

Let us now move on to the Moon—the Sun become Moon. In the process of evolution this meant that the spirits of form also put aside their astral body, with the I now their lowest principle. To describe them we would say: Where man has the physical body as his lowest principle, the spirits of form living around the Moon had the I as their lowest principle, then Spirit Self, Life Spirit, Spirit Man, and an eighth, a ninth and then also a tenth principle. And they thus presented their I to the outside. This is very strange, but that is how it was. They presented nothing but Is to the outside, literally brimming over with Is. All activity in the surroundings of the Moon was as if you were to meet entities that revealed all their individual nature, their very own character to you. This was coming from the atmosphere of the Moon. Just think of all the Is present here in your physical bodies being suddenly released from the physical bodies; no physical body, ether body, astral body but only your Is as the lowest principle. And imagine you were able to express yourself throughout space. Think yourselves on the old Moon and your Is out in the world but in such a way that they would be embedded into the spiritual substances, with only the lowest principles of the spirits of form having an influence from the air. This would give you an idea as to how the spirits of form expressed themselves as nothing but Is acting in from space. They had given the astral body which they had had on Sun to humanity, so that on the Moon human beings consisted of physical body, ether body and astral body.

To get a really good grasp of this let us make a small sketch. Let us imagine that this is Saturn man, a human being with the first beginnings of a physical body. We have to think of entities hovering above him that are the spirits of form. They have an ether body, astral body, I, Spirit Self, Life Spirit, Spirit Man and two more principles.

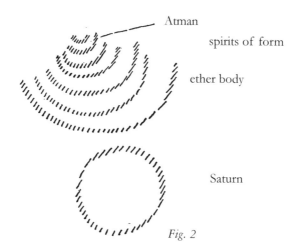

Fig. 2

Then we must think the next stage. In the Sun, human beings had a physical body and an ether body. The ether body had come to them in that the spirits of form poured out their ether body, keeping only their astral body, so that they now had an astral body, an I, and the rest up to a ninth principle.

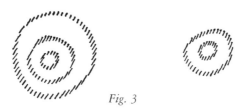

Fig. 3

Now we move on to the Moon. We have a human being consisting of physical body, ether body and astral body, and the astral body came into existence in that the spirits of form sacrificed their astral body. They now had the I as their lowest principle, then Spirit Self, and so on up to a tenth principle. Everything we call 'human being' had thus gradually flowed down from the surroundings of the planet, had been put together from outside. Everything inside had once been outside and had entered into the human being.

Let us now follow evolution on Earth itself. At the beginning of that evolution human beings had the beginnings of a physical body, an ether body and astral body. The spirits of form came across from the Moon.

Their lowest principle was the I; they now sacrificed this as well, fructifying the incipient human being with it, so that the I was a fructifying power as it presented on Earth, a power that was now flowing out from the spirits of form. And the spirits of form kept the Spirit Self or Manas as their lowest principle. So if we wanted to describe them we would have to say: Above us, in the surrounding Earth atmosphere, the spirits of form held sway. Their lowest principle was Spirit Self or Manas in which they lived and moved,[19] having sacrificed the I which was acting in all directions and which they still had on the Moon. This dripped down and fructified the human being.

Now we will consider the progress of man on Earth. It is possible to say at which point the I was dripping in, but today we'll just take a general view. Human beings were given their I. This I would, of course, first encounter its astral body which was like an enveloping aura. It first flowed into this, penetrating this astral body. This was at the time we call the Lemurian age. During that age, over long periods of time, this I first entered into the astral body to fructify it. Let us put this further developed human being before our mind's eye.

At that time the physical body did not consist of bones, flesh and blood the way it does today. It was a very soft early form, with no cartilage either, but with something like magnetic currents running through it. So the physical body was there, then the ether body as the next one, and then the astral body fructified by the I. We have to think of this fructification as something like a hole, an incision developing in the astral body, like an invagination. This is truly the case, that something like an opening developed at the top of the astral body as the I flowed in, an opening going as far as the ether body (see Fig. 4). This was of great significance and had a powerful effect, and the consequence was that a first, dim perception of a physical outside world developed. At earlier stages human beings perceived nothing but their own inner life. It was as if they were hermetically sealed off from the outside. They perceived only themselves and what was going on inside them. Now, however, their eyes were opened to a physical world outside. Yet they were not yet completely independent. Much was still regulated by others, by divine spirits that they were connected with. Not that they were able to see everything around them right away, as is the case today.

With only the astral body opened they did also only perceive with this body. It was a very dim clairvoyance so that when human beings moved across the ground in those primordial times they would perceive what was there outside their bodies in so far as they felt like or dislike, found it useful or harmful. As they moved along they might, for instance, have perceived a bright red colour image rising up as an auric colour image; for only their astral bodies had been opened. They would know that when a red image rose up there would be an entity nearby that was a threat to them. And if the image was bluish red they would know that it was safe to go there. They would let themselves be guided by those dim clairvoyant perceptions. They perceived soul qualities only, not yet able to perceive what exists in present-day plants, for example. They perceived only the soul qualities in other human beings and in the animals, which also included the group souls. This, then, had been the first fructification with the I.

This I or self gradually configured itself more and more. The fructification element entering into the astral body came to penetrate it more and more so that the I was present more and more in feelings of inclination and disinclination in the astral body. As the I spread in the astral body the element I have called the 'sentient soul' in my book *Theosophy* developed. It was the sentient soul which arose there. It was as if the fructifying I spread its power over the whole astral body and this brought about the sentient soul.

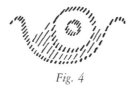

Fig. 4

Here it is important to add the following. We have now seen a fairly normal process of evolution. We have seen the spirits of form let their lowest principle, the I, send in its rays on old Moon, and when the Moon had become Earth they gave up this I and fructified man with the I. We know that certain spirits remained behind on the Moon, not having completed their evolution on the Moon. What does this mean? It means that they did not progress to the level where they were able to let their I stream forth and fructify man. They were not able to do this. They were still at the old Moon stage when they influenced the Earth's atmosphere with their I. These spirits remained behind around humanity and they acted in the way the spirits of form did on the Moon; they acted in this way on the Earth. In the Earth's atmosphere man was surrounded by I spirits that had not yet given away their Is. They now endeavoured to do on Earth the last thing they had to do on the Moon. This exposed humanity to influences that would not have been theirs in the normal course of evolution. These influences of the I spirits radiated into the human astral body. This was remodelled by the instilled I of the spirits of form. At the same time the I spirits which had not reached the level of the spirits of form radiated in powers that were less elevated than they should have been in normal evolution. These lesser powers caused man to separate into a higher and a lower part. Thanks to the I coming in from the spirits of form we thus have an I destined to be selfless, and thanks to the influence of the backward I spirits we have the other I destined for self-centredness, egotism. This was the I which did not yet want to let go of instincts, desires and passions. These entered in and penetrated the astral body, and so we have two things in the human astral body—selfless drives that seek to be elevated and passions full of self-seeking. They have entered into human beings under the influence of the I spirits and have become anchored in them.

We will now look at further evolution. We have seen how the astral body was wholly penetrated with the power of the I that dripped down into it. The next thing was that the ether body was also taken hold of by this power and it, too, developed a kind of hole open to the outside world. To draw this we have to have a physical body at the centre, then an opened-up ether body wholly filled with the power of the I, and then the astral body, also filled out completely with the power of the I. So we now have the power that wants to go outside in the ether body. The ether body is opening up to the outside world (Fig. 5).

Fig. 5

We are now approximately in the first and second third of the Atlantean age with regard to configuring the human being. An old clairvoyance still persisted but not such that only things useful and harmful, liked and disliked would be seen in images. Something like living dream images appeared and remained for a long time. For the ether body is the vehicle for memory, and with no disruption as yet from the physical body these people did hold on for a tremendously long time to the images they took in from outside. At that time memory was a particularly outstanding power of the soul. You can read in *Cosmic Memory (Atlantis and Lemuria)*[20] how people were in this respect at that time. They still did not see the outside world completely but in a kind of dim clairvoyance. This was more comprehensive, however, than perception with the astral body. It was more comprehensive, letting everything arise like a dream in tremendous images that had definite form and did already correspond to external objects; before that the images had merely served to tell human beings what they should do, going in one direction or another. They had not as yet seen the external objects.

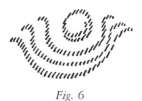

Fig. 6

We move on now and come to the last third of the Atlantean age. The power of the I then took hold not only of the astral body and the ether body but also of the physical body (Fig. 6). The potential for an outward bulge developed in the physical body. The physical body was made to project, with the ether body and the astral body around it. Let us consider it in general terms at present; we will get to know the realities in the lectures that follow. In a way there had thus been such a kind of projection. The physical body took in the I. The point where the I was taken in was between the eyebrows—I have spoken of this a number of times. With this opening which developed as the physical body was penetrated with the I we have to think especially of the physical senses opening up. The I penetrated the eye, the hearing; there was not just one opening but a whole series of openings. All this happened in the last third of the Atlantean age, and it was only with this that the physical human body was remodelled into what it is today.

We call the remodelled ether body of the early Atlantean age 'the rational or mind soul', and the remodelled physical body 'the spiritual soul'[*]. This is in evolutional terms what you find described in my *Theosophy*, the way it is today. Here you can see how things gradually developed.

Then the physical body, too, was open to the outside, and human beings at last got to know the outside world in real terms. There followed the conscious remodelling of the astral body. Before, all remodelling had been more or less unconscious, for it was only now that the spiritual soul existed. To visualize this condition we have to think of it like in the diagram, with the astral body, the ether body and the physical body opened up. In relating to the outside world human beings developed a powerful new element that entered into them. This was everything the I developed in dealing with the outside world, everything it learned from dealing with the outside world. Now envisage everything which the I thus developed getting bigger and bigger—and this truly was the case, putting it in general terms but clearly in accord with the actual process—and this new configuration which human beings gradually developed surrounding the astral body and united with it and then in the course of evolution remodelling this into the actual human Manas or Spirit Self (Fig. 7). This is the work man is doing

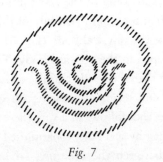

Fig. 7

---

[*] Often translated as 'consciousness soul' but we know from George Adams that Rudolf Steiner suggested calling it 'spiritual soul' in English. Translator.

today, remodelling his astral body into Manas or Spirit Self through the faculties gained in dealing with the outside world. We are still in the process today. Because the spirits of form have given up their I, instilling it into human beings, we have these spirits of form around us everywhere as entities with a Manas, Spirit Self, as their lowest principle. Wanting to look for these spirits of form in the world around us, for their lowest principle, we find it in the fifth principle we ourselves are gradually developing. The human wisdom we develop, which would have to make us wiser and wiser, we would have to find expressed as the lowest principle of the spirits of form in our environment. Let us consider the things made by more sublime, higher spirits around us, things in which we do not yet have a part. Looking at part of a thigh bone—I have often said this—where trabeculae going in different directions make a marvellous structure, we have to say to ourselves: great wisdom has made the smallest amount of matter achieve the greatest measure of stability here. The wisdom which human beings gradually gain lies hidden in there. Humanity will gradually learn to engineer bridge structures that will be as wisely arranged as the way in which the thigh bones act as piers to support the upper human body. The whole human body is so wisely organized, a reflection and revelation of wisdom, and we meet this wisdom everywhere when we go out into the world of nature. Consider the lodges built by beavers. We see beavers get together at times of the year when the water falls sharply and create a structure at a particular angle in the water that will dam the water up, making it fall less sharply. All of it is so correct technically as if they had all the aids provided by mathematics and other science at their disposal. Everywhere in the world around us we find everything full of wisdom, impregnated with it, a wisdom we ourselves will be impregnated with when we have fully developed our Manas. This wisdom which we find everywhere is one of the principles belonging to the spirits of form. These spirits also have Buddhi and Atman where we have our ether body and astral body, and then their eighth, ninth, tenth and eleventh principles. So you see these are most sublime spirits we look up to, and when we see the wisdom in the world around us we are seeing only the lowest principle of these most sublime spirits. Compared to them we are like an animal, a lower form of life, crawling around on a human being and seeing only the outside of the physical body. Do forgive the analogy. We crawl around on the ground and see the wisdom which for the spirits of form is as the physical body is for us. One such spirit is the one we call the creative spirit influencing human beings; for this creative spirit has instilled its I into man.

In exactly the same way as we rise to Manas in the way I have described we will one day rise further in the course of evolution by remodelling the ether body. We will then make the Life Spirit, Buddhi, part of ourselves. We have Manas or the Spirit Self as wisdom impregnated into the world around us. Just as this is a lowest principle of spiritual entities, the spirits of form, so spirits are also connected with the Earth whose lowest principle is not Manas, our fifth, but the Life Spirit or Buddhi which is our sixth principle. The atmosphere for spirits whose lowest principle is equal to our Life Spirit is here around us. And just as it is true that at the beginning of Earth evolution the I was instilled into human beings as a deed done from outside, so it is true that at a particular point in time during Earth evolution the first impression and influence appeared for the spirits which then gradually instilled the full power of the Buddhi into human beings. At the time when the I dropped down, in the long distant past, not much was to be seen of such Is in human bodies even after two thousand years. It all happened gradually. This power of the I only came fully into play after many thousands of years. We should never imagine that the instillation of the I was the kind of event where one might say: 'Nothing special happened there; I do not accept it; it was an event like others that went before.' If some kind of strangely 'enlightened' spirits had lived on Earth two thousand years after the instillation of the I and if they had established a materialism, let us say, at that time, they would have said: 'Well, there are the odd ones among us who insist that a special power has come from heaven and that it has taken all humanity forward; but that is a dualism of the worst kind; as monists we have to declare that this is something that did exist before!' These things evolved slowly and gradually.

At the beginning of the Lemurian age the instillation of the I brought a mighty leap forward, with the possibility of developing the Spirit Self or Manas only following later. And there was also to be an event of fundamental significance that would enable man to develop not only Manas as part of the whole human being but also the Life Spirit or Buddhi. This event was the deed on Golgotha, the coming of the Christ on Earth. It may well be that there are people who deny this today; but this event was an influence from the surrounding world just as much as the other was due to an influence from the surrounding world. We see therefore that we can grasp world evolution in its spiritual aspect if we look into the depths of this world. We learn gradually to raise our eyes not only to material existence; instead we discover spiritual entities and their actions wherever we look in the universe, and with theosophy, as we call it, we get to know the deeds of these spirits. We are alive and active and we are within the spiritual entities and their activities.

The next time we will go into the human organism in more detail and consider how those points truly evolved, having considered them in more general terms today.

LECTURE 5

BERLIN, 16 MARCH 1908

THE last time we considered the evolution of man in conjunction with the evolution, the development, of the cosmos in quite general terms. We can look at these things from many different angles. When we turn our eyes, made sharper by spiritual study, to the dim, distant past we find events no less manifold than those in our immediate present; and we should not think that having character-ized evolution with a few concepts and ideas we have fully grasped and presented the matter. On the contrary, it will be necessary to characterize the times from that dim distant past to the present day from many different angles. We will then get a clearer and clearer picture. We must not let ourselves be led astray by apparent contra-dictions that may be found here and there. These apparent contra-dictions arise because mentally, too, we can look at things from all kinds of different angles. We may walk around a tree, for instance, and gain an image of it from many different sides. Each of those images would be true. There may be a hundred of them. This is, of course, merely an analogy; but in a way it is perfectly right to look at the periods of Earth's evolution from all kinds of different angles.

Today we are going to look at the evolution of our Earth in con-junction with our human evolution from a different angle, and we'll take more note of the human being. We are going to describe the developments that present to the clairvoyant eye as it looks back into what we call the Akashic Record or Chronicle.[21]

We have said several times that our Earth before it was earth went through a number of embodiments. First came the Saturn time, the Sun time and the Moon time and only then our actual Earth time.

If we take just another brief look back at the time of old Saturn we recall how it was said that on old Saturn fire, heat, was the only one present of the four elements and physical states we know on Earth today—solid or earthlike, fluid or watery, airy and fiery. We have the right idea of that first embodiment of the Earth if we consider that Saturn did not yet have gases in it, nor watery parts, let alone anything of an earthy nature. If you had visited old Saturn, as it were—if you could already have been the kind of human being we are today—you would have found no kind of liquid or other matter as you approached old Saturn but a sphere that would have consisted of heat only. It would have been like walking into an oven. You would have been sentient of it because you would have entered into a different heat zone. Old Saturn thus consisted merely of fire or heat.

The Sun, which was the second embodiment of our Earth, had heat condensed to a point where we speak of a gaseous or airy state. The Moon then showed our substances in a watery state; and I have told you before that on the old Moon part of its substance, the Sun substance, separated out, and when it had separated out all Moon entities suddenly went through a mighty condensation.

Today the main point for us is to see clearly that at any further stage of evolution the earlier stages have to be in a way recapitulated first. Looking back on the evolution of our Earth itself we thus have a kind of Saturn evolution in the beginning, a recapitulation of the Saturn state; we then have a kind of Sun evolution, a recapitulation of the Sun state; then a kind of Moon evolution, a recapitulation of the Moon state. And it was only after this that the present embodiment of our Earth's evolution began. When our Earth came out of the pralaya state, the twilight state which it had gone through after being Moon, it, too, was initially a ball of fire. I did describe for you how the other planets separated off. For the moment we'll say that the Earth was a sphere containing nothing but fire, heat substance. The potential for the human being existed within this heat sphere consisting of fire. Just as the first beginnings of man existed on old Saturn, so man was also present when the Saturn state was recapitulated on Earth. There were no other realms. Man was the first-born of Earth's state. No plant world, no animal world, no mineral world existed when the evolution of our Earth began, and essentially our Earth, too, was made up solely of human bodies when it began to evolve.

But what difference was there between the old Saturn state and the state of our present Earth when it recapitulated the old Saturn state? It was quite a considerable difference. The human bodies—which were at this point emerging the way fresh plants unfold from their seed—had gone through the three earlier stages of evolution. They were a great deal more varied and complex in form; for all the powers that had been active on Saturn were present during this first Earth state. And the old Sun and the old Moon were also in there. They had united at the beginning of Earth evolution and had all become one body again. Powers of Saturn, Sun and Moon were acting together in it. Because of this the first human being at the beginning of Earth evolution was much, much more complex than the human being on old Saturn. In Saturn everything had been undifferentiated, everything was still Saturn man. Now in the newly arisen Earth, Saturn, Sun and Moon were together; the earthly human being arose in his first, highly complex beginnings.

At that time, when the Earth was emerging, rising, as it were, from the darkness of cosmic space as a space of glowing heat, the earliest human forms in this space of glowing heat were heat entities themselves. Looking back with a clairvoyant eye on the human being as he then existed, you would first of all find this early beginning of man as if the whole heat sphere had many, many currents in it. These currents moved towards the Earth's surface (this would be on the newly emerged Earth), going down into this surface and there forming masses that were hotter than their surroundings. The human being differed from his environment merely in that one would feel that certain areas were hotter. It will be easiest to show you what existed as the human being at that time if I show you the human organ which had its first beginnings at that time.

Think of a newborn infant. At the top of the head is a spot that is still very soft. Now think of it as really open, and think of a current of heat entering into this opening from outside. Think of this current not as dense, material in terms of bloodstreams, but as streaming energy, and as going down and creating a kind of centre at the point where your heart is today, running in individual vessels but not blood vessels. There you have the first beginnings, in heat, of the human being. The human heart with its blood vessels, the blood circulation, developed from this later, as evolution progressed. And the organ which existed for a long time in human evolution, and then vanished, was a luminous heat organ which at that time was also in its first beginnings. Much later in Earth evolution human beings had such an organ. The spot where the head is still soft in the infant marks the place, as it were, where a kind of warmth organ went out from human beings when they were not yet able to see things in their environment. When they were still sea human beings, unable as yet to perceive things the way they do today, when they were still floating in the ocean, they had to know above all what the temperatures were, if they might move in a particular direction or not. With this lantern-like organ they were able to perceive if they might go one way or another. Human beings still had this organ in the third space of time, in the Lemurian age. As I mentioned on an earlier occasion,[22] the legend of the Cyclopes—human beings with the one eye—goes back to this form of human eye. It was not an actual eye, and it is not correct to call it an eye. It was a kind of temperature-sensing organ which showed where the individual might go. So we would have something of a beaker-like organ that opened out into the first beginnings of a heart at the bottom and was surrounded by something like tentacles, so that at the top you had something like a flower. That is how this organ was at that time.

Something very important then happened in the course of Earth evolution. The uniform heat matter became differentiated and air matter arose, with part of the former heat matter persisting as heat matter. Here you have to take note of a law, however, and it is necessary for you to be really clear in your mind if you want to consider these parts of the human being in the course of evolution. Wherever the heat matter condensed to air light would also arise. Heat matter was still dark matter, with no light in it. Yet when part of this heat condensed to gas or air in such a cosmic sphere, part of this was able to let light penetrate. That is how it was.

We now have the Earth in its second state of evolution. All other aspects went parallel to this. We have an Earth consisting partly of heat, partly of air, and luminous inside. And all this was indeed also reflected in human evolution, human development. The temperature-sensing organ which before had been merely in its beginnings actually began to give out light. The human being was like a kind of lantern; he shone. A few decades ago people might still have been amazed to hear that there are luminous creatures. Today it need no longer amaze one, for scientists know that deep down at the bottom of the sea, where light no longer penetrates, creatures exist that are luminous, giving out their own light. That is how human beings began at that time to give off light.

Then something most peculiar showed itself in this human form. The first beginnings were evident—they would continue to develop gradually—of using the air which was available; the beginnings of a breathing process developed. We see, therefore, how a kind of breathing process was added to the existing heat process. It is most important that we clearly understand that the breathing process began when air was incorporated into the Earth. All it meant was that air came to be attached to the heat matter and this then had air bubbles in it. That was the effect of the air. But it was also connected with something else, for the action of light existed as well, and this was evident in that the first beginnings of a nervous system, an internal nervous system, appeared. Note, please. It was not a nervous system in physical form, and the whole consisted more in lines of energy that had progressed to a degree of condensation. You have to think of the whole in gaseous form, with only extremely fine air currents possible in it, like lines of energy.

So we now have the potential human being, most subtle, wholly etheric, still a heat entity, an air entity, with the first beginnings of a nervous system. If you think a little about this you will realize that this was the stage in our Earth evolution when the Sun was still in the Earth. Of course it was still in the Earth! Think what this cosmic body would have looked like in cosmic space to someone looking at it from outside. All the entities we have just been describing as early human entities would individually let light shine out, and this light would become the total light streaming out into cosmic space. You see, this really was a Sun shining out into cosmic space. If you had been able to examine the

Saturn stage you would have found that you could have approached it
without seeing it; it made itself known only through heat. Now,
however, you have a Sun body, inwardly warmed, but sending its light
out into cosmic space.

Then the time gradually came which I characterized for you as the
Sun separating out. All the higher spirits connected with the Sun, spirits
that had given human beings the abilities we have just been discussing,
all these spirits with their more refined substance separated out. The
Sun went out. It was not yet shining, did not yet give light; it left the
Earth.

We now have a cosmic body in this stage of evolution of our Earth
that consists of Earth and Moon, for our present-day Moon was still
within the Earth then. Then something most remarkable happened. As
all the finer powers had gone away with the Sun, a rapid condensation
followed—relatively speaking, of course. The former lines of energy
were now showing a quite dense configuration. And as the finer substances went away we see the gaseous state condensing into water. The
whole now consisted not only of fire and air but also of water. The
luminosity had gone away with the Sun. It had grown dark again on
Earth; the entities on it had merely kept part of the luminosity within
them.

This was an interesting stage in human evolution. I told you that
with the light came the beginnings of a nervous system. This nervous
system is a creation of light. In all your nerves you have nothing but the
original light that shone in. Now the light, the Sun, had gone out into
space. With this, the mass condensed rapidly. It did not immediately
turn into the kind of nerve mass we have today, but it grew denser than
before, it was no longer merely a fine etheric mass. And, most important
of all, whereas before it had let its light shine out, it was now shining in.
It means that this early human nervous system had the capacity to
generate inner light images—visions arose, clairvoyant consciousness.
So the Sun was departing from the Earth, leaving it without light, as it
were. But the entities on Earth generated an inner light. Before, they
had shone the light on one another from outside. Now they had lost the
ability to shine. The Earth was no longer Sun, but inwardly the sphere
of conscious awareness was illumined, just as today you illumine your

sphere of conscious awareness with the whole world of dreams when asleep. At that time, however, this whole sphere of conscious awareness was filled with light in an infinitely more significant, living way.

We now come to something else which is important. Just as light arose when air did, so a counter-image now developed as air condensed to water. Water relates to sound, tone, as air does to light. Sound can of course pass through the air, causing it to vibrate. This makes it audible. But sound arose, appeared on Earth—meaning sound as such—side by side with the development of water. And just as light activity streamed through the air, so rays of sound were vibrating through all the water to which the air had condensed—we now have Earth consisting of heat, air and water. At this point rays of sound were most of all vibrating through our Earth in the parts where it had grown watery. Harmonies of the spheres, sounds were streaming into the Earth from cosmic space in all kinds of sound harmonies. These effects of sound on the water had a most important effect. You have to imagine, of course, that that original water, the fluid water on Earth, contained all the substances which today have separated out as metals, minerals and so on. Above all it is interesting to turn the spiritual eye to that ancient time and see how all kinds of forms developed from the water as sound created configurations in it. Sound created configurations in water. It was a most wonderful time in the evolution of our Earth. At that time something happened to the highest degree which also happens if you spread fine dust on a metal plate and draw a violin bow down a side of it; this will produce Chladni figures.[23] You know the regular figures which arise. This is how the music streaming in from cosmic space created infinite configurations and figures, and the substances dissolved in the water, being watery themselves, obeyed the cosmic harmonies and arranged themselves accordingly. The most important product of substances dancing to the cosmic music was protein, protoplasm, the basis of all living matter. Materialists may reflect as much as they wish on the mechanical combination of protein from oxygen, nitrogen, carbon and so on. The original protoplasm, protein, developed from the cosmic material that took shape with the harmonies of cosmic music. And in the sphere of life substances were arranged according to that cosmic music. That protein-like substance, the protoplasm, was now developing around the fine structures and into them, penetrating everything. Water coagulated to protein by cosmic harmonies followed the lines I described earlier as heat lines and gradually turned into the development of blood. In the nerve lines the coagulated water settled as developing protein. Initially the protein was like a kind of enveloping form, cartilaginous glue one might say, to give protection on the outside. All this truly developed as substances danced to the music of the spheres.

And this existed before there was even a single cell. The cell is not the origin of the organism. The spiritual principle which I have now described for you was the origin, initially as heat entity, then more hinted at in energy lines, and then substances arranged themselves according to the harmony of the spheres and were laid down along these lines of energy. The cell came relatively late, the last thing to develop. The cell as a last secretion had to come from something that already had life. Organisms never developed from cells, for cells only arose from something that had life. Anatomical things are always only a consequence of putting things together.

All this was there at the beginning of the stage where the Moon was still in the Earth and the Sun had already gone out. But for as long as the Moon remained in the Earth the protein that had developed was progressively hardening, and if the crudest substances and spirits had not left the Earth it would in the end have gone as far as the mummification I have described. The last things still to develop out of essential human nature at that time were the nerves that go to the sense organs. But the sense organs had not yet opened up. They had been developed from within but were not yet open. So now the Moon departed together with the crudest substances. The consequence of this stage of development was that human beings were gradually able to progress to a higher state in that their senses were opened, with the two bodies that were now outside keeping one another in balance. They had built up the human being during the time when they were bound up with the Earth; now they were acting from outside, opening man's senses and making him into the seeing and hearing human being we have before us today.

The departure of the Moon came in about the middle of the old

Lemurian age. There we have a human being whose sense organs had not yet opened but who had a mighty gift of clairvoyance. I described this for you—man was able to fill his sphere of consciousness with all kinds of colour and heat phenomena from inside, all of real value and significance. But he was not yet perceiving objects in space around him. This would only begin once the Moon had left the Earth.

If you consider the brief sketch I have given of that old Earth evolution you will see that human beings as they are on Earth today really had their beginnings from the heart. The heart was not there as the kind of organ it is today. That developed only much later; but the potential for the heart arose from the fire. Then, born from the air, came the breathing system, and born from the light the nervous system. There followed the mass of protoplasm integrating into the organs and this finally made the whole of it into living matter as cosmic sounds coagulated the watery substances. Condensation to the earthy state came in the last part of Earth evolution when the Earth was still together with the Moon substance. And the mineral world, as we usually call it today, developed only shortly before the Moon departed. The earthy element developed from the fluid state at that time. Protein is somewhere between solid and fluid. But the earthy principle, the solid state, really only developed at that late stage. What brought this about? It developed because the elements themselves grew progressively more material under the influence of condensation—for all of it was a constant process of condensation. Think of the beginning of Earth evolution. What did the heat matter do then? It gave you the principle that is now pulsing in your blood for your bodily nature. This was not the same heat as before. When we speak of the first heat state of the Earth you should not think of the kind of heat you get when lighting a match. That is mineral fire and mineral heat. We are speaking of the fire, the heat, that pulses in your blood; that is living heat. So there actually is not only the mineral heat which develops outside in space, but also another, living heat which is inside you. This existed at the beginning of the Earth, and the first beginnings of the human being evolved from it. Continuous condensation did however also make this living heat into lifeless heat. This was also connected with the condensation process that occurred when the Sun departed and the Moon was together with the Earth. And this heat, the mineral heat, initially was a combustion process.

Here we come to an important aspect and I'd ask you to give it serious consideration. We might initially speak of a state of heat, of fire, but we should not speak of a combustion process. That would not be right. We should speak of nothing but the warmth we feel pulsating in the blood. Heat arising through external mineral combustion only appeared when the Sun had departed and the Earth was alone with the Moon. And with this combustion, which did not exist at all before that, the material separated out within the Earth mass which in occultism is called 'ash'. Ash is produced when you burn something. The ash was deposited in the developing Earth when this was alone with the Moon. We have reached the point where the cosmic sound, coming in and forcing the substances to dance, led to the integration of the proto-plasmic masses. We now have entities where masses of fine protoplasm had earlier on gathered along the energy lines, similar in outward appearance to the form of present-day protein. Denser masses existed as if for protection, surrounding those entities like a kind of outer skin of glue. What was missing? Hard bone substance! If I may put it in popular terms, everything was still a mass that was more like glue, and the mineral principle was missing altogether in those entities up to the time that I have now been describing to you. You have to consider how different these entities were. Today there is nothing in your physical body that is not also full of mineral substance. The human body of today has only developed quite late. Today the human body consists not only of bone but also of muscle and blood. And this mineral mass is integrated into all of them. Think the mineral mass away, with the whole Earth and its entities still without mineral mass. Then a com-bustion process resulted in mineral ash being deposited, ash of many different minerals. Ash constituents thus came to be deposited in all directions in human beings who had so far only achieved the density of glue. They took up the ash as they had earlier taken up protein, inte-grating it in their own way, taking in mineral elements ranging from dense bone to liquid blood. You can easily imagine what came to be deposited there—everything that remains behind as ash when the body is burned or decomposes. The principle that truly remains behind as ash is the one that was the last to come into existence. Everything in you that does not turn into ash existed earlier; the ash was only made part of it later. Someone who looks at the ash remaining when a body is cremated with a seeing eye has to say to himself: 'This is the mineral substance in me; it was the last of the earlier constituents to be absorbed.' The mineral principle was thus the last to develop in the course of Earth evolution, and the other realms then made it part of themselves, though before that they had consisted only of other substances.

Now we may also ask what caused the ash to become integrated? After all, we are all the time carrying this ash about with us, but it is dispersed in us and will be left behind when our dead body is cremated or decomposes. How did the ash penetrate into these lines that were filled with protein substance?

We saw that originally there was fire; the potential for the heart developed from this. Then the potential for a breathing system developed from the air. Light became integrated into it and became the potential for a nervous system. Sound then came and created living substance by making substances dance. What made the ash principle, the mineral element, flow into this substance? It was the thought which makes sound, tone, into word which pushed the ash into the human bodies. In Atlantean times, when vapour and mist surrounded everything, the things human beings said were not the one and only articulated language for they were able to understand the language of soughing trees, trickling wells. Everything we have today by way of articulated speech and everything expressed by it made up the dance of the substances; the tone, the musical quality in it, made substances into living matter. The meaning, the significance of words pushed the ash resulting in the combustion process into this living matter, and as the skeletal system grew more and more dense towards the end of the Atlantean age human beings were more and more filled with thoughts, with self-awareness. Intellectualism lit up, and they came to be more and more self-aware.

The things we have in us are created from outside—first the potential that will ultimately be the heart, then our nervous system with the potential for breathing, then the organs that arise from living substance as the glands. In the course of Earth evolution, the sequence is therefore the reverse of what it was before.[24] Then the skeletal system is integrated, the solids are filled with ash, and man gains self-awareness. That is how evolution went within our own Earth embodiment. We have now almost reached the end of the Atlantean age.

If you compare this with the things we were considering earlier, you will see that first there was always the principle which was the last to take effect; for the 'word' which penetrates into matter was there first of all. The principle which gave man his I was there first of all. If you seek to understand what has been said today, full of light, you will also easily find here the facts for the first verses in John's Gospel. On one of the next evenings[25] we'll really have to show how our reflections, going far out into cosmic space, are beautifully given in John's Gospel and also in the first verses of Genesis. All these things are found again as we thus consider the course of world evolution. And one thing will become really clear to you. When we consider the facts, this human evolution looks different from what it seems to materialistic fantasy, imagining that man has arisen from crude matter, and that his faculties of mind and spirit developed from this.

So you see that the actual mission of Earth evolution, the sphere where love comes to expression in man, had its first beginnings in the organ of heat or warmth we have. That was the first to appear. The spiritual appears in the form of energy lines before the organic does; the organic is later integrated under the miraculous influence of cosmic music, and only then is the whole as if integrated through and through with mineral matter, with solids, with the word or the thought. The part which is most dense develops last. Human beings evolve out of the spiritual sphere, also as we consider the course of Earth evolution. Human beings have their source and origin not in matter, but in the spirit. This is something every true contemplation of the world has always shown. Matter only became integrated into the human being after the powers of the spirit. This is becoming more and more evident as we consider these things.

LECTURE 6

BERLIN, 24 MARCH 1908

ANYONE who gives careful consideration to the last lecture given here, thinking it through and recalling how the recapitulation of certain stages that have been gone through before comes at a later stage—a Saturn, a Sun and a Moon state gradually arising on our Earth, for instance, with our Earth state only fully developing after this—might feel impelled to say the following.

He might say: 'It was said in a number of earlier lectures[26] that the first beginnings of the physical human being had gone through something like a kind of sensory system, as if this first beginning of the physical human being on Saturn had consisted in primitive, elementary sense organs. A glandular system would then have developed on the Sun, the nervous system on the Moon, and all of this was later recapitulated on Earth. How can we reconcile this with the things that were said here the last time? You said that the first thing to emerge on Earth was the first beginning of the blood system, a kind of human being showing degrees of heat. Then, with the Earth state condensing to the airy state and light being added, a kind of nervous system with inward perception developed. You went on to say that all this was still in a subtle etheric state, and was then filled with a kind of protein-type substance which differentiated into the individual substances under the influence of cosmic sound, the cosmic tone. If I now assume,' that person might say, 'that the glandular system did after all only begin as this organic matter was deposited, this would mean that on Earth there would first have been a kind of temperature system, though this would be in fine etheric energy lines; then would have come the glandular system, which in a sense would already have been of organic matter, and finally the mineral would be deposited in this, as was said the last time. If these consecutive states of Saturn, Sun and Moon have been like this and if they were recapitulated on Earth, it is strange that it was not a sensory system first also on Earth, followed by a glandular system, a nervous system and finally a blood system. But it was described the other way round last time, first blood, then nerves, glands, and finally the solid deposits, and it was stressed that only the last of these did finally open the senses to the outside. Some might say that this recapitulation principle had a raw deal because the last time it was presented in a kind of reverse order rather than what one might have expected with a proper recapitulation that was exactly the same.'

It has to be admitted that if someone wanted to speak of those situations in a purely intellectual way, describing them as mere repetition of what had gone before, he would probably have given a description that would have been the opposite of what truly happened. For the rational mind would conclude that first the events on Saturn, the Sun and then the Moon would be recapitulated in a stereotyped way, and in that case the blood system would be first. I have stressed on several occasions that in occultism you go wrong as a rule and may make the most awful mistakes if you do not base yourself on the occult facts but depend purely on the intellect, on any kind of logical conclusion. When you follow the evolution of Saturn, Sun and Moon in the Akashic Record you actually have to say that the beginnings of a kind of sensory system were established on Saturn, a glandular system on the Sun, a nervous system on the Moon, and blood was added on Earth. If you go further into the occult facts the situation is that a kind of blood system came first on Earth, followed by a glandular system, a nervous system, and only then did the sensory system appear in the configuration that proves useful on Earth. Speaking of recapitulation we would with regard to the facts indeed have to speak of a recapitulation in reverse. The things said on earlier occasions and those said in the last lecture were not based on speculation but correspond to the facts and there you do actually get this kind of reversal, which makes the recapitulation a great deal more complex.

We also should not be content with the assumption that it was a simple reversal. The blood system, as it first emerged in its early potential on our Earth as a kind of warmth human being, the way I described it in the last lecture, truly was at the same time also a kind of sensory system. It was a system of warmth and perception. Human beings were, as it were, all blood or warmth human beings. There was no blood substance in them but etheric lines of heat energy, and these lines, later to become the blood system, were in their first beginnings very much a kind of sensory system. It was only in its first beginnings and was itself a sensory system. And the system of nerves and light was first a kind of glandular system on Earth. And the later glandular system was only able to integrate as the other systems, the blood system and the nervous system, which by then had been integrated, moved ahead in their evolution. This advance came as follows. With the nervous system evolving as a kind of glandular system, something remained behind of the blood that would later be the first beginnings of the blood. But at the same time the blood system itself was in this second state changing into a kind of nervous system; and when that was achieved and the glandular system was integrated in the third stage, the two earlier systems were again the first to change, so that the blood system was indeed advancing by one level and the nervous system also by one level. Thus there were constant changes, transformations. Evolution was extremely complicated, and it also is not the case that you can be content with the idea of recapitulation in reverse. For that reversal was again only partial; the blood system was a sensory system which later became transformed, and it was the same with the nervous system, and so on.

So you see what happened so that human beings would be able to reach their present level. It is certainly not easy for the rational mind, and it needs patience and time to find one's way into this complicated process of evolution. But this is just a kind of introduction I wanted to give for those who have been busily reflecting once more on the things that were said the last time.

Today something very different will be needed. We need to consider the evolution of human beings themselves on Earth from a very different angle, so that the essential human being will come wholly alive for us. Looking back once more, for this purpose, to the previous embodiment of our Earth, the old Moon, the human beings on the old Moon had a physical body, an ether body, an astral body, but not yet the individual I which they have now on Earth. Studying the state of conscious awareness of such a Moon individual we find that it was indeed radically different from that of a human being on Earth. The condition of the earthly human being is well expressed in what we may call his or her individual nature. This term tells us much about the characteristic nature of an earthly human being, for there was no individual nature as yet on the old Moon. We have seen that this individual nature did only gradually develop fully on Earth, and that in earlier times human beings still felt themselves to be much more part of a whole group. We need not even go far back in the regions where we ourselves are at home, and even going back to the early centuries after Christ we will find the last echoes of a most ancient state of mind. The ancient Cherusci, Sicambri, Heruli, Bructeri[27] did not feel themselves to be individuals the way people do today. They felt themselves to be part of their tribe. When they said 'I', this meant something completely different from what it means today. Today someone saying 'I' means his individual nature, what he is within his skin. In those past days people felt towards their tribe like a limb feels itself to be part of our body. They felt themselves to be primarily one of the Sicambri, Heruli, Bructeri, Cherusci and only secondarily an individual person. You will find it easier to understand many of the conditions of those ancient times if you take note of this radical change in individual nature, realizing that certain kinds of blood feud, family feud, tribal feud are fully explained by the common thinking of the tribe, the state of mind of a kind of group soul. People felt themselves to be groups of the same blood, and if someone was killed, revenge would be taken on the whole tribe of the murderer as though it were he. If we go even further back, to the classic times of the Old Testament, we know that the individual Hebrew wholly felt himself to be a member of the whole Hebrew nation, as it had streamed down in its generations from Abraham's day: 'I and my Father Abraham are one!'[28] With this the member of the tribe felt secure and appreciated. If we go even further back to far, far distant times on Earth we find the group soul quality to have been much more marked. Individuals would recall from memory what their forebears had done, all the way to the original ancestor. The memories of descendants would go back through centuries.

In our time people will not normally remember what their fathers did unless they had seen it with their own eyes. They no longer remember what their ancestors lived through. Their memory covers only their own lives. In ancient times human beings remembered inwardly, through their memory, not only things they had lived through themselves but also those their ancestors had known because they were of the same blood, not because they knew these things but because memory continued on beyond birth. And we know that the age of those ancient patriarchs,[29] of Adam and the ancestors of the Hebrew nation who followed him originally signified nothing but the length of memory, how far one was able to remember back through the line of ancestors. Why did Adam and the other patriarchs live so long? Because one would refer not to a single individual but remember far back through the generations, just as today we remember the days of our youth. They would use a common term for this. The individual did not come into this. They would remember not only the days of their own childhood, but those of their father, their grandfather and so on, through the centuries. The whole of this memory would be summed up in a single word, 'Adam', if you like, or 'Noah' perhaps. In those ancient days the separate individual did not rank the way it does today. Memory extended beyond father, mother, grandfather, and so on. And a common term would be used for the whole of it. The way we see things in this materialistic age this may seem clumsy and unreal, but anything known in a well-grounded psychology, where one knows to reckon with the facts, would have to be put like this if one goes to the very bottom of the facts.

There we realize whilst still here on our Earth that human beings had a kind of group consciousness attached to their group soul. If we were to go back to the old Moon, when humanity did not have such a limited I embedded in group consciousness, but in fact had no I at all, where they still consisted of physical body, ether body and astral body only, we would find that conscious awareness was not less on this old Moon but encompassed tremendous, large groups, and comprehensive group souls were the foundation of the human race on the Moon. These group souls on the Moon, putting individual Moon people on the Moon as if they were parts of them, were wise souls. When describing the animal group souls on Earth we did also see wisdom to be an outstanding characteristic. The group souls on the Moon implanted the wisdom we know and admire today in our planet's previous embodiment. And if today we marvel at the way in which every piece of bone, heart and brain, every plant leaf is filled, imbued with wisdom, we know that that wisdom came down in droplets from the group souls that were in the atmosphere of the old Moon, just as clouds let rain come down today, and became part of all life forms. These took in the wisdom as potential and let it emerge again when they arose once more on Earth after pralaya. All-encompassing group souls, full of wisdom, thus existed on the Moon.

However, there is one quality which we find to an increasingly greater degree on Earth as Earth evolution progresses but would not find in the Moon entities. This is love, the drive that brings creatures together of their own free will. Love is the mission of our planet Earth. This is also why the Moon is called the 'cosmos of wisdom' in occultism, and the earth the 'cosmos of love'. Just as today we on Earth admire the wisdom which imbues it, so will the entities on Jupiter one day come face to face with others from whom the scent of love will come to them. They will be tasting and smelling the love from those around them. Here on Earth wisdom shines out to us; on Jupiter it will be the love which is going to evolve from purely sexual love to be Spinoza's love of God[30] here on Earth. Its scent will arise just as today plants give off their different scents. The degrees of love will stream out as the scent that will rise from the cosmos which will be the successor of Earth, the cosmos we have called Jupiter. That is how conditions change in the course of evolution, and always where there is any kind of progress in evolution the entities will have part of this.

Then the entities connected with that particular stage of planetary evolution will rise to ever higher levels of evolution. Today the human beings on Earth are the instruments, as it were, for the evolution of love. Before, the animal world developed these different forms of love as retarded forms, and in so far as love does show itself in animals, simple reflection would show that these were all stages that preceded human love, a love that is growing more and more spiritual. Man, instrument for the evolution of love on Earth, will be capable of taking in a still higher quality when he has evolved as far as Jupiter. In the same way the spirits that let wisdom rain down from the Moon's atmosphere were capable of higher development as the Moon became Earth; they rose higher. These spirits which at that time had the power to imbue the entities on the Moon with wisdom were after all exactly the same as those which at the point in Earth evolution when the Sun separated from the Earth had developed so far that they were able to go out with the Sun and make the Sun their sphere of activity. The spirits which on the Moon had been the spirits of wisdom,[31] of wisdom raining down (these were different spirits of wisdom from those we spoke of in connection with Saturn), those spirits or at least a large number of them chose the Sun for their sphere of activity. Only the spirit that we refer to as Yahweh or Jehovah had at the end of Moon evolution reached full maturity and became the lord of form on Earth, governing the Moon powers.

We have however also been referring to other spirits that had not gone all the way through full Moon evolution but had stopped, as it were, halfway between human and divine existence. We have been characterizing them in many different ways. We have pointed out that at a certain stage of its evolution the Sun made Venus and Mercury split off to provide a sphere of activity that would suit those spirits. We have also been considering how spirits had a part in the progressive evolution of man which, like those on Venus and Mercury, came to be the great teachers of humanity in the mysteries. Today we'll add to this from another point of view.

It has already been mentioned that if the powers and the spirits that left the Earth with the Sun had stayed connected with the Earth in their original way human beings would have had to develop at a speed so fast that they could not have coped. They could not have achieved their evolution at all if the spirits of wisdom had stayed connected with the Earth the way they had been connected with the Moon. They had to move away and act from outside if humanity was to have the right measure of time for their evolution. Otherwise human beings would be old practically as soon as they were born, going through their development at too fast a rate. I can also picture this for you in another way.

These spirits, which had developed as far as Sun existence, were not interested in human beings going step by step through the different stages of life, through childhood, youth, maturity and old age, slowly and gradually gathering earthly experience in their bodily nature. All they were interested in was an evolution that was complete, arriving at spirituality. If they had stayed connected with the Earth, the bodies would have atrophied in a way, burned up. The mind and spirit would have gone ahead in rapid evolution without garnering the fruits of mastering earthly existence. Not garnering the fruits of mastering existence of Earth, the spirit would have gone into rapid development and human beings would have lost everything they could learn on Earth. Above all the imprint of love into the cosmic evolution would have remained hidden. For love to develop on Earth, the body must first have reached a certain level of development. Love had to be brought in in its lowest form, which is sexual love, so that it might evolve through the different stages; finally, when the Earth in its perfection has reached its final stage love will be ennobled and raised to be purely spiritual love in human beings. All lower forms of love are training for the higher love. Human beings on earth are meant to develop love so that at the end of their development they can give it back to the Earth; for everything evolved in the microcosm will ultimately be poured into the macrocosm. Human progress will be a further development of the macrocosm. The wisdom that flowed into Moon human beings shines out to earthly human beings as wisdom present in their build. The love which is step by step implanted in human beings on Earth will pour out its scent to the Jupiter entities from the whole realm of Jupiter. This is the road which the individual cosmic powers have to take.

The starting point for our Earth mission—imprinting love—is thus facing the following two directions. The spirits of wisdom, the creators of wisdom, who let wisdom flow into the Earth realms on the Moon, were not for themselves as spirits of wisdom on Earth interested in the human physical body. In so far as their interest was only in the wisdom, they handed over the specific Earth mission to the spirits of love. These are a different class, and as spirits of love they were initially also able to join in development on the Sun for a time. So we have two things in Earth evolution—an inflow of love, which is something new, in a way, and an inflow of wisdom that acts from outside, because the spirits that are above all interested in wisdom have withdrawn to the Sun sphere of activity. It is most important that we get the right idea of this collaboration between spirits of wisdom and spirits of love, for it reflects an infinitely important difference. If I now seek to put what happened there in human words, the difference is that the spirits of wisdom leave the individual human beings as they develop between birth and death wholly to the spirits of love, whilst they themselves take on the governance of the individual spirit which goes through different individual natures or individual spirits in the course of reincarnations.

Considering the human being as a whole you now have the two regiments under which human beings are within cosmic government. Between birth and death they are in a living body which may be said to make them truly into entities that stand firmly on their two feet, and because of this everything they develop inwardly is governed by the spirits of love. The eternal individual who is born with the human being, dies, is born again, dies again and so on, is in a way governed by the spirits of wisdom. But you must not make this into a rigid system, saying, 'You maintain therefore that the individual human spirit is under the influence of the spirits of wisdom and the individual nature is governed by the spirits of love.' If you were to make this into a rigid system it would again end in sheer nonsense. For concepts are valid only if we grasp their relativity, knowing that every concept has two sides to it. If you thought that this one life between birth and death had no significance for all later lives, it would be permissible to make it a rigid scheme. But if you consider, and I have always stressed this, that the fruits of every single life on Earth, that is, the fruits of everything gained under the influence of the spirits of love, flow into all evolution, into the sphere governed by the spirits of wisdom, and if on the other hand you understand that everything that there is in the human body up to the astral body is governed by the spirits of wisdom—we have previously described how the things learned on Earth must be refashioned and transformed—it is after all the spirits of wisdom that act on the essential human being because he has a physical body, an ether body and an astral body. And because the individual nature, which the human being develops under the element of love, will remain once it has been developed, the spirits of love are through the element of wisdom influencing anything developed in the individual human life. That is how they work together. Then the governance of these spirits is divided again in that everything by way of individual nature is immediately, directly subject to the rule of love, and everything that happens between birth and death is indirectly subject to the rule of wisdom.

So we see how the human being's individual nature and his individual spirit are part of different currents and streams. This is important for the following reason. If the spirits of wisdom we are referring to now had presumed to take on the governance, as it were, evolution would have been effervescent, vehement, we might also say that the individual would have known all kinds of perfection from all incarnations packed into a single incarnation. As it was, the contribution the spirits of wisdom were to make was spread out over all successive incarnations on Earth. A specific term is used for this in occultism. If the spirits of wisdom had stayed involved in the evolution, human beings would have gone through all stages of development to the spiritual stage at a fast rate, burning up their bodies. However, the spirits of wisdom refrained from taking human beings to such a vehement evolution. They went away from the Earth in order to orbit it, to moderate the time periods which otherwise would have been vehement. Occultists therefore say that these spirits of wisdom became 'spirits of the orbital periods'. The human being's successive incarnations were regulated in consecutive orbital periods regulated by the movements of the stars. The spirits of wisdom became spirits of orbital periods. They would have been capable of using their powers full of wisdom to take human beings away from the Earth, but human beings would have had to give up garnering the fruits that can only ripen in periods of time. The fruits of love, of learning on Earth, could not have been won. The secrets which spirits have and must take to heart if they are to garner the fruits of love, of experiences on Earth, were not known to those spirits of the orbital periods. That is why it says in the Scriptures: 'They covered their faces before the Mystic Lamb.'[32] For the 'Mystic Lamb' is the Sun spirit which knows the secret not only of moving the spirits away from the Earth but of releasing the bodies from the Earth, making them spiritual once they have gone through their many incarnations. The Sun spirit whom we call the Christ has the secret of love. And because he takes an interest not only in the individual spirit but in every single individual on Earth, we call him the 'great sacrifice of the Earth' or the 'Mystic Lamb'.

Thus some became spirits of orbital periods and regulated the successive incarnations. The Christ became the centre in so far as human individuals were to be hallowed and purified. Everything human individuals can add to their individual spirit as their fruit is gained in that they have a connection with the Christ spirit. Looking to the Christ spirit and feeling connected with it purifies and ennobles the individual. If Earth evolution had proceeded without the coming of the Christ, the human body, if we put it comprehensively, would have remained evil. It would have had to connect with the Earth and would have been subject to materiality. And if the spirits of wisdom had nevertheless not refrained from making human beings spiritual right at the beginning of our actual Earth evolution, the following might have happened. Either the spirits of wisdom would right at the beginning of Earth evolution—that is in the Lemurian age—have torn the human being out of the body and guided him towards rapid spiritual development, quickly burning up their bodies (in that case the Earth could never have achieved its mission), or the spirits of wisdom might have said: 'We do not want this, we want the human body to develop fully; but we are not interested in this, and so we leave it to the late-born, to Jehovah, the Lord of Form.' Humanity would then have been mummified, dried up. The human body would have remained Earthbound, however; it would never have progressed towards being spiritual.

Neither of those ways was chosen but a middle position was created so that a balance might be established between the spirits of wisdom and the last-born of the Moon, the Lord of Form, who was the starting point for the activity of the Moon. This middle position was prepared for by the coming of the Christ who is above wisdom, and the spirits of wisdom humbly cover their faces before him. He will redeem humanity if human beings fill themselves more and more with his spirit. And when Earth itself reaches the point where the human being is wholly spiritual, no dry ball will drop out of the evolutional process, but human beings will with everything they have been able to gain from evolution take their progressively ennobled human form to complete spiritualization. And we see human beings growing more and more spiritual. If we were to look at the original human bodies of the Lemurian age—I will never describe the human body on Lemuria in a public lecture—we would find that they present as the utmost extreme of ugliness. The human body as we know it today only developed its form gradually. And human beings grow more and more noble as love purifies them more and more. But humanity will evolve even beyond the present-day human face. Just as the human body has grown more and more spiritual than the Lemurian race, so the human face will grow more and more spiritual. Today we are in the fifth race. Good and noble things living in the soul are evident in the human face today. In the sixth race the human face will be luminous with inner goodness. Human beings will have a very different physiognomy then, so that the outer form will show how good and noble they are, and the face will show what inner qualities of soul they have in them. Nobility of mind and goodness in the human soul will be imprinted in the physiognomy until by the end of Earth time the human body will be wholly filled with spirituality, in complete contrast to others who have remained attached to materiality. They will present the image of evil and remain behind at the mineral standpoint. This will come, and so will the Last Judgement, as it is called, separating good and evil souls. This is the spiritualization of the human body or, in popular terms, 'the resurrection of the body'.[33] We merely have to understand these things in occultism using sound common sense; there can then be no attacks made against them. The 'enlightened' will not be able to understand, however, that matter as we know it might one day be something other than matter. The 'madness of materiality', as we may call it in the best sense of the word, means people would never be able to imagine that matter could one day turn spiritual, that is, that one day something will happen which we call the spiritualization, the resurrection of the body. But that is how things are, and the process of Earth evolution is just so, and the meaning of Earth evolution and the position of the Christ within Earth evolution thus arises.

If we were to look just at the things considered so far today we would get a strange picture of our Earth's evolution. It would be that a balance is indeed maintained between the spirits of form and the spirits that have become spirits of the orbital periods, the actual spirits of light. They would be in balance because from the Mystery of Golgotha onwards the Christ is in charge of further Earth evolution, and what was to come would indeed be a successive ascent. But things are not that simple. We know that spirits remained behind, spirits that had not achieved the full maturity of wisdom evolution and therefore were not interested in handing the rulership over to the stream of love. They wanted to continue their influence and let wisdom continue to flow in. They influenced human beings, and so we cannot say that their activity on Earth was unfruitful. They gave human beings freedom. Where the Christ principle has brought love, these spirits, which we call the luciferic spirits, brought freedom for the individual. They made it possible for people to choose between good and evil. The remaining behind of certain spirits does also have a very good side, and everything, progress or staying behind, is divine by nature. So there were spirits of the orbital periods that guided the progressive incarnations, the individual spirit that goes through all incarnations. So there were spirits of love under the guidance of the Christ principle and they prepared this individual spirit so that the individual may gradually move on into a realm of love. We can characterize this realm of love we have in mind as follows.

A profound error that continues to be widespread today is that the well-being and well-doing of one person does not depend on the well-being and well-doing of all other people on Earth. People will not admit this directly, but in practice everything centres on the fact that the way we live today the individual lives at the expense of others, though it is widely believed that the well-being of the individual is independent of the well-being of the others. Future evolution will mean developing full community in the spirit, that is, the belief will begin to prevail on Jupiter that there is no well-being and well-doing of the individual without those of all others, meaning actually the same well-being and well-doing of all other individuals. Christianity is paving the way, and exists to do so. A community spirit first arose on Earth through the love which is bound to the blood. This had overcome pure egotism. It was then the mission of Christianity to ignite the love in human beings that was not bound to the blood, that is, they must find the pure love where the well-being and well-doing of one is unthinkable without the well-being and well-doing of the other. The realm of love will be such that where originally blood relationship was the bond between people, now every individual will see every other one as a relative, never mind the common blood. This is indicated in the words 'If any man come to me and he does not hate his father, and mother, and wife, and children, and brethren, and sisters ... he cannot be my disciple.'[34] Anything else is not true Christianity. This is how we can characterize human evolution to a higher stage. This goes in cycles, however, and is not successive. You can get an idea of these cycles by simply considering the following.

You see a civilization arise in the first part of the post-Atlantean age which was the Brahmanic civilization, coming to a culmination and falling into decadence—coming to that culmination in shunning materiality and seeking salvation in this, but it had to go into decline because it sought civilization in the sphere where matter was not given recognition. Then you see a new cycle with the ancient Persian civilization conquering the globe because they did acknowledge matter, though as a power that resists human beings and is conquered by human work; this civilization also came to its culmination and then fell into decadence. But a new civilization arose, the Egypto-Chaldean-Assyrian-Babylonian, not merely giving recognition to matter but penetrating it with human intelligence, where the movements of heavenly bodies were studied, buildings were erected according to the star wisdom gained, and human buildings on Earth followed the laws of geometry. Matter was now no longer a resistant mass; it was recast and reshaped to be spiritual. The pyramids reflect what people read in the stars. When the Egypto-Chaldean-Assyrian-Babylonian civilization had fallen into decadence the Graeco-Latin civilization followed. In Greek art human beings reshaped matter by making it reflect their own image, overcoming matter through beauty. That had not been the case earlier on, that human beings imprinted their own image on matter in Greek sculpture, architecture and drama. Individual human nature was glorified in Greek art as the most sublime expression of beauty. And we see how the concept of the individual's rights came in with the Roman civilization.

Once again it is totally perverse scholarship to say—common sense will tell us at first glance—that the concept of rights had existed before that. Hammurabi's code[35] was something very different from the jurisprudence established in Rome. That was a truly Roman product, for jurisprudence emerged where the individual created his image also in the sphere of rights; there the human being was wholly the individual. Do study and compare the last will and testament in Roman law with anything to be found in Hammurabi's code, where the individual nature of a human being was wholly within a theocracy. The 'Roman citizen' was a new element in the cycle of humanity's evolution. In the fifth, Germanic civilization the human being had to enter even deeper into matter. Overcoming the forces of nature, the triumphs of technology were the consequence. We have, however, gone a little bit beyond the lowest point in this evolution. A new cycle will come when human beings will have fully grasped theosophy as it appears today. We see how every cycle in civilization comes to its culmination and then goes down again, and how every new cycle has the task of taking civilization further ... [gap in text].

... The firm equilibrium gave human beings the certainty that they could be released from the Earth; and the striving up and down is what we call striving for actual freedom, something the luciferic spirits had inculcated into humanity. The Christ principle and the luciferic spirits thus work together in world evolution and determine civilization. It does not matter that in the early times of Christianity the luciferic principle was excluded, with reference made only to the Christ principle. Humanity will undoubtedly conquer freedom in full devotion to the Christ principle; for the Christ principle is so all-embracing that it can only be grasped by those who seek to encompass it at the level of greatest wisdom.

Let us go back to pre-Christian times. We find that the religions that existed were a preparation for Christianity. We do see religions in ancient India and Persia, but these were just for the nations that they were born out of. They were national, tribal, racial religions for the nations where they had arisen, for in a sense they were still coming from the group souls and connected with them. With the Christ religion an element came into human evolution that truly was the element of Earth evolution. Initially Christianity was such that it did immediately break through all earlier religious principles. It was absolutely going against the words 'I and father Abraham are one'.[36] Initially it opposed the idea that you may feel at one with anything that is only a group of human beings. Instead the soul dwelling in every individual must be able to feel at one with the eternal ground and origin of the world known as the 'father' who dwells in every soul, and this is put in words as 'I and my father are one'.[37] And Christianity opposed the words 'In the beginning there was light'[38] with the words 'In the beginning there was the word'. This marked one of the biggest steps forward in human evolution. For when light emerges we speak of something outwardly visible, in so far as one may speak of light. Because of this the ancient writings contain a genesis where the physical is presented as a revelation of light. But the 'word' is something that comes from the inside. And before there had been all the revelation of light there was that of the human being 'which was, is and shall be'[39]—that is what is meant by the innermost nature of the human being. In the beginning there was not light but the word. John's Gospel is a document that cannot be put on the same footing with the others, for it adds to the others, taking them from the temporal to the eternal.

Christianity thus is not a religion that might be tribal but a religion for humanity if rightly understood. When the Christian feels at one with the 'father', soul meets soul irrespective of which tribe one belongs to. Thus all barriers will have to go down under the influence of Christianity, and the Jupiter state must be prepared for under the influence of this principle. This is why Christianity began as a religion, for humanity was based on religion. Yet religion is something which in the course of human evolution will have to give way to wisdom, insight. In so far as religion is based on faith and does not have full insight aglow in it, it is something which will have to be replaced in the course of humanity's advance. In the past, human beings had to have faith to arrive at knowledge; in future full insight will shine out, and people will know and from there rise to recognition of the most sublime spiritual worlds. Humanity evolves from religion to wisdom aglow again with love—first wisdom, then love, and then wisdom aglow with love.

We may ask: When religion has become insight, when human beings will no longer be given religion in the old form so that they will only be directed towards the wisdom that guides evolution on a basis of faith, will Christianity also cease to exist? No other religion will then exist that is based on pure faith. Christianity will remain, for although it was religion in its beginnings it is greater than all religion. That is Rosicrucian wisdom. In its beginnings the religious principle of Christianity was more comprehensive than the religious principle of all other religions. But Christianity is even greater than the religious principle itself. When the shells of faith drop away, it will be wisdom-form. It can shed the shells of faith completely and be wisdom religion, and spiritual science will help to prepare humanity for this. People will be able to live without the old forms of religion and faith but they will not be able to live without Christianity. Christianity is greater than all religion. Christianity exists to break through all religious forms, and the Christianity that lives in human beings will still be there when human souls have grown beyond all merely religious life.

LECTURE 7

THE last time we were here I was able to conclude by saying that Christianity was more all-encompassing than anything that was within the religious element and that in future times, when humanity will have outgrown the element we have grown accustomed to call religion, in those future times, I said, the subject matter of Christianity, freed from the old-style religious element, would have become a spiritual factor in civilization. Christianity is thus able to overcome even the form which, in the light of civilization as it has developed so far, we are quite right to consider the form of religious life.

Since I gave that last lecture all kinds of cultural life have passed before me. As you know, a little bit of cultural work lies between that time and today—in Sweden, Norway and Denmark.[40] The week before last I had to speak in Stockholm as well as in other places in Sweden. You will understand what I mean when I tell you that in those Nordic countries, where the population is small and there is so much room for people that they live further apart than people do in our northern European countries—we just have to remember that the whole of Sweden has a population equal in number to London on its own—that in those regions there is so much room that the old Norse gods and the spirits of the spiritual world that surround life there still enter into things. It would be reasonable to say that for those who know something about the spiritual the situation is in some respects such that the spiritual countenances of those old Norse gods still appear in every corner, countenances that appeared to the spiritual eye of the Norse initiates in days when the Christian idea had not yet been poured out over the world.

In those regions, rich in legend not only in the poetic but also in the spiritual sense, one would find another symptom right at the heart of things. Between the days when I spoke in Stockholm I also had to give a talk in Uppsala. In the library at Uppsala—right in the middle of all the manifestations of a spiritual kind from the time of the old pre-Christian gods—quietly lies the first old Gothic Bible translation known as the Silver Bible,[41] the four Gospels translated by the Gothic bishop Ulfilas (Wulfila in Gothic) in the fourth century. Through a strange sequence of events in the Thirty Years War it was taken as booty from Prague to Sweden and is now kept right in the midst of the entities that flit through the spiritual atmosphere of that region—in memories if in no other way. And as if it was only right and proper for that document to be in that place, the strange fact gradually also emerged that eleven pages were once stolen by a collector. His heir had such a bad conscience about it after a time that he had the eleven pages sent to Uppsala again, where they are now together again with the other pages of the first translation of the Bible into Gothic.

One of the lectures I had to give in Stockholm was on the key idea in Wagner's *Ring of the Nibelungs*.[42] Crossing the road one would see posters on the columns of the opera house: 'Wagner: Ragnarök— Twilight of the Gods', the last night of a performance of the *Ring of the Nibelungs*. These are genuine symptoms that interweave in a strange way—the world of Norse legends, always with profound tragedy at the base of it, indicating that one day the one would come who would take the place of this Norse world of gods and spirits. I have on a number of occasions drawn your attention to it that this mood in the world of Norse legend is evident even in the medieval form, with Siegfried killed in the one spot where he was still vulnerable, and this points prophetically to the spot that will later, in someone else, be covered by the cross, as if to say: Here is a spot where something is still missing. That is no mere poetic reference but something that has come up from deep down in the inspiration of that world of legend. This tragic element lies both in the Norse legend and in the mystery on which it is based—that in time to come the Christian principle would take the place of the Norse gods. In the mysteries of the north attention was everywhere drawn to what this twilight of the gods really meant. At the same time it is characteristic—once again I mean more than just a poetic image—that memories of the old gods exist peacefully side by side in people's minds with the Christian ideas that have been brought there, have migrated there. It is like a symptom, I feel, this Gothic Bible at rest in the midst of the memories of the past.

We may also feel that it is a symptom, a pointer to the future, when in the country where the gods of the twilight period were as alive in people's memories as possible, and now arise again in the form given by Richard Wagner, rising outside a religious life that moves within narrow limits. Anyone who is able to interpret the signs of the time even a little will see the first star beginning to shine out in Richard Wagner's art, how Christianity in its most profound idea steps outside the narrow frame of religious life into the wide sphere of modern spiritual culture. One would literally like to listen and hear how the religious idea of Christianity emerges in Richard Wagner's soul itself, how it breaks the religious bonds and grows into something more all-embracing. Looking out from the Wesendonk Villa on the shores of Lake Zurich on Good Friday in 1857, seeing the first flowers of spring come up, and the first beginnings of *Parsifal* coming to him,[43] this was such a transformation of the religious idea that had been there initially, broadening out into a wider plane. Having first elevated his mind to the prophetic announcement of Christianity that shone out so powerfully in his Nibelungs text, his *Parsifal*[44] later let this Christian idea emerge fully, gaining a wider horizon. This made it the starting point for a future when Christianity will be not just religious life but life in insight, in art, in beauty in the comprehensive sense of the word.

This is what I wanted to say today, picking up on what was said the last time, something that can lead to a real feeling for what Christianity can be for humanity one day. Let us now give some consideration from the depths of human evolution to the relationships between religion and Christianity. The time when we are doing this is also not inappropriate for conjuring up these things before the mind's eye.

We are just about to celebrate the great symbolic festival which we may say is the festival for the spirit's victory over death. We are about to

celebrate Easter, and we may perhaps recall how we sought to understand Christmas out of the depths of the mysteries.[45] If we take a higher
point of view and consider Christmas on the one hand and then also
Easter, which will be followed by Pentecost, the relationship between
religion and Christianity really comes before the mind's eye in a truly
wonderful way if we look at it in the right way.

We'll need to go quite a long way back for the basis of this study, but
it will also show us what is truly preserved in such festivals and what
they may awaken in our souls. We are going to go a long way back in
human evolution, though not as far as we have done in the last lectures,
neither in time nor in space. But the thoughts we have been having are
going to be a help because they have shown us the process of Earth
evolution and how it is connected with the evolution of the spirits in the
heavenly spheres. Today we'll only go back to about the middle of the
Atlantean age. That was the age when the forebears of present-day
humanity lived in the west of Europe, between Europe and America, on
the continent which today is the floor of the Atlantic Ocean. The Earth
was different then. Where we have water today it was land, and that is
where the ancestors lived of the people who today represent European
and Asian civilization. If we cast the mind's eye on the inner life of these
antediluvian Atlantean people we find it to be very different from the
inner life of post-Atlantean humanity. We know from earlier studies
how enormously everything has changed in the course of Earth evolution, also in the human soul. Everything has changed in human consciousness, including the alternation between the waking state during
the day and sleep at night.

Today it is normal for us to enter into the physical body and ether
body with our astral body and I when we wake up in the morning. As
we enter we use our eyes to see, our ears to hear and the rest of the
instruments of our senses to gain impressions of the sense-perceptible
world around us. We enter into our brain and nervous system and make
deductions based on those sensory perceptions. That is our daytime life.
At night we withdraw our astral body and I from the physical and the
ether body. And when we go to sleep, with our physical and ether body
lying in bed, all the impressions gained of the world of the senses and
daytime life drop away. Pleasure and pain, joy and sadness, everything

that is our inner life drops away. Dark is the life around us during the night.

It was not like this in the middle of the Atlantean age. The conscious life of that time presents an extremely different picture. When human beings entered into their physical body and ether body in the morning, they did not perceive the definite, clearly defined images of the physical world outside. The images were much more indefinite, roughly the way street lamps appear to have an aura in dense fog today, rainbow-coloured forms. This gives you a bit of a comparison to get an idea of what Atlanteans would see in the middle of their era. However, those colours around objects, not permitting the sharp outlines we know today, and the sounds made by objects were not yet the sober colours and sounds of today. Those coloured margins, which also existed around all life forms, reflected something of their inner life. Entering into their physical and ether body, those human beings would therefore still perceive something of the spiritual nature of anything around them, whereas today we perceive physical things only in their firm outlines and surface colours. And when human beings left their physical and ether body at night there was no silence and darkness all around them. The images they would perceive would at most be a little different but hardly any fainter than by day. The only difference was that they would perceive outside objects from the mineral, vegetable, animal and human worlds during the day. But at night, when they had risen from their physical and ether body, space would be filled for them also with such colour images and sounds, and all kinds of impressions of smell and taste of everything around them. But those colours and sounds and impressions of hot and cold which they received were the garments and covers of spiritual entities that had not descended as far as physical embodiment, of spirits the names and ideas of which have come down in legends and myths.⁴⁶ For legends and myths are not 'popular inventions' but memories of the visions which people of earlier times had had when in those states; for they perceived spiritual things by day and also by night. During the night people truly were surrounded by that Norse world of gods, a world preserved in legend and myth. Odin and Freya and all the other figures in Norse legend are not inventions. They have truly been experienced in the spiritual world by that early humanity, just as we experience other people around us today. And the legends and myths are memories of something which early humanity knew in everything they lived through in their dim, clairvoyant state.

When this state of consciousness, which had developed from an even earlier one, came to grow more and more, the Sun would be in the sign of the Scales at the time which we now call spring. And moving on in the age called Atlantean we see how the state we have today was gradually developing. The impressions gained when astral body and I were out of the physical and ether body at night grew progressively more dull and inconsiderable. The daytime images grew more and more distinct when human beings were in the physical and ether body. In short, we may say paradoxically, night became night and day became day more and more for human beings.

Then came the flood on Atlantis, and the post-Atlantean civilizations which I have described so often for you arose—the old Indian civilization in which the Holy Rishis themselves taught the people—to old Persian, the Chaldean-Assyrian-Babylonian civilization, then the Graeco-Latin and finally our own civilization. To describe the mood today in which people lived in the post-Atlantean and partly also in the last parts of the Atlantean ages we find it to be such: everywhere peoples, including those who had gone east and settled there as descendants of the Atlantean peoples, still had the old memories, the old legends and myths that told of human experiences in an earlier age, in the earlier state of conscious awareness in Atlantean times. The peoples had brought these treasured legends with them from the Atlantean age, and they would preserve and tell them. This lived in them, and the earliest inhabitants of the north still very much had a feeling for the power that spoke to them from the legends and myths, for the oldest of the ancestors would remember that their forebears had once seen the things that were told for themselves.

Something else was also preserved among those peoples, something which they had not lived through themselves but which the initiates of those early times, mystery priests and mystery sages, had known. They had been permitted to look with the eye of the spirit into the very depths of world existence which are now being explored in spiritual science. They had been permitted to do so because the states of soul of human ancestors who were initiates were exactly like those of the folk soul which in those early times still lived right in the midst of the spiritual world. It may have been dim but that clairvoyant state did still exist in those early days. People thus preserved the legends, folk tales and myths, the broken strands of which showed what earlier experiences had been, and the most ancient wisdom preserved the things seen in the mysteries, things cultivated in the old days—a comprehensive view of the world which could then be brought to immediate, individual conscious awareness in the mysteries for the people who were being initiated. In the ancient mysteries artificial ways had to be used to evoke the states that had been natural in early times.

Why was that state of spiritual perception natural in those early times? It was because the relationship between physical and ether body was still different. The present relationship developed only in the last parts of the Atlantean age. In Atlanteans, the upper part of the ether head and various other parts of the etheric body still projected far beyond the physical head, and the ether head only moved gradually into the physical head, doing so completely only towards the end of Atlantis. Then the ether body coincided almost completely with the physical body. This coincidence of the physical and ether parts of the head evoked the later state of conscious awareness for human beings after the Atlantean age—the possibility of perceiving physical objects in clear outline in the present-day sense. The fact that human beings can hear sounds, perceive smells, see the colours on surfaces, where they no longer bear witness to the inner spirituality of things, all this was connected with the physical body and the ether body coming more firmly together—a state that gradually developed in those times.

In yet earlier times, when the ether body was still partly outside the physical body, the part of the ether body that was outside could still receive impressions from the astral body, and those impressions were the perceptions one had in the old, dim clairvoyance. This was only fully taken away from human beings when the ether body entered completely into the physical body. In those early, pre-Christian mysteries the state that had been natural on Atlantis had to be artificially produced by the initiator for the initiand. There we see that the initiands in the mystery temples were treated in such a way that the astral body would receive the relevant impressions and then the ether body would be partly lifted out by the initiating priest. This put the physical body into a lethargic sleep, a kind of paralysis, for three and a half days. Then, with the ether body free, the astral body was able to impress on it all the experiences which the earlier Atlanteans had received naturally. There the initiands of old were able to see things that were then no longer merely preserved in writing or tradition, but which now became individual experience for them.

Let us think of what initiands would go through there. The mystery priest would take the ether body partly out of the physical body and guide the impressions of the astral body into this. The initiands then experienced the spiritual worlds so powerfully that they would bring memory of it back with them into the physical world. They had witnessed events in the spiritual worlds. They could bear witness of this and had been raised above all the things that were otherwise divided up according to peoples and nations, for they had been initiated into the principle that unites all peoples—original wisdom, original truth.

That is how it was in the ancient mysteries. And it is also how it was in the movements of which I was able to speak to you with reference to the Christmas mystery when the things that were the real characteristic of the later state of conscious awareness vanished before the initiate's eyes. Do consider that the essence of post-Atlantean conscious awareness was that human beings were no longer able to see into the inner nature of a thing, that there was a boundary between them and the inner nature of the thing, and that they saw only the surface of things in the physical world. For initiands, things that had become obscure and were no longer transparent to the conscious mind of post-Atlantean times became transparent and clear. When the great moment came they were able in the Holy Night, as we call it, to see through the solid Earth, and were able to see 'the Sun at midnight', see the spiritual element of the Sun 'at midnight'.

Essentially therefore, this pre-Christian initiation was like calling up again something that had been natural for people in ancient times, the natural state of conscious awareness that people had had in ancient times. Human beings had then gradually grown out of this memory of ancient times. We have seen how humanity did bit by bit grow out of those old memories as one civilization followed another, and progressively lost the ability to experience anything when out of the physical body.

Early on in the post-Atlantean age, in ancient India, in the Persian, Chaldean and even in the Egyptian civilizations many people had not yet linked their ether body so firmly with the physical body that they were unable to receive impressions from the spiritual worlds that were like atavistic remnants from an earlier time. But during the Graeco-Latin age all these remnants of an earlier time faded away, as it were, and there was less and less opportunity to perform the old initiation in the same way as before. There was also less and less opportunity to preserve memories of the ancient original wisdom for humanity. We are progressively coming closer to our own fifth age which seen with the inner eye was something very special within the evolution of humanity.

In the fourth period, that is in Graeco-Latin times, the situation still was such that we may say the possibility continued to exist to remember things humanity had once seen in the old, dim clairvoyance, yet on the other hand some people fully inhabited the physical body and were therefore completely closed off from the spiritual worlds. The whole of our life shows that in our fifth post-Atlantean age human beings have entered even more deeply into the physical body. The outer sign of this is the appearance of materialistic ideas. They came up first in the fourth age, for the ancient Greek atomists.[47] Then they vanished, but came up again and again until they gained so much strength in the last four centuries that people have lost not only the positive old memories of the spiritual worlds but also belief in the spiritual worlds altogether. That is how it is. Human beings have entered so deeply into the physical body in this fifth age that they have even lost faith. Many people have completely lost this belief in the existence of spiritual worlds.

Let us now ask ourselves how the evolution of humanity proceeded from a different point of view. Looking back to that ancient Atlantean age, which we have tried to bring to life, we can say that human beings were then still living with their gods. They believed not only in themselves and the three realms of nature but also in the higher realms of the spiritual worlds, for in Atlantean times they had been their witness. The difference between night-time and daytime consciousness was not great. They were still in balance, and one would have been a fool to deny something which could actually be seen around one, for they saw the gods. Religion in the present-day sense was not yet possible then, as there was no need for it. To the Atlanteans the content of today's religion was simply a fact. Just as you do not need a religion to believe in roses, lilies, rocks and trees, so the Atlanteans did not need a religion to believe in gods, for the gods were real to them, fact.

However, these facts were progressively disappearing. The facts of the spiritual worlds were coming to be more and more of a memory, partly preserved in things traditionally told of the olden days, things that the forefathers had seen, and partly preserved in legends and myths and in things that clairvoyant individuals with a special gift were still seeing themselves. Above all, however, these facts of the spiritual worlds were preserved by the priests in the mysteries. The Hermes priests in Egypt, the priests of Zarathustra in Persia, the Chaldean sages, the Indian successors of the Holy Rishis were preserving nothing but the art to initiate human beings and make them witness again of things which earlier generations had seen quite naturally in the world around them. And depending on the nature of a nation, with their special abilities and sentience, depending on the climate where they lived, the things preserved in the mysteries came to be the religion of peoples, one religion in one place, and another in another. But the original wisdom was behind all these religions as the great oneness of the all. This original wisdom was the same, uniform, irrespective of whether Pythagoras cultivated it in his school or the disciples of Hermes in Egypt, the Chaldean sages in Asia Minor, Zarathustra in Persia or the Brahmans in India taught it— the same original wisdom everywhere, but graded according to the needs and the particular circumstances in the religions of nations as we know them in different regions. There we see religious culture coming into being.

So what is this religious culture? Religious culture is the way I have just described of mediating the spiritual worlds for human beings who no longer have their own instruments for perceiving the spiritual world. Religion came to be the message from the spiritual world for all those for whom the spiritual world could no longer be a fact. Spiritual life thus became a culture in religious form around the globe. It lived in this way in the different periods of civilization, from ancient Indian, ancient Persian, Egypto-Chaldean, Graeco-Latin to our own times.

Human beings have entered fully into the physical body so that they might know and experience the outside world with their physical senses, and take the experiences gained out there into their spirituality in preparation for further stages of evolution. But now, since we have entered wholly into the physical body and have passed the midpoint in our post-Atlantean civilizations, we are in a very special situation. Not everyone but many people are already in this situation. All evolution within humanity proceeds in a strange way. Up to a point it will progress, and then it will go in the opposite direction. When evolution has gone down to a certain point, it will rise again and arrive at the same stages again, but in a higher form, so that humanity does today face a strange future, a future—and everyone who knows of this profoundly significant fact in human evolution—where the ether body will gradually come looser again, having been immersed in the physical body where it perceived everything that can be perceived in the physical world today in clear, sharp outlines and forms. The ether body has to come looser again, has to come away again, so that human beings may rise to spirituality and be able to perceive things in the spiritual world. Humanity has actually reached the point again today where the ether bodies of a great many people are loosening again.

Now we come to something very strange. We are literally touching on the secret of our civilization in considering this fact. We have to think of the ether body gone down deep into the physical body and now having to go back again. It has to take everything it was able to perceive with the physical senses back with it. But because the ether body is coming loose again, everything that was physical reality before will gradually have to grow spiritual again. Human beings have to take with them into the future the awareness, the certainty, that the spiritual is also present in the physical. For what would otherwise happen to them? The ether body would leave the physical body but they would only keep their belief in the physical world, not being aware that the spiritual has a reality in the physical which departs with the ether body, being the fruit of experiences gained in the physical body. It might then happen that those human beings cannot connect with this departure of the ether body.

Let us accurately and firmly stick to the point where the human ether body is fully inside the physical body and beginning to go out again. Let us assume that the individual lets his ether body go when this has lost its belief in, his awareness of, a spiritual world for as long as it lived in the physical body, that it has thus cut off its connection with the spiritual world when in the physical body. Let us assume it has gone down so well and firmly into the physical body that it has not been able to retain anything but the belief that the physical body is the only reality. And when the ether body goes outside in the time that follows, inevitably so, the individual is unable in this state to hold on to the fact that awareness of a spiritual world exists. He will then not perceive this spiritual world. This is something humanity may have to face in the near future, that they will not recognize the spiritual world which they should experience with the loosening of the ether body, taking it to be imagination, fantasy or illusion. And the people who have descended into the physical body in the craftiest way—well, to be polite let us say in the most subtle way—and become materialistic scholars, that is, have acquired the most rigid concepts of matter, these people are most in danger of having no idea as the ether body loosens that there is a spiritual world. They then consider everything they experience of a spiritual world to be illusion, fantasy, daydreams.

Let me give you just one example. A book on psychology[48] has recently been published by a German professor. The aim is to show that the soul is really completely identical with the brain, merely showing its functions from another side—now from the outside, now from the inside. The inner aspect, he writes, is feeling, the forming of ideas and will, and the outer aspect is the brain's anatomy and physiology. You will find a strange statement in this book; it says that if there were an independent soul one would surely have to assume that this independent soul must increase or reduce its powers with all the impressions a person receives. But, he continues, there is the law of energies which says that all energies we take in from outside must also go out again, pointing out that all the heat energy we take in is also given off again. As this was therefore subject to the general law of energy, and one can see that anything going in also comes out again, one must conclude, it says, that there is no independent soul in there that intervenes but that the processes are wholly material which come into play in there and then flow out again.

There is no intention to voice any kind of negative criticism of such a book and of the things of this kind taught in the lecture halls of our official science, for people cannot help thinking up such theories; they are subject to the most dreadful suggestions. In reality it is just as intelligent to investigate how much heat enters into human beings and comes out again, concluding from this that they have no soul, as it would be if someone took up a position in front of a bank's offices to investigate how much money goes in and comes out again, and then wanted to conclude, once all the energies, that is, moneys, had come out again, that there are no bank staff in there. You find this kind of thinking almost anywhere today in everything considered to be the official psychology. And it is tremendously suggestive in its effect on people today. It is the age when the very people who want to be the leaders of humanity and believe they are working with a science free from bias are the ones who have entered most fully into the physical body. As the ether body was entering into the physical body they completely lost all awareness that there is a spiritual world, and it has to be said that these scientists will more than anyone suffer the fate which I must now describe to you. For what can the future destiny of these people be?

If people are to live their lives in the right way in future, when the ether body is looser again, they must have an awareness of what presents to this ether body and what then corresponds to humanity. And to have an awareness of the insight into the spiritual world which presents itself it will be necessary that human beings preserve that insight beyond the point where they are wholly immersed in the physical and sensual. The link between religious life and life in insight must never be lost. Humanity initially lived among the gods; they will rise again to a life with the gods. But they will need to recognize them. They will really have to know that the gods are real. When the ether body is loosened again human beings will no longer be able to remember the earlier times. If someone has lost all awareness of the spiritual world in the middle periods, if he has solely and only come to believe that life in the physical body and all one can perceive when in the physical body are the only reality, he will hang in the air in all future times. He won't know his way about in the spiritual worlds, having lost the ground under his feet. He will then be in danger of 'spiritual death', as it is called; for everything around him is then unreal, illusion, and he will have no awareness of its reality. He will not believe in it and he will die off. That is the real death in the spiritual world, something that threatens if people are unable to bring awareness of the spiritual world with them as they enter the spiritual worlds.

How will the Christ idea live in human beings in future? In future times people will look back on our time, when human beings lived in physical bodies, just as people of the post-Atlantean age now look back on Atlantean times when human beings were still living with the gods. They will feel that they have gained victory over everything experienced in the physical body. When they then rise again to the spiritual plane they will point down to the physical as something that has been overcome. This is what we should feel in a great prophetic act as we look to the miracle of Easter.

Future humanity has two possibilities before it. One is that they remember the time when they had their experiences in the physical body, and say to themselves: 'We are now in the world of illusions; life in the physical body was the reality.' The people look at the physical left behind as if it were a grave, and in the grave they see a corpse; yet that corpse, physical as it is, is to them true reality. That is one possibility. The other possibility is that human beings also look back on experiences they had in the physical world as a grave, but in such a way that they will say with deep feeling to those who believe the physical to be the only true and real thing: 'He is not here, for he is risen, as he said.'[49] The empty tomb and the risen Christ—that is the mystery of prophesy; and we thus have the mystery of prophesy in the Easter mystery.

The great synthesis[50] of the Christmas mystery as a recapitulation of the ancient mysteries and the Easter mystery as the mystery of the future, the mystery of the risen Christ, that is what the Christ wanted to show to humanity. That is the mystery of the Easter festival. The future of Christianity will be such that the Christian idea is not just something like hearing about the spiritual worlds, not just something like religion, but that the Christian idea will be something professed, an impulse in life. It will be something people profess because they will see in the risen Christ what their own lives will be in all future times, a deed of life, because the Christ is not only something they look up to, someone who may perhaps offer comfort and solace, but is the great example they will follow in overcoming death. To be active, to live, in the spirit of Christianity, seeing not only the comforter in the Christ but the one who goes before us and is in the deepest sense connected with our essential nature at its deepest, whose life we imitate—that is the Christ idea for the future, which may be present in all knowledge gained, all art, all life. And if we want to recall everything to be found in the Easter idea, we shall find in it a symbol for the Christianity of true deed and true life.

When people will for a long time have had no need of religious messages to tell them of the gods of ancient times because they will be living among the gods again, the Christ will be the one to make them strong and robust in finding the right standpoint in the midst of the gods. There will then be no more need for religion in order to believe in gods; human beings will see gods again as in earlier times when they had no need for this because they were living among gods. Then they had no need to believe, and they will have no need to believe in the gods for they'll see them again when they go to be among these gods, strengthened and made robust with all that Christianity has been able to give. They will then be spiritual themselves among the spirits and able to do their work among those spirits. In the not too distant future human beings will see again how the physical world loses its significance for them and physical things fade away, as it were. The reality of that world will fade, even if human beings will still be on Earth for a long time. But when physical things are going to lose their significance and importance and fade away, human beings will either see the importance of the physical vanishing and be unable to believe in the spirituality, which will then rise up before them, or they will be able to believe and preserve an awareness of this for the spirituality of the future—and in that case they will not know spiritual death.

To come face to face with a reality that one does not perceive to be such is to be shattered in the spirit. Human beings would come to live in spiritual disruption when the spiritual worlds appeared before them as the ether body loosened and would not be able to recognize them as such. Today some people could already be aware of spiritual worlds but they are not, and those worlds will then strike back—as is evident in those people's nervous state, neurasthenia, pathological fear of disease. These are exactly the repercussions of non-awareness of the spiritual world. If you feel this you will also feel the need for a spiritual movement that grows beyond mere religion and preserves belief in the human being, the whole human being, that is, including the spiritual human being, and offers full insight into the spiritual human being. To recognize the Christ is also to recognize the spiritual human being.

To live into the future of humanity with the Christ idea is to overcome even Christianity as a religion and take Christianity forward to perception of the widest horizons. Christianity will enter wholly into art, broadening it and giving it life; it will provide powers of artistic creation to the richest degree. Richard Wagner's *Parsifal* is a preparation for this. Christianity is going to enter wholly into all life and activity on Earth, and when religions will have long since ceased to be necessary for humanity, humanity will be strong and robust under the influence of the Christian impulses which in the past had to be given to humanity when it was in the middle of the fourth period of civilization. In Graeco-Latin civilization the Christ came to be among human beings. Humanity had to go deep down into the depths of material life, and it must be taken upwards again to recognition of the spirit. This impulse was given with the coming of the Christ.

Sentience of this should live in our souls in the days when we have the Easter mysteries around us in symbolic form, during the Easter season. For the Easter mystery is not merely a mystery of remembrance but also a mystery of the future, of prophesy for human beings who will gradually free themselves more and more from the bonds, traps and snares of a life that is solely physical and sensual.

LECTURE 8

TODAY I want to talk to you about something which is a bit outside our subject matter so far, though it also adds to it, for some of the things said in past lectures will be repeated, and in a sense can be seen in a better light.

We know that human beings, the way they are now, have gone through a long process of evolution, having evolved through different planetary stages to the level they have now reached. We also know that in future they will progress to yet higher levels of evolution. We have already been considering the thought that in the past, when man was still in a state of dim conscious awareness on old Saturn, spirits also existed that were at the level human beings have reached today; and spirits then also existed that were far above the level humanity has reached today. We know that today, too, some spirits have reached a level of evolution which humanity will only reach in future. We may therefore look up to a hierarchy—that is the term used in occultism—of spirits higher than human beings, always one level above that of man. The spirits which are immediately above man we call 'angel' or *Angelos* in esoteric Christian terms. Angels are thus spirits for us that had reached human conscious awareness at the Moon level, the planetary precursor of our Earth, and are today one level above man. Human beings themselves will have the level of conscious awareness at the Jupiter level of existence which today belongs to the spirits we call angels or *Angeloi*. So this is the first level of spirits above man. We do know the levels that follow from other contexts. We know that moving up from the angels we have the 'archangels or *Archangeloi*. Then comes the order of 'Elemental Powers' which we also call 'Archai', next the 'Powers' or 'Authorities', 'Exusiai'; then the 'Virtues', 'Dynamis'; above them the 'Dominions' or 'Kyriotetes'; then the 'Thrones', the 'Cherubim' and the 'Seraphim'. It is only beyond and above the Seraphim that we speak of the actual 'Godhead' in Christian terms. Genuine occultists, true spiritual scientists or esoteric Christians do not share the common view that human beings might look up directly to the highest Godhead; we have the whole sequence of spirits which in Christian terms we call 'angels', 'archangels' and so on in between. In a sense we have to say it is a refusal to make the proper mental effort when people say today: 'Really, why should there be this whole succession of spirits? Human beings can enter into a direct relationship with the Godhead.' Theosophists and occultists cannot go along with this; for the spirits are absolutely real, and today we want to say a few things about the mission, the work, of these spirits for world evolution, and of their special characteristics and qualities.

First of all let us try and get an idea of the nature of the angels. It will be easiest to get an idea of the conscious awareness of these spirits by remembering that external physical human awareness today covers four natural worlds which we are able to perceive—mineral, vegetable, animal and the human world itself. We may thus define human conscious awareness as encompassing four worlds perceptible to the senses. Everything human beings perceive through the senses, whatever it may be, belongs to one of these four worlds. If we now ask ourselves what kind of conscious awareness the angelic spirits have, the answer is that in a sense it is a higher form of conscious awareness, and it is characterized as a higher form in that it does not go down as far as the mineral world. Angelic awareness does not extend down to the nature of the stones, of minerals. Instead it covers plants, animals, human beings and the angels' own world, which plays the same role for them as the human world does for us. We may say, therefore, that these angels also have awareness of four worlds—the plant world, the animal world, the human world and the angelic world.

It is a characteristic of angelic spirits that they do not have a physical body and therefore also none of the organs of the physical body—no eyes, ears, and so on. They therefore do not perceive the physical world. Their lowest part is their etheric body. This means a certain relationship to plants. They are able to go down as far as the plants in their conscious awareness. They are able to perceive plants. But they perceive a void where we see a mineral, just as we have described it[51] for human beings during the Devachan state, when human beings also perceive a void where a mineral takes up space here on the physical plane. The angels thus perceive a void everywhere where we have the physical world. On the other hand their conscious awareness extends up to a level that human conscious awareness cannot yet reach.

We know, however, that even today people relate in certain ways, some being leaders and others being led. I am specifically referring to children and the adults who educate them. Children need to be led until they are as mature as the adults who bring them up. At the present stage of evolution human beings are growing into their Jupiter state of awareness. This will be the same as the angels have today. Angelic awareness being as it is, the angels are the guides, the leaders, of humanity, preparing human beings, and there is a close connection between the faculties gradually developing in human beings and the task and mission of the angelic spirits. What is developing in human beings for the rest of their earthly existence? We have spoken of this on a number of occasions. We said that human beings have a physical body, an ether body, an astral body and an I, and that they are currently in the process of transforming their astral body so that it will gradually come to be wholly Spirit Self. Human beings are also working on their other bodies, but the essence of existence on Earth is to develop the Spirit Self completely. The angels have developed their Spirit Self; it was already developed when existence on Earth began. In the hierarchy of evolution the angels are therefore the spirits that guide the work human beings must do to transform the astral body into Spirit Self.

We now ask ourselves: 'How do they do that?' We remember we said that when someone dies he first has the 'long tableau of memories' of the life that has just passed away. This stays for two or three days; it is slightly different for different people. As a rule it continues for as long as the individual could manage without sleep in that life. People vary greatly in this. Some are used to sleep always after twelve hours, when their eyes will close; others can stay awake for four or five days, and the memory tableau will last that long. The tableau persists for as long as the individual was able to manage without sleep. Then the ether body dissolves, only an extract remaining as the fruit of the past life. This is taken along for all the time that follows and is made part of the individual's essential nature, and he will be able to develop his physical body on the basis of it in his next incarnation. He will be able to make his next body more perfect because he will be able to use the fruits of his past life. The individual thus has this essence of life and will create his next body from it in the new life.

We also know something else. We know that human beings not only create this body of theirs but that they are not inactive in the Devachan. It is wrong to think that human beings have to concern themselves only with themselves. The world is not based on such egotism. It is designed in such a way that human beings have to share in the work on the Earth on every occasion. In the Devachan they shared in the work of transforming the Earth's surface. We ourselves know that the soil on which we stand here today, for instance, looked very different just a few centuries ago. At the time when the Christ Jesus was on Earth, there were vast woodlands here; completely different plants and animals lived here. And so the face of the Earth is changing all the time. On the physical plane, human beings are busy building cities, and so on, using the forces effective in the physical world. From the Devachan they work with the powers that change the physiognomy of the Earth, including the plant and animal worlds. The result is that in a new incarnation they find a soil which presents a very different picture, so that life always offers something new. It is not for nothing that we are born into a new incarnation, but so that we gain new experiences. Human beings contribute to the reshaping of the Earth, but cannot do so without guidance. They cannot determine the incarnations that follow, for in that case they would not have to experience first what is going to happen in future. And the guiding spirits that instruct human beings to share in the work of transforming the Earth using the powers of the Devachan, establishing harmony between individual human beings and the Earth's evolution so that it will be in accord with those individual natures, these spirits are the angels. They cannot work on the stones, on the solid

Earth's crust; for their awareness does not extend to the stones. But it does extend to the plant world on Earth. There they can work, not creatively but to transform.

And that is indeed how it is. Such an angelic spirit is working with every human individual, guiding and directing them in the work of developing the Spirit Self in the astral body until it is fully developed. That is why in some Christian teaching one speaks of guardian angels. This is wholly in accord with the reality and its laws. They are the spirits that establish harmony between the individual human being and the course of Earth evolution until at the end of that evolution human beings will themselves have come far enough to take over from their angels, for by then they will have the conscious awareness which the angels now have.

You will now find it easy to understand that the conscious awareness of archangels does not extend as far as the plant world but only to the animal world. Plants do not exist for them, as it were. They are too inferior a world, insignificant. In the animal world they still have points to which they can relate; they do perceive the animal world. They have no ether body; their lowest principle is the astral body. Animals also have an astral body, and so the archangels do definitely influence the astral bodies of animals. They also perceive the human world, the world of the angels and their own world. The archangel world is the one they say 'I' to, just as the human I is there for human beings. These spirits also have an important mission and you will understand that with their conscious awareness two levels higher than that of human beings their mission can be at a very high level. The conscious awareness of archangels is at such a high level that they have fully developed the Buddhi, the Life Spirit, and are thus able to direct and lead in Earth evolution from an insight that corresponds to the Life Spirit or Buddhi. This is evident in that these archangels are in the first place the directors and leaders of whole nations. The spirit of a nation, the common spirit of nations, is in real terms one of the archangels. You will now also find it understandable that the nations which still had an awareness of such a spiritual relationship did not look up directly to the highest spirit of all but rather to the nearest spirits that were their leaders and directors.

Take the ancient Hebrew nation. They venerated Yahweh or Jehovah as their highest god. But for them this Yahweh was of the order of 'Authorities'. It was a sublime spirit in which they recognized their god. But they would say: 'The one who directs and leads us at the behest of and as the actual arch-messenger of Jehovah is 'Michael', one of the archangels—his name means 'he who stands before God'. In ancient Hebrew he was also called 'the face of God' or 'who is like God', because someone belonging to the Old Covenant, when looking up to God, felt that Michael stood before God and reflected his essential nature, just as the human face reflects the essential nature of a person. This is why he was called 'the face of God'.

When we speak of the spirit of a nation we are in occult terms not speaking of an incomprehensible conceptual element. Speaking of the spirit of a nation in the present materialistic age, people don't really mean anything by this; they are referring to an abstract, superficial sum of a nation's characteristics. In reality there is a spiritual representative, known as an archangel, who directs and leads the nation as a whole. This spirit extends down to the animal world. The nations also used to be sentient of this. After all, it is easy to be sentient of it out of a nation's instincts. One nation lives in one place, another in another. Depending on the different regions where they lived they had to avail themselves of one kind of animal or another, and this, the nations felt instinctively, had been allotted to them by the spirit of their nation. Its influence extended as far as the animal world, so that the ancient Egyptians, who were certainly sentient of this, would say: 'When we look at the development of plants, this is where angels are active; when we consider animals, they are allotted to us by the spirit that guides the whole nation.' They thus saw the power which guided the animals to them as a sacred power, and the way they related to the animals reflected this awareness. They would not speak of archangels; but their sentience was like this. That was the actual sentience which the Egyptians connected with the animal world; and behind this is the fact that if there was awareness of the whole of this spiritual connection these spirits would be represented not by images of earthly animals, but by images of animals such as the sphinx, winged animals, and so on. You can see these in the pictures produced by the different nations. It was as if the guiding archangels shone in. You can therefore see the esoteric expression of the guiding archangels presented in the different groups of animals. Many of the ancient Egyptian images of their gods were based on this idea that the archangel, the spirit guiding the nation, extended down as far as the animals. This is essentially the mission of the archangels, though they have another one as well.

Today Uriel, Gabriel, Raphael and Michael are legendary names still known to people. You only have to look up the Book of Enoch[52] to find the names of other archangels as well. One of them was Phanuel;[53] an important archangel who had the mission not only of guiding a particular nation but also something else. We know that initiation consists in the individual endeavouring to rise to higher and higher levels of conscious awareness, rising to these even now, during life on Earth. The people in the initiation centres knew full well that this also needs powers to guide and direct it. They therefore put the initiands under the protection of the archangel called Phanuel. He was the protector who was called upon by those seeking initiation.

Other spirits at this level have other tasks. The whole of world evolution has behind it a sum of powers led by certain spirits. There is an archangel called Sariel (or Saraqael) in earlier times,[54] whose mission it is to eradicate particularly widespread vices in a city or a whole region and transform them into virtues. If you know about this you can see how the principle given the general, abstract name 'providence' is truly guided. Once you make the effort to get to know the spiritual worlds, do not be content with general abstractions but go into details of this kind. For the most sublime spirits of which human beings may still have some idea guide the course of world evolution through intermediaries like those we've just got to know. This is what we may call the different tasks and missions of the archangels.

We now come to the order of the Archai. They are yet higher spirits, the conscious awareness of which does not reach down to the animals. When the initiate ascends to deal with the Archai he does not communicate the forms and figures of the animals on Earth to them from his human conscious awareness. For their conscious awareness only goes down as far as the human world. They also know the realm of the angels, that of the archangels, and their own realm. They say 'I' to themselves, and human beings are the lowest entities they perceive.

Human beings are to the Archai as stones, the mineral world, are to human beings—the lowest realm. This tells us that they guide the course of humanity from a very high level. Human beings sense it now and then that there is such a thing as a 'spirit of the age' who is different for the different time periods. We have spoken of the 'spirit of the ages' here on a number of occasions, saying, for instance, that in the first post-Atlantean civilization, among the ancient Indians, the spirit of the age consisted in people being aware that they were longing to be back again in the ancient Atlantean times when they dimly perceived higher realms around them. This then developed into the yoga system which they hoped would take them to the higher worlds again. In that ancient state of consciousness people did not think much of the real world around them, of the physical plane. This was maya, illusion, to them. The ancient Indian civilization was very little interested in the physical plane. This may seem strange to you, but it is true. If the ancient Indian civilization had persisted there would never have been railways, telephones and such things which now exist on the physical plane. It would not have seemed at all important to concern oneself a great deal with the laws of the physical world and so populate the physical world with all the things we see as the achievements of modern civilization.

Then came the spirit of the Persian age. With it, human beings got to know matter as an element which resisted, which they had to work on. They joined forces with Ormuzd, a good spirit, against Ahriman, the spirit of matter. But the Persians did take an interest in the physical plane. There followed the spirit of the age which on the one hand came into its own in the Babylonian, Assyrian and Chaldean and on the other in the Egyptian civilization. Human science was established. Geometry was used to make the Earth suitable for humanity. People sought to learn about the movements of the stars in astronomy, arranging events on Earth according to those movements. In ancient Egypt they very much followed the stars in their social life. People took their guidance from the secrets they discovered of the stars. Where the ancient Indian sought to find his way to the gods by turning all his attention away from the real world around him, the Egyptian studied the laws that pertain to the real world around him in order to see how the will and the spirit of the gods was reflected in the laws of the natural world. That was yet another age. So there is a particular spirit for each age, and evolution on Earth comes about in that the spirit of one age takes the place of another. That is the case in every instance. Human beings rise to the views of their age without knowing that behind the whole course of time are the spirits of the ages. People are not aware that here on Earth they are but the instruments, as it were, to bring the spirits of the ages, which are behind them, to expression. Consider Giordano Bruno.[55] If he had been born in the eighth century he would not have been the person he was in the age when the spirit ruled to whom he then gave expression. He was the instrument of the spirit of his age, and that is also how it has been with the other spirits. If Giordano Bruno had been born in the eighth century, the spirit of his age could not have come to expression the way it did through Giordano Bruno. We see from this how human beings are the instruments of the spirits of their ages, the guiding spirits of great time spans and also of the 'spirits of views and opinions' for shorter time periods. Those are the Archai. They reach down as far as humanity. They are not guiding anything that brings humanity together with other natural worlds; for their conscious awareness does not extend as far as the animal world. The orders according to which human beings organize their lives, found states, sciences, till the soil—everything that comes from human beings—this progress of civilization from beginning to end is under the guidance of the Archai. They guide humanity in so far as human beings are involved with other human beings.

I have also been able on an number of occasions[56] to draw your attention to the way in which certain spirits from the hierarchies lag behind, not having ascended as far as the others, having failed to reach the required level, as it were, in world evolution. You'll easily under-stand also that there are spirits that could and should have reached the order of Exusiai during Moon evolution but only got as far as being Archai. These are different Archai from those that rose to being Archai in the regular process of evolution. So there are Archai that are really masked Exusiai on Earth. We are now getting to know various things from a different angle, having learned about them already from another angle. Behind the Archai others are hiding which could actually be Archai already; and among the Archai that are really not rightfully there is the spirit—though only for those who see something like this from the spiritual-scientific point of view—which we rightly call 'Satan'. Satan is the wrongful prince of this world, the rightful one being one of the Exusiai, Yahweh or Jehovah. The wrongful one belongs to the order of Archai. He expresses himself by throwing the spirit of the age into confusion all the time for humanity, always going against the spirit of the age. That is the true nature of the spirit which is also called the 'spirit of darkness' or the wrongful prince of this our Earth, wanting to guide and direct humanity. You will now understand that the coming of the Christ had profound meaning. His mission was to cast light on all evolution that followed, and he had to fight that wrongful prince of this world. Behind this lies the most profound wisdom, put into words in this wonderful part of the gospel.[57]

You hear inferior things about Satan today not only from people whose thinking is materialistic but also from others who still have certain old notions lurking in their minds which, however, are mistaken notions. People have been talking about Satan in a rather derisive way. Even those who like to give recognition to other spirits—Satan they like to deny, saying that he does not exist. This is because even in medieval times people had the most peculiar views about Satan, saying: 'He actually is one of the Exusiai who has lagged behind; if he is a spirit from the ranks of the Exusiai he is lagging behind.' Where are the Exusiai spirits? They are reflected in whatever spirit is manifest in the world. Satan was called a spirit of darkness, but people would say that darkness was merely a negation of light. Light, they would say, is real, darkness is not. This was also meant in spiritual terms. Spirits manifesting in the light were thus said to be real; but Satan, manifesting in darkness, was not considered real. That is about as intelligent as saying that coldness is merely a lack of warmth; it is not anything real in itself. If we reduce warmth more and more, it will get colder and colder, but however much warmth we take away, the coldness is not real they'd say; let us not think of winter, therefore. But although coldness is a negation of warmth, we do feel it when there is no heating. Satan thus is perfectly real, even if he is but a negation of the light.

We have now come to very elevated spirits, the Exusiai. One of them is the spirit which in other contexts we knew as Yahweh or Jehovah,[58] and his companions as the Elohim. The spirits of light belong to the order of Exusiai. We know that Yahweh had six companions that separated off the Sun for themselves. Yahweh himself went with the Moon which reflects the light of the Sun on to the Earth; but he is a companion of the other Elohim. If you now attempt to construe the conscious awareness of these Exusiai in analogy to the above, you will say to yourself that these spirits are no longer concerned with individual human beings. The individual is guided by the spirits we have called angels, archangels, Archai, up to the level we called 'spirits of the age'. The whole scene in which humanity is embedded, the guidance and direction of the planet and all that happens on it, is now in the care of the Exusiai. For, as we said, the whole of humanity's present-day evolution could not have happened if there had not been the Sun powers rushing forward and on the other hand the Moon powers slowing them down. The Exusiai no longer have anything to do with individual human beings but only with groups of people. They guide the outer powers and spirits that configure the planet, powers and spirits human beings need if they are to go through their evolution on this planet. Ultimately we look up to a sublime spirit which goes beyond anything we have just been considering, and that is the Christ spirit which brings something to the Earth that has nothing to do with individual human beings but with the guidance of the whole of humanity. And human beings must find their way to the Christ themselves, for only the Exusiai still force them to accept guidance. They must come to the Christ of their own free will.

We have now got an idea of the lowest levels of the hierarchies above human beings, of angels, archangels and a little also of the Archai and Exusiai. To the Christ, an even more sublime spirit, we can only look up with some slight idea.

We can make an opportunity on some other occasion to consider what may be said of the Thrones, and so on. Today I wanted to tell you something of the whole spiritual structure of which we are part, concentrating on angels, archangels, Archai and Exusiai.

LECTURE 9

BERLIN, 13 MAY 1908

THE subject of this lecture is one which it is important to consider from the viewpoint of life in the spirit. We will be able to speak of how someone professing to take the spiritual-scientific point of view can also speak of other spiritual approaches, how he can relate to developments in present-day humanity and to the issues of today altogether. I intend to speak to you in broad outline about the development of religious ideas in post-Atlantean civilization up to the present day.

In doing so we will remember things mentioned on previous occasions—that the idea of religion is really something that has meaning only in post-Atlantean times. There could be no such thing as religion, as we call it, before the great Atlantean flood, for religion presupposes that human beings do not have a direct perception or view of supersensible worlds, or at least that the major part of humanity does not have such perceptions. Religion means humanity being connected with the supersensible at a time when the supersensible is not perceptible to the majority of human beings but can only be conveyed to them in various ways, through prophets, seers, sages, mysteries and so on, as has been the case for the last millennia. Before the great flood on Atlantis, when our forebears mostly lived in the region of old Atlantis, all human beings still had more or less direct experience, perceptions, of the supersensible. At a time when human beings were themselves living in the spiritual world, where they learned things at any time just as present-day humanity does in the physical world, there was no need for religion. Towards the end of Atlantis supersensible experiences were extinguished for by far the greatest majority. The clear perception through the senses which we have today took their place. What remains of the ancient Atlantean period?

If we go back to prehistoric times and study the legends and myths, letting the ancient Germanic teaching about the gods come alive in us, we find that details of the supersensible worlds were in the form of images. They were not images or personifications people had thought up, fantasies, as the theorists say, but genuine memories of that earlier time when human beings still knew what they had learned. The legends of Wotan, Thor and so on are such memories. And what has essentially remained for humanity in post-Atlantean times is a kind of memory religion in the truest sense of the word. This was most advanced among the peoples living in southern Asia, the Indian peoples; it made itself felt in a different form in Europe. In India the memory of the time when humanity, every individual, still perceived things in the spiritual world makes itself known as a longing for that world. Reality was felt to be illusion, maya, and people yearned to be back in those earlier times. The element which in individual people produced the ability to penetrate into the supersensible worlds was called yoga. Not all peoples had sages among them who were able to achieve yoga. Other peoples had to be content with memories, especially the peoples of the north. Their initiates did also penetrate into the spiritual worlds, and did also have direct experiences in the divine world, but Nordic nature made it difficult for them to penetrate in greater numbers. Norse mythology developed as a result.

There is one thing, however, which we'll find people have in common, have retained in the post-Atlantean age, and that is an echo of the much more developed power of memory which existed in Atlantean times. Memory then developed in a very different way from today. People would remember further up, to the lives of distant forebears. They knew of things such a forebear had gone through centuries before, knew it the way an old man today remembers his young days. Memories like these gave rise to something we may call the ancestral religion, ancestor worship. Ancestor worship, veneration of the ancestors, was indeed the first religion. The memory had in a sense stayed alive. This liveliness of memory was so great that some individuals who were unable to attain to yoga did achieve a spiritual condition where the common ancestor of a nation would appear to them in a dream or a mental state.

That common ancestor of an ancient tribe was no mere myth or legend; it was something that appeared to human beings from time to time, appearing in their mental state of awareness, something that would accompany a nation. The different peoples migrating through Europe had many different experiences. But one experience would always be very much alive to them and they would tell others who had trust in them about it and believed them—it was the appearance of the ancestor who counselled them from the realm of the spirit, who was connected with them. He would come at particularly important moments, would be there in cases of doubt. Ancestor worship was something that was certainly alive to people, thanks to the physical qualities of the ancestors.

This ancestor worship continued to develop into a kind of religious system. This had been worked out by certain initiates but also proved acceptable for many non-initiates. Religious systems of this kind appeared in various regions, for instance in the Brahmanism of ancient India. We find the last echoes of them in Vedanta philosophy, but earlier philosophical systems also show last echoes of this ancient pantheism. It was a kind of esoteric pantheism in ancient Brahmanism. It also showed itself in the actual system of the Egyptians, and among the Hebrews. In real terms we can imagine that a more comprehensive idea arose of the divine spirit which flowed and streamed through everything. The ancestor had merged into the spiritual foundations of existence, had become a kind of original spiritual power.

In anthropomorphism, as we may call it, we have a special development of esoteric pantheism. Here the different gods were envisaged in images that were like human beings. The Greek system of religion came into this category, for example. But you are taking quite the wrong view if you think that for the educated Greek there was no uniform spiritual world behind his gods. When we speak of angels, archangels and so on, or of the different spiritual entities altogether that are above man, as we have done in looking at cosmic evolution, what we are saying is very similar to what was said at that time, when people spoke of Zeus, Athena and so on compared to the one and only cosmic spirit. One and the same idea of the world was behind this system. Pantheism is the spiritual ground of things; the gods were then given human form.

If we ask ourselves why it is that esoteric pantheism, which was still much more abstract, changed into the world of the many Greek gods, we have to see in it a profound basic need of humanity altogether, a profound principle in human evolution. Looking at the transition from Egyptian to Greek civilization we see this principle coming into its own most beautifully. All thinking about Greek times has something tremendous, something symbolic, to it. The pyramids of Egypt and the sphinxes are magnificent, tremendous creations of the human spirit that point in a slightly abstract form to a spiritual ground and origin which they did not yet dare to develop. But the Greek spirit showed the ability to impress the spiritual into the images created. This shows a tremendous step forward which may be seen everywhere. It is expressed in its purest form when you follow the transition from Eastern to Greek architecture, seeing the architectural concept in its pure form. In the whole of human evolution, that thought emerges most clearly in Greek architecture. Nowhere else do we see that thought flow so utterly and completely into physical form. We see how everything is placed in the world according to the great cosmic laws.

Perhaps there was just one other time in human evolution when architectural thoughts were created and that was the idea of Gothic architecture. Comparing the Gothic idea with the Greek idea in architecture, we have to say: In Gothic architecture we are not really dealing with pure architecture but with just a suggestion of a mystic element entering strongly into feelings. Gothic architecture did not develop the thought fully. A Greek temple on the other hand is the dwelling place of the god and must be wholly seen as such. For you need to think of the god being creative in space, his powers flooding the space, creating a body for himself, as it were, weaving a garment for himself, and that is the Greek temple. When we see it before us we know that it is the dwelling place of a god. A Gothic cathedral is not; it is a house of prayer. We cannot think it without the visitor in it for whom it has been built, the atmosphere created. Think of the Greek temple put there all by itself, life given to it only by the god; that is the whole of it. It is not to be taken or meant symbolically. The devout believer is part of the Gothic temple. And if you know that space is not empty but has powers moving in it, if you know that powers crystallize in a space and if you sense these powers, you will feel that in the Greek temple something crystallized out from the dynamics of the world. If you have a feeling for this which is so powerful that you are able to perceive these spirits, you will know that powers rush through the space. The Greeks knew of the life in a space. You'll find it easiest to grasp how the thinking, the feeling and the will intent grew concrete if you compare Romanesque with Greek architecture. Then we see how the Romanesque column, for example, is lifted out of its spatial function as a support. Romanesque architecture is also great, but much of it is decorative, including those very columns for which there is no deeper motivation. What is lacking is the feeling for this, a feeling for space. The column is there but it does not serve a purpose. All this is connected with the stages in the evolution of the human mind and spirit. That anthropomorphism was necessary to prepare humanity for understanding the man of god, the god dwelling in the human being himself. That, however, is the Christianity which occultists also call theomorphism.

In Christianity the different figures of the gods come together in the one, living form of Christ Jesus. This needed a great, tremendous deepening of humanity, a deepening that made humanity able not only to think the living form of space we see in Greek sculpture, but to rise to the thought of seeing inwardness in outward form, to the belief that the eternal truly lived on Earth as a historic figure in space and time. That is the essence of Christianity. This idea marked the greatest step forward for humanity on Earth.

We only have to compare—and we are allowed to make this comparison—the Greek temple, a dwelling place of the god, and the element that would later be the Christian church, as it showed itself in its purest form in Gothic architecture, and we shall see that there actually had to be a step back in outer form if one wanted to represent the eternal in time and space. Something achieved in a later art by bringing the inner to expression in the outer was absolutely under the impress of the Christian stream. Basically we have to say that we can see that architecture was at its most beautiful where one was still able to cleave with all one's soul to the external forces that flooded the space.

So we see how religious thought grew more and more profound in post-Atlantean times, how people were looking for pointers to the supersensible. It will not be difficult to see pointers in everything said here to the longing which people had to penetrate into the outer form, somehow to have the supersensible held fast in the outer form. That was the goal with the earliest ground and origin of art. We have come to our own time, as it were, with Christianity. From what has been said about the evolution of the post-Atlantean age in connection with various other things you will see that humanity's development was more and more towards inwardness, deepening. There was also growing awareness in the different races of inwardness, deepening, in the outer aspect.

We would like to say that in the images of the Greek gods we see how something that lives inwardly in human beings was pouring out into the outside world. In Christianity the most important impulse in this direction is given. We see the element which to this day we call 'science' arise with Christianity. For the element to which we give this name today, grasping the thoughts that are the ground and origin of existence, only began in Chaldean times. Now, in our time, we are truly living in a time of great change in human evolution.

Let us now take an overview of the things we have been considering in outline, asking ourselves why all this happened, why humanity evolved to impress the inner on the outer. The answer is that in evolving their organization human beings were compelled to do this. The people of ancient Atlantis had perceptions in the supersensible world because their ether bodies had not yet been drawn completely into the physical body. One point of the ether head did not yet coincide with the corresponding point in the physical head. Complete penetration of the ether body with the physical body is the reason why human beings are now forced out more into the outside world.

When the gates to the supersensible world closed, humanity needed a connection, a link, in their artistic evolution between the world perceived through the senses and the supersensible world. Before, in Atlantean times, they had no need of this, for they could then still get to know the supersensible world from direct experience. People only had to be told about the gods and spirits when they had lost those powers of perception, just as you only have to tell people about plants which they have never seen. That was the reason why religion evolved in post-Atlantean times. Why did a spirit of the supersensible kind such as the Christ have to appear in a finite individual, in Jesus, and walk on Earth? Why did the Christ have to be a historical person? Why did human eyes have to be drawn to this figure? We have said that human beings were no longer able to see into the supersensible world. What had to happen so that the god would be an experience for them? He had to become sense-perceptible, incarnate in a body perceptible to the senses. That is the answer to this question. For as long as human beings were able to perceive things in the spirit, for as long as they were able to perceive the gods there in supersensible experience, no god would have needed to become human. Now, however, the god had to be present in the sense-perceptible world. The disciples' words to affirm this fact arose from those feelings: 'We thrust our hand into his side ...,'[59] and the like. So we see how the coming of Christ Jesus himself becomes clear to us from the nature of post-Atlantean humanity, we realize why the Christ had to reveal himself to the senses. The most powerful historical fact had to be perceptible to the senses so that humanity had a point of reference to connect them with the supersensible world.

Merely knowing things turned more and more into veneration, an adoration, of the outside world. We have reached a high in this today. Christianity was a strong support against thus giving ourselves up completely to the senses. Today Christianity must be deepened through theosophy to give human beings a new understanding. We need a supersensible deepening of knowledge, of wisdom itself, if we are to understand Christianity in all its depths. We are thus moving towards a spiritual view of Christianity. That will be the next level, a theosophical or spiritual-scientific Christianity. Search for knowledge focused wholly on the material world will progressively lose its connection with the spiritual world.

So what is the task of spiritual science? Can a person seeking the spirit look to the established science of today? That science will gradually go more and more in the direction of post-Atlantean evolution, focusing more and more on superficial, physical and material aspects, progressively losing its connection with the spiritual world. Whichever science it may be, consider how it was in earlier times. Then there were still many spiritual elements in it.

You will see how everywhere, in medicine and in other fields, the connection with the spiritual has progressively disappeared. You can see this everywhere. And it has to be like this, for progress in the post-Atlantean age is such that the original connection with the supersensible world must be lost more and more. Today we are able to predict the course of science. Outer science will not be capable of spiritual deepening, however many attempts are made at this. It will more and more turn into a higher kind of instruction in technical skills, a means of mastering the outside world. For a Pythagorean, mathematics was still a means of looking into the way the higher worlds related to one another, into world harmonies; for people today it is a means of developing industry further and so to master the outside world. Made secular, non-philosophical—that will be the future of external science. All humanity will have to gain their impulses from spiritual evolution. And this spiritual evolution follows the course that leads to spiritual Christianity. The science of the spirit will be able to provide the impulses for all life in the spirit.

Science is turning more and more into technical instructions. Life at the universities is slipping more and more into technical college life, and that is rightly so. Everything spiritual and cultural is going to develop into independent humanities that need to be outside science. Science will then appear in a completely different context, a completely different form. There it will be necessary for humanity today to connect again with the great experiences of supersensible worlds. You will see that it is necessary if you understand what will develop if this does not happen. The ether head has now entered into the human being; the connection between ether body and physical body is now at its height. Because of this the percentage of people who gain supersensible experience is the lowest ever. But the course of human evolution goes forward in that the ether body will go outside again of its own accord. This has already started. The ether body goes outside again, grows more independent and free, and in future it will be outside the physical body again as in early prehistoric times. The ether body has to loosen again, something which has already started. But human beings have to take along in their ether bodies the things experienced in their physical bodies, particularly the physical event on Golgotha which they must experience physically, that is, in a life on Earth. Otherwise something will be lost for ever—the ether body would go outside and not take anything of value with it; people like this would continue to have empty ether bodies. But the ether bodies of those who have gone through spiritual Christianity will have an abundance of things that have been gone through in the physical body.

The danger is greatest for people who have been led astray by science to turn away from spiritual truths. But a beginning has already been made with the ether body moving out. Nervous states are a sign of this. They will increase progressively if people do not take the greatest event in the physical body outside with them. There is still plenty of time for this, because for the masses it will be a long time yet, but some individuals have already reached this point. Yet if there were to be someone who has never gone through in the physical what is the greatest event in the physical world, who has never known the depth of Christianity and taken this into his ether body, he would have to face spiritual death, as it is called. For emptiness of the ether body will lead to death in the spirit.

The Atlantean needed no religion, being clairvoyant, and living experience of the supersensible was a fact to him. All human evolution started from such an age. Vision of the spiritual world was then lost. *Religere* is to 'link', and religion is to link the sense-perceptible with the supersensible. The age of approaching materialism did need religion. But a time will come when human beings will once again be able to learn things in the supersensible world. They will then no longer need religion. The new kind of vision presupposes that human beings bring spiritual Christianity with them. That is the basis for the statement which I would ask you to remember as something particularly important: Christianity started as religion but it is greater than all religions.

What Christianity gives will be taken along into all future times and will still be one of the most important impulses for humanity when religion no longer exists. Christianity will remain even when human beings have overcome religious life. The fact that initially it was a religion is connected with human evolution, but as a world view Christianity is greater than all religions.

LECTURE 10

BERLIN, 16 MAY 1908

THE last time I had to point out to you that now, in this period of our branch's development, some things will be said[60] for advanced theosophists, and it has already been stated that the term 'advanced theosophists' does not refer to any particularly theoretical, detailed knowledge of theosophical teachings. It means something we can understand if we consider that when life has gone on for some time in a theosophical branch this does signify something for the human soul. In this theosophical branch life you do not only gain ideas and concepts on essential human nature, higher worlds, evolution, and so on, but—more than the individual will actually be aware of—you gain a certain sum of feelings, of sentience, that differs from anything people bring with them when they first join. These feelings, this sentience, mean that you are calmly and without tension learning things and listening to descriptions, accepting them as something that is not fantasy or dreamt up, things you would probably have laughed at before coming to theosophy, making fun of them. Many of our contemporaries today would no doubt make fun of these descriptions as sheer fantasy. This sum of feelings, this sentience, is something much more important than the details of theosophical teachings as our souls gradually become used to them. For they do indeed gradually make us change. People who have developed such feelings and sentience concerning other worlds, worlds that are indeed present in our own world, continually pulsing through us but not perceptible to the physical senses, such people with feelings and sentience relating to other worlds, as indicated, are what is meant here with 'advanced theosophists'. It is not your theoretical knowledge which comes into this but your heart, your feelings, if we want to look at this without bias the way we did the last time and are doing today. We would be deceiving ourselves if we were to speak only of the abstract theories that go as little as possible against sound common sense; we would not have the will that is needed so that gradually we truly learn about the worlds that we need to learn about.

The subject we want to talk about a bit today is one that should introduce us to other spirits that exist—spirits that are below us, if we see ourselves as spiritual entities—though we have not been saying much about them on earlier occasions. In our theosophical studies we have always focused on man as microcosm. In order to understand man, however, to learn about human evolution, we have had to look up to other spirits, to higher spiritual entities which in the evolution of our planet Earth have played a role like the one which human beings play on Earth today. We have seen that before it entered into its present state this Earth was something which we call the old Moon, and we explained that certain spirits that have higher faculties than human beings have today, faculties that humanity will only have in future Earth stages, were at the human level then on the Moon, when conditions were different. These are the angels or Angeloi, the spirits of twilight. The archangels or Archangeloi or fire spirits which are two levels above humanity today, went through their human stage on the old Sun. The Asuras, the spirits of individual nature, the Archai, far above humanity today as far as good or bad attributes are concerned, have gone through this stage on the old Saturn. We have thus been taking a closer look at a whole number of such spirits as time went on, spirits involved in the whole evolution of the Earth and the whole of our life and existence. We have got to know a number of such spirits that we must look up to in some respect. For someone who considers such spirits clairvoyantly, a significant difference is apparent between them and humanity.

When we consider the more detailed differentiation of human beings we divide them into the physical body, which we call the actual bodily nature, the etheric body and the astral body. We distinguish the soul from this bodily nature and differentiate it into sentient soul, rational soul and spiritual soul. The third principle in essential human nature is the spirit and this is only in the early stages of development today. Human beings will fully develop it in future stages of evolution. These three parts of essential human nature—body, soul and spirit—by and large make up the threefold nature of a human being.

If we now look up from the human being to those higher spirits of which we have just been speaking, we may say that they differ to some extent from human beings in that they have not developed the more material bodily element, which is the lowest. So we do not see the more material bodily element which is perceptible to the senses. Looking at the lunar spirits, or angels, as they are called in Christian esotericism, spirits that went through their human stage on the Moon, it will be evident from various things we have said that we cannot say they have the more material bodily aspect which human beings have. Instead they have the higher principles which humanity will only develop in time to come. We are therefore able to say that they differ from human beings in that they are spirit and soul, whereas human beings are threefold, having spirit, soul and body. So we have predominantly been considering the spirits in the cosmos which actually are human, having spirit, soul and body, and the spirits that are above humanity, having spirit and soul.

The occult observer will, however, also be aware of other spirits, very much hidden at the present stage of human evolution, but playing a role in the evolution of the cosmos. For there are also spirits where someone who investigates the world with a clairvoyant eye will not discover the principle which in human beings we call 'spirit'. They consist essentially of body and soul. You do know a whole group of such spirits from our studies so far, namely the animals. They have body and soul. We know, however, that these animals are connected with their group souls up above, or their group Is, and these are spiritual by nature. The individual animal we see before us has only body and soul, but it continues on, as it were, into higher worlds where it connects with spirituality. I have several times used the comparison which is permissible with regard to animal group souls: If there were a screen here and I were to push my ten fingers through ten openings in the screen, and if you were seeing not me but only my ten fingers, you would rightly conclude that the movement of my fingers must come from an entity that is behind the screen. That is how it is with animals and their group Is. They exist, and the animal gradually continues on into them. Different animals that have the same form are connected with these group Is of theirs. We can therefore only say that animals have body and soul when speaking of the part of animal nature which constitutes the individual animal here on the physical plane; we are in that case ignoring the continuation into the astral.

But there are also other entities, entities that also have only body and soul and are no longer visible to the physical eye. They are very often called 'elemental spirits'[61] in the different theosophical teachings, but that is as clumsy as can be, for they are entities which exactly do not have spirit, entities without 'spirit' which we do better to call 'elementals', not 'spirits'. We shall see later on why their bodies are not visible. For the time being, when we are not giving more than a kind of definition of these entities, let us say that they do, in a way, have body and soul, and that they are below human beings. These entities are, of course, said not to exist in our age of enlightenment, for at their present stage of development people are unable to perceive them. If you want to perceive them you must have achieved a certain level of clairvoyant awareness. If something is not perceptible to the senses this does not mean that it does not have an effect in our world. The activities of these entities, which have body and soul, definitely play a role in our world. The things they do are distinctly perceptible, it is only they themselves which are not perceptible.

It will be necessary for us to get an idea of such elementals, though our senses do not perceive them. They exist in various forms in the spiritual space that accommodates us all, and are also referred to as 'nature spirits'. They are altogether given all kinds of names. But those names are not what matters. What is needed is that we get an idea of them. Here we come to something which truly challenges your feelings and sentience, for I would like just for once to speak quite openly of how such entities present to the clairvoyant eye.

Different entities exist in different places on Earth. You can see them for instance if you go to depths where there has never been any growth, any kind of life form, where everything has always been mineral by nature. In places where metals or rocks are found you will find entities there which initially bring themselves to your notice in a strange way, as if something were flying apart. We find that they have been crouching together in enormous numbers and when the soil is opened up they burst apart as it were. And the important thing is that they do not only burst apart, fly apart, but also grow in bodily size. Even in their greatest size they are still smaller than human beings. The enlightened people of today do not know them. But people who have retained a certain natural feeling, some of the power of clairvoyance which all people once had, a power that had to be lost in the process of gaining external, object-centred awareness, people like that are well able to tell you of such entities, and they have given them all kinds of names, such as goblin, gnome, and so on. These entities differ from human beings in that they are not visible in their bodily nature the way human beings are, and also very much in that there'd be no point in ascribing any kind of moral responsibility to them. They do not have the moral responsibility, as we call it, which human beings have. Anything they do is done as if automatically. Yet the things they do are not at all different from anything the human rational mind, human intelligence does. They actually have 'wit', as we call it, to the highest degree, and anyone who is in touch with them can easily get a taste of their wit, for they may play all kinds of tricks on people. Any miner who has retained some sound natural feeling may discover this on occasion—a miner of metals, not of coal.

Using the methods of occultism, these entities can be studied to establish their constituent principles just as human beings can. Looking at the human being we have the physical body as the lowest principle, then the ether body, astral body and the I. And the principles that gradually develop as the I works on these we call Spirit Self or Manas, Life Spirit or Buddhi, and Spirit Man or Atma. The essential aspect for the present-day human stage are the four levels of physical body, ether body, astral body and I. We thus say that the I is the highest level, the physical body the lowest. It would be very wrong, however, to insist in an abstract way that this physical human body has nothing to do with the human I. In the physical human body we have the instrument for the human I. We have seen that this human body is a highly complex structure. We also said that the I has its physical instrument in the blood system, the astral body in the nervous system, the ether body in the glandular system, and the physical body itself in the physical organs functioning in a purely mechanical way, so that we have to consider that everything by way of inner human experience happening in the astral body comes to material expression in the nervous system, everything happening in the ether body has its material reflection in the glandular system, and so on. The physical human body thus gives us an image of the fourfold nature of man.

Take the human physical body as you have it before you, and take everything this physical body is as the instrument of the thinking, intelligent I. You'll best see what is meant if you consider that the I itself stays the same from incarnation to incarnation, but the instrument is developed anew with every incarnation. The parts where human beings have the advantage over the animals by way of a finer material organization, above all therefore the organization which reveals human intelligence, have come about in that over a long period the I slowly and gradually learned to work on the astral body. For we do know that the astral body of every human being consists of two parts, one part which it brought along with it from the cosmos, a part on which the I has not done any work yet, and another part which the I has already trans-formed. These two parts of the astral body have developed to a certain degree in every individual. The higher nervous system, especially the brain, is the external, material reflection of work done on the astral body from the I, though largely unconsciously so. Human beings have a much more developed and perfected forebrain because this forebrain is the reflection, the revelation, of the astral body worked on and trans-formed from the I. But it is nevertheless the astral body which comes to outward expression in the nervous system.

It will be easy to see that the moment any principle in our organism is reconfigured it will be necessary to change all the rest of the organism. Why can human beings not walk on four feet? Why have their fore-limbs been reconfigured into organs to work with? Because they have been working on their astral body and that brought about the necessary reconfiguration of their forelimbs into organs for work. And the form of the brain in the human body is another result of this inner work. The outer always is a real revelation of the inner. Everything we see in the physical body in its present stage of evolution is a specific result of spiritual evolution.

You will realize now that everything that exists in the material terms, including its form, is a result of the active principle which is behind this material world. When we have entities before us like those I have described, entities lacking the possibility of reconfiguring their astral body, for they lack spirituality—they do not have an I to work on their astral body—this astral body, which nevertheless is the sum of such inner experiences as an astral body is able to have, must come to expression in a material form. This material form of such an entity which is not aglow with I cannot be visible in the physical world at our stage of evolution because it is one degree below our visible matter. Take good note of what is meant by this.

If you want to be clear about the nature of your physical body you say: 'One can see the physical body.' You cannot see the ether body because it is one level higher in its substantiality. Nor can you see the astral body; it is one level above the ether body. Substantiality lies not only above but also below physical matter, and it too is not visible as only a band in the middle is visible of all matter—exactly the one that is physical matter seen with physical eyes. And just as the substantial principle continues in an upward direction in the physical basis of the etheric, of the astral, so does it continue downward and there becomes invisible again. Having considered the differentiation of the human being, we will now also be able to envisage the differentiation of these other entities.

We have seen that when we look at human beings, starting from below, they have first of all their physical body, then their ether body, their astral body and their I as the fourth principle. The entities we now call elementals do not have the I and, because of this, also do not know responsibility. They have a principle instead that is below the physical body. Call it 'minus one', if you like. Principles three, two, one and minus one are therefore developed in them. But we can go still further. There are not only entities that start with the astral body and have developed minus one in addition, but also entities that begin with two, having only the ether body principle, then the physical body principle, then minus one and also minus two. Finally there are entities where the highest principle is the lowest found in human beings. They start at one, and then have developed minus one, minus two and minus three. We can get a yet clearer idea why these entities are not visible. For you might object that having a physical body they must surely be visible. If human beings did not have their higher principles but only a physical body, this would look very different. When people die, the physical body is on its own; but it crumbles away then, goes apart into all possible atoms. That is the natural human form. It is the way you know it today because it is penetrated from above by I, astral body and ether body.

The entities we call gnomes or goblins do have a physical body, but they lack I, astral body and ether body. The gnomes, as we call them, are the very entities that have the physical body as their highest principle. They have three principles below the physical body, with the result that their physical body may be much less visible than the human physical body. As the powers of these entities are below the physical plane, even the principle of the physical body can never be physically visible to ordinary eyes. If they are meant to have material substance that is approximately physical, they can only have this under tremendous pressure, which is what happens when external matter presses them together. Their bodily nature is then under such pressure that they crouch closely together in large numbers and develop in the dreadful way I have described. Generally speaking the process which develops if you take away the pressure from outside is one of dissolution that happens at tremendous speed. The process which you can see in human beings after death happens at tremendous speed in the case of the goblins when you remove the soil. Because of this they can never be visible, even though they do have a physical body. For someone who is able to see through this physical earth they have a small physical body.

This physical body, which they possess as a power principle, does, however, have something in it which is similar in structure, in organization, to the human instrument for thinking, the human instrument of intelligence. People who create gnomes, having some feeling for nature, are quite right to make the heads particularly characteristic. All the symbols they draw have a kind of reality. You find a kind of intelligence in these gnomes that seems downright automatic. It really is as if you think of your brain taken out and not penetrated by the higher levels of existence; it would then not be working exactly like higher development either, but against higher development. This is why we have the entities we call gnomes before us in this way. We will then also be able to cast light on the entities that are lower than man.

In connection with the more profound task set for us we must now form an idea of how such entities have arisen in the course of evolution. This is connected not only with past evolution but specifically also with future development. That is the point of this. To learn about this let us give some consideration to human evolution. We know how human beings progress from incarnation to incarnation. We know that they bring the fruits of their previous incarnation into every new incarnation. Human beings thus play a part in creating both their form and their abilities as well as their destiny for every new incarnation. The actions they have engraved in the outside world come back to them as their destiny. Things they have engraved in themselves in an earlier life come back to them as their abilities and talents. They thus play a creative part in their external destiny as well as their internal organization. So we now ask ourselves: 'Where do the things that take us to a more perfect level come from?' Compared to earlier conditions of humanity, every average person today has reached a higher level in this respect. We achieve ever higher perfection because of the things we have acquired in progressing from incarnation to incarnation. It is not for nothing that we perceive the world, see things with our eyes, hear things with our ears, for in every incarnation we gather certain fruits of life. We take these with us after death, and the active principle in them develops into the germinal powers that play a role in our development and progress in the next incarnation.

Now there are various possibilities. The scales may tip to the one side or the other. The ideal situation would of course be that human beings make proper use of their life in every incarnation, leaving out nothing where they can learn and experience, and nothing that may bear fruit for later incarnations. Instead they would ideally take along everything they have made their own earlier. This does not happen as a rule, however. Human beings go astray in the one direction or the other. Either they do not make proper use of their life, to gather everything that may be gathered. Certain powers remain unused, therefore, and human beings take less with them into their new incarnation than they could have. Or they enter too deeply into their organization, melding too much into their incarnation, their bodily nature. You know there are two kinds of people. Some want to live wholly in the spirit and not descend all the way into their bodily nature. Down-to-earth people call them dreamers, idealists, and so on. Others again descend too far into their bodily nature; they do not only gather what they may but actually meld into their incarnation. They find it comfortable, they like to be one with their incarnation. They fail to preserve the element that continues from one incarnation to another. They let this sink down into something that is merely intended to be an instrument for the very core of the eternal human being.

I have said on a previous occasion that there is an important myth, an important legend, which shows us what can happen to people who go down too deeply into the temporal and transitory in an incarnation. If we take the extreme situation we may imagine that there may be someone who says 'What do I care about anything I take with me in the core of my eternal being into another incarnation. I want to be wholly in this incarnation here and now; it suits me, I like it, and I do not care what will happen later.' Where would it end if this attitude were to take radical form? It will end in the kind of character who sits at a corner in the road as one of the great guides and leaders of humanity walks past. And someone who does not want to know as far as the future is concerned will reject such a teacher, a great guide of humanity: 'I don't want to know about you who wants to guide the core of my being in future incarnations to the point where humanity will have reached perfection. I want to be wholly bound up with the form I have here and now.' Such an individual, who rejects such a guide of humanity, will return in the same form as he did before. And if the same attitude continues in him he will reject the guides of humanity in the following incarnation, and he will always return in the same form. When others who have been listening to the great guides of humanity, and preserved the soul with the core of their eternal being, return in a more advanced race, the individual who did not want to know about the great teacher and guide, rejecting him, will always return in the same race, having been able to develop only the one form. That is the idea behind the story of Ahasver who must always return in the same form because he refused the hand of the greatest guide, of the Christ.

The possibility thus exists for human beings to meld with the essential nature of one incarnation, rejecting the great guide, or to go through the change into higher races, to greater and greater perfection. Race would not grow decadent, would not decline, if there were not souls that cannot move forward and do not want to move on to a higher form of race. Look at races that have survived from earlier times. They are there only because souls were not able to rise higher there. I cannot discuss today what is meant when we say that the human being 'melds with the race'. A whole range of races have come into existence and fallen into decadence in the course of Earth evolution. Think back to Atlantean times. The Atlanteans advanced through the races; the races have vanished but the human souls have moved on into other, higher races. But the possibility exists for those who want to stay put, to meld with the race, to go down 'thanks to their own gravity' and be wholly material. There are 16 ways of melding with the race. One calls them 'the 16 ways to perdition'. Human beings who move forward will, however, be able to advance to higher and higher levels.

So we see that it is indeed possible for a human being to meld so much with the one incarnation that he lags behind in evolution, as it were. The others are then at a higher level when he returns in a new incarnation. He will have to be satisfied with an inferior incarnation, as it has remained for him from some decadent race or other. This need not make anyone afraid. Today the way ahead is not such for anyone that they could not catch up again, without having to drop out of evolution. But we do have to take note of this possibility.

Let us take the most extreme case. Someone melds as closely as possible with the essence of one incarnation. He cannot do so all at once, for he is not strong enough to do it all at once, but he would be able to do it over a period of 16 incarnations, going astray 16 times. Let us assume that he was able to do this. The result would be as follows. Earth and the souls on it do not wait, they progress. However, as the material is always also reflecting a soul element, such a person will finally get to a point where he has no possible way of getting a body for himself. For it is indeed possible that there are no more bodies for souls that have melded too closely with bodily nature. Those souls then lose the possibility of incarnating and will find no other occasion. Consider what they are losing, even if it is only possible in exceptional cases for this state to develop fully in the future evolution of the Earth. It is only for quite unusual people that occasion might arise during Earth evolution to be so much inclined towards evil that they would not find any possibility of incarnating, there being no bodies available that would be bad enough for them. They would then also lack something else which reflects normal evolution. Let us assume such an entity were to remain on Earth. When the Earth changes into Jupiter—later events always being the consequence of what has gone before—it would not find suitable bodies there either, for such entities are too good for bodies available for the subordinate natural worlds and too bad for the bodies which human beings will then have. This means that they must now create a body-less existence for themselves, that they really cut themselves off from the course of human evolution. It is the price to be paid for not making good use of life. The world is there around them. They have not made use of the world around them to enrich the core of their inner being through the senses and achieve ever new perfection. They are not moving ahead with world evolution but stay behind at a certain level. Entities like these, staying behind at such a level, will then appear in later periods of time, retaining the character more or less of the earlier period of time; for they have melded with this. They do not present in the forms and figures of the later period but as subordinate nature spirits in that later period, similar to the way described earlier.

In the second half of Jupiter evolution the human race will yield quite a number of such new nature spirits, for humanity will have developed the fifth principle of their essential nature, Manas, at the Jupiter stage. Those who have not used the opportunities given on Earth to develop that fifth principle will appear in their evolution on Jupiter as nature spirits with four basic principles, the fourth being the highest of these. Human beings will have five, four, three and two on Jupiter, but these entities will have four, three, two and one, something which cannot attain to outer form. That would then be the destiny of human beings who have not gradually developed the higher ones of their basic elements by making use of life on Earth. They will be nature spirits working invisibly, as it were, in a future period of evolution. The same happened with our present-day nature spirits in earlier periods of evolution, only that this is, of course, always changing depending on the character of the individual periods of evolution. The nature spirits on Jupiter, originally human beings, will have some degree of moral responsibility because we have that also here on Earth, and this will make them different from the nature entities in Earth existence.

Let us recall what I said about how Jupiter will differ from our Earth. We described the nature of Earth as the planet of love, compared to the nature of the Moon, which we called the planet of wisdom. Love is gradually evolving here on Earth, and the wisdom we find all around us evolved on the Moon. Love sprouted forth in its lowest form in Lemurian times; it changes, moving to higher and higher levels, until the highest, spiritual form will be reached. In Jupiter existence, the inhabitants of Jupiter will look at love the way human beings on Earth look at wisdom. When earthly human beings look at the wisdom that exists all around them, in a thigh bone, for instance, with its marvellous structure, how trabecula fits together with trabecula, they have to say to themselves: 'People with the greatest engineering skills today cannot produce something like the structure which cosmic wisdom has achieved in part of the thigh bone.' The whole of planet Earth is crystallized wisdom in this way, wisdom developed on the Moon. And love is developing in the same way here on Earth. Here we admire wisdom in every flower, for instance; the inhabitants of Jupiter will feel love coming to them like scent coming from all entities on Jupiter, just as the wisdom which is like a secret quality in Earth coming from Moon existence speaks to us here and now.

Thus the Earth is progressing from stage to stage. The Earth is the cosmos of love. Every planetary state has its own mission, and we'll only understand the mission of an age when we really take in this insight. Love will prevail throughout Jupiter just as wisdom prevails on our Earth. And just as the destructive powers in the wisdom come from Moon entities that lagged behind, so there will be destructive powers of love on Jupiter. These will be placed right in the midst of the general tissue as the ugly figures of Earth entities that lagged behind; they will be nature spirits with egotistical love and will make demands on love. They are going to be absolutely horrendous, disastrous powers on Jupiter. Individual human beings remaining behind—that give rise to disastrous natural forces. The lagging behind of individual human beings creates the destructive forces in nature. So we see how the world is woven in its useful as well as its harmful parts. We have a moral element woven into the world process.

	Physical body and above	below
gnomes	1	3
undines	2	2
sylphs	3	1
salamanders	4	0

All nature spirits configured in the way shown in the table, having one principle which human beings also have and three principles below human beings, are called 'gnomes'. Those called 'undines' have two principles below the human ones, and the 'sylphs' share three principles with human beings and have one below the human level. All of them lagged behind in earlier planetary ages and have not gained a spirit like the one that is now unfolding in man. They are below man, 'sub-spiritual', and consist of body and soul only. These entities are two-part and we call them gnomes, undines and sylphs.

But what are 'salamanders', you will ask. Gnomes, undines and sylphs are entities that have lagged behind in earlier states of the Earth. The salamanders have, in a way, come into existence in that they have partly, but only partly, developed the fourth principle. They have not got so far with this that they might assume human form. So where do salamanders come from? I am going to explain this to you as we come to the end. For if you understand this fourth kind of entity you will understand many of the secrets in the natural world around us.

Looking back through human evolution we find forms that are more and more spiritual. We know that the different animal genera were gradually put outside like brothers that were retarded in the progress of human evolution and remained at earlier levels of evolution. Human beings have reached the height they have because they were the last to emerge with their physical nature. The other entities came to be as they are because they were not able to wait, because they pushed their way into physical incarnation at an earlier point. Animals have group souls; these exist only on the astral plane, but work into the physical world. In the animal world we see the wisdom which the Moon has contributed to our evolution spread by the group souls to exist most comprehensively in the animal forms. Humanity must not consider wisdom to be theirs and theirs only. They do create their civilization with it, but wisdom exists in the whole of planet earth to a much greater degree than this. Someone who is proud of the human race may marvel how far humanity has advanced in wisdom. The new inventions make this evident. Just think of all the things told to pupils in school about everything human wisdom has achieved. Paper will be one of the things. Yes, paper is an achievement of human wisdom, but the wasps were able to make paper long before them. A wasps' nest is made of exactly the same material as proper paper. It is made just like human paper but out of the process of life. We can go through the whole of nature and we would everywhere find wisdom prevailing. Think how much sooner the group I of wasps invented paper than human beings did. Individual wasps do not do this, but the group soul does.

We see, therefore, how human wisdom is woven, imprinted, into the whole essential nature of Earth. We could go through the Earth bit by bit and would indeed find this wisdom everywhere. But the relationship of the animal to its group soul is only what it really should be up to a point, if I may put it like this. How does the group soul relate to the individual animal?

Think of the group soul of some insect species or other. When an individual insect dies it means the same to the group soul as it would for you if you lost a hair or cut a nail. The new animals which always develop are merely new replacement parts of the animal group soul. You are thus able to trace animal lines a long way up and you'll find that the part which is on the physical plane seems like a cloud that is always dissolving and reforming. Physical existence metamorphoses, and the group spirit only renews the part into which it continues down below. This continues until a particular stage is reached. Then something new arises. In the higher animals—more and more so as you come to the higher ones—something happens which is not at all like what I have just been describing.

Take apes, for instance. An ape takes too much of the group spirit into the individual which is down below. In lower animals everything goes back again to the group spirit, but the ape has grown too complex and therefore holds some of it back in its physical form. Too much of the group spirit has come down into it and it cannot all go back. That is the group spirit as it progresses. In lower animals it merely creates a part; it then draws the whole entity in again, produces a new one, draws it in again, and so on. It is the same with lions. But if you take an ape, for instance, the group soul does produce it, but the ape takes something from the group soul which cannot go back again. When a lion dies, the physical element dissolves and the soul principle returns to the group spirit. In the case of the ape, the part it has tied off from the group spirit cannot go back. In human beings, the I is such that it proceeds from incarnation to incarnation, capable of developing further because it is able to take up a new incarnation. That is not so with an ape. But the apes also cannot go back again. This is why apes make such a strange impression on naive people; they are in reality entities separated off from the group spirit. They cannot return to the group spirit but they also cannot reincarnate.

Marsupials are another kind of animal that tear something away from the group spirit. The principle which remains of these seemingly individual animal souls but is not able to reincarnate is the true origin of a fourth group of elementals. These are the separated-off parts of animals that cannot get back to the group spirit because they went beyond the normal point in evolution. Such I-like entities remain behind from numerous animals, and these are the salamanders. They are the highest form of nature spirit, for they are I-like.

I have now introduced you to the nature of a number of entities which we will gradually get to know in more detail. So far we have just got to know the nature and ground of their existence and how they relate. They are active in our world, and the traces of their activities can be perceived. Today we also want to gain an idea of these 'elemental spirits', as they are called. The salamanders are certainly also coming into existence in a strange way today—we may certainly say so—when certain human natures of a particularly low kind, which do, however, continue to incarnate, leave behind part of their low nature. Those are particularly bad elements, these natures that have remained behind from certain low human beings in our evolution. They are partly left-behind human natures staying on as a kind of nature spirit in the world where we exist. Much that is present in our spiritual space and becomes perceptible to people in a peculiar way—you'd never dream of this, not even of its existence—is only too evident in the traces it leaves. These spirits all have a partial relationship with human beings, and they intervene in human evolution, mostly in a destructive way. Many a bad element in civilization, seemingly natural today, will only be comprehensible to human minds when people know the disruptive, retarding powers they are dealing with in such a case.

The consequences will show themselves in many signs of decadence in our civilization. Our Theosophical Society has only come into existence because this is clearly seen by those who know how to interpret the signs of the times, and insight is the only thing to bring a sound quality to our world. People who have no insight have to let these things influence them, often developing all kinds of fancy ideas about them. Only those with insight into the activities of these spirits will be able to perceive the usefulness of the theosophical movement and realize the profoundly spiritual nature and soundness of the theosophical movement. It seeks to free human beings from the spirits that hold them back in civilization. Without this, our civilization would grow completely decadent. In the immediate future people will know all kinds of horrid phenomena in civilization; they will also find that people who cannot find their way about will call those who properly identify the phenomena dreamers and fanciful. The world will more and more take a form where people who know the spiritual, true reality are called dreamers and fanciful, whilst the real dreamers and producers of fantasies themselves declare reality to be sheer folly. True progress in our civilization is, however, that people gain full insight into those hostile powers. It is insight which out of the theosophical stream can make the words come true which the guide to Christian life addressed to his followers: 'You will perceive the truth and the truth will make you free.'[62] But it needs a truth that also truly and fully encompasses reality to make human beings wholly and completely free.

LECTURE 11

BERLIN, 1 JUNE 1908

IT was a bit daring for us to enter into a field last time where we turned our attention to some spirits that certainly exist as spirits in our reality but in a way do nevertheless drop out of the regular course of evolution. Their real significance was exactly that in a way they do drop out of evolution. The field was that of the elementals. We look at the elementals, though enlightened minds in our present age do, of course, consider this to be the most extreme kind of superstition. Yet it is exactly because of the position they hold in the cosmos that they will play a significant role in the not too far distant future in our evolution. We have seen how such elementals arise as irregular, tied-off parts of group souls. We merely have to recall what we said at the end of our last meeting and the essential nature of such elementals will immediately be there before our mind's eye. We referred to one of the last kinds of elementals to develop. We pointed out how a group soul exists for every type of animal or, to put it crudely, a sum of animals that have the same form. We said that these group souls are, as it were, playing the same role in the astral world as our human soul does in the physical world—providing, of course, that it is endowed with an I. The human I really is a group I that has descended from the astral to the physical plane. This has made it an individual I. Animal Is are still on the astral plane in the regular way today, and the individual animals we have here on the physical plane have only physical body, ether body and astral body on the physical plane, whilst their I is in the astral world, but in such a way that animals which have the same form are the members, as it were, of the group soul of these animals. With this we can also imagine how birth and death as we call them in human life today do not have the same significance for animals. The group soul or the group I lives on when an individual animal dies. It is like, if such a thing were possible, a human being losing a hand and having the power to attach the hand again. His I would not say that it had died with the loss of the hand but would feel as if it had renewed a member. The group I of lions thus renews a member when an individual lion dies and another replaces it. We can see, therefore, that birth and death simply do not have the significance for the group soul of animals which they do for the human being in the present cycle of evolution. The group soul of the animals knows changes, metamorphoses, knows of members being tied off, as it were, members which then extend into the physical world, of the loss of these members and their renewal.

We had said, however, that there are certain animal forms that go too far in the tying-off, and are no longer able to send everything they have drawn down onto the physical plane back again to the astral plane. When an animal dies, everything that drops away in that case must merge completely into the surrounding world. The element that fills the animal with spirit and soul, on the other hand, must flow back into the group soul, to be extended again and grow into a new individual. There are certain types of animal that cannot send back everything to the group soul, and the things left over, tied off, torn off from the group soul, then lead an isolated existence as elementals. Our evolution has gone through many different forms and stages, with such elementals tied off at every stage. So you can well imagine that we have quite a large number of such elemental species around us in the supersensible world, as we call it.

When an enlightened individual says, for instance, that there is no such thing as the elementals called sylphs, or also lemurs,[63] which people speak of, we would have to give an answer that does indeed sound strange and paradoxical. You do not see these things because you refuse to develop the organs for gaining insight that would get you to acknowledge the existence of these spirits. But go and ask the bee or, in other words, the soul of the hive. This would not reject the existence of sylphs or lemurs. For the elementals that are given those names are found in quite specific places, which is where the animal world touches in a way on the plant world, and even there not everywhere but in places where that touch is made under particular conditions. The animal does come in touch with the plant world when an ox eats grass; but that is a sober, regular contact which is wholly in the regular process of evolution. The contact between bee and flower is written on a completely different page in world evolution, and that is because bee and flower are much further apart in their organization, and come together again subsequently, and because a truly marvellous power develops when bee and flower come in contact—though this is only something for occultists.

One of the interesting observations in spiritual, supersensible worlds is the peculiar aura which always develops when a bee or another such insect drinks from a flower. The peculiar, unique experience which the bee has when it drinks from the flower is felt not only in the masticatory organs or in the body of the bee but the sharing of tastes between bee and flower spreads out into something like a small etheric aura. Such a small etheric aura arises every time the bee sucks, and whenever something like this arises in the supersensible world the spirits that need something like this will come. They are attracted by this, for to put it crudely—we have so few really apt terms for such subtle things—they find nourishment there.

I have said on a previous occasion that we should not really be touched by the question someone may ask, which is: 'Where do all these spirits come from that you are talking about?' When occasion arises for particular spirits they will always be there. When someone spreads nasty, evil sentiments around him, these sentiments will also be something that lives around him and attracts spirits which are there, waiting, just as a physical entity is waiting for food. A comparison I used on one occasion was that there are no flies in a clean room; but they will be there as soon as there are all kinds of food residues in the room. That is how it is with the supersensible entities; all you have to do is to provide food for them. The little bee sucking the flower creates a small etheric aura and this brings those spirits, especially when a whole swarm of bees settles on a tree and then departs, with the taste sensation found there in their body, as it were. The whole swarm is then enveloped in this etheric aura and at the same time filled with the spirits we call sylphs or lemurs. These spirits are present especially in boundary regions, where different worlds are in touch, as it were. And they have a definite role to play, for they are there not only when that subtle etheric aura develops, and they do not merely feed but, feeling hungry, they show their hunger in that they guide the animals concerned to the relevant sites. They are acting as guides, in a way.

We see therefore how spirits which, we may say, have given up their connection with other worlds, worlds they had been connected with earlier on, have gained a strange role in the exchange. They have turned into spirits for which there is good use in other worlds. But when they are used in that way, a kind of organization is set up and they are then subject to higher spirits.

When we started today I said that in the not at all distant future human insight will need to know about these spirits. Science will follow a strange course in the not too far distant future. It will get more and more sensual and physical, we might say, being limited to description of the outer facts perceptible to the senses. It will be limited to the crudely material, though we still have a strange transition stage at present. We have had a period of truly crude materialism in science and this is not that far behind us. Today crude materialism is at most seen as a possibility by people who take the layman's point of view, although the number of those who endeavour to put something else in its place is small. We see a whole range of abstract theories evolve where rather embarrassed reference is made to something supersensible, something more than bodily. The course of events and the power of external sense-perceptible facts will, however, completely upset exactly these strange, fantastic theories that are developed by people who are dissatisfied with physical science today, and the day will come when learned people will find themselves in a peculiar situation with regard to these theories. Everything people dream up about the all-being and all-ensouled nature[64] of one world or another, all this speculation will be completely upset and people will have nothing to hand but the purely physical, sensual facts in the fields of geology, biology, astronomy, and so on. The theories produced today will be short-lived, and anyone who is able to see even a little into the special progress of science will see that there will be the most absolute desolation of a purely physical horizon.

Then the time will also have come when a relatively large number of representatives of humanity will be ready to acknowledge the super-sensible worlds of which we speak today in spiritual science or the theosophical philosophy of life. A phenomenon such as the life of bees brought together with the things we are able to know from super-sensible worlds provides a wonderful answer to the great riddles of existence. And these things are of tremendous importance also in another respect. It will be more and more essential for humanity to understand the nature of group souls. This will play a major role also in the purely outward evolution of humanity. Going back through thousands and thousands of years we find that human beings them-selves still belonged to a group soul. For human evolution on our Earth goes from group soul nature to the individual soul. Human beings are progressively advancing as their souls, endowed with I, move down into the physical world where they have opportunity to be individual. We can look at various stages in human evolution and see how the group soul gradually became individual.

Let us go back to the first third of Atlantean civilization, for instance; human life was very different then. Our souls lived through very dif-ferent events in the bodies in which we were then incarnated. One event which we may look at plays a role in life today, for individuals as well as for human beings as social individuals, and has gone through a mag-nificent change from those times. It is the alternation of waking and sleeping.

In the old days of Atlantis you would not have known the same alternation of waking and sleeping as we have it today. What is the characteristic difference when we compare it to present-day humanity?

When the physical and the etheric bodies lie in bed and the astral body is rising out of them with the I, conscious awareness as we know it today sinks down into an indefinite darkness to the extent to which astral body and I go out. In the morning, when the astral body enters again with the I into the physical and the ether body, the astral body and the I are again using the physical organs and conscious awareness comes alight. This state of waking daily in the conscious mind, sleeping nightly in unconsciousness, did not exist in those earlier times. It was rather, if we may use the term—not quite in accord with conditions then, but we need it for describing the state in which the human being was connected with his physical body—it was such that during the day, when it was day for human beings and they had entered into their physical body in so far as this happened at that time, they would not at all see the physical entities and things around them in the kind of clear outline we know today. They would see everything in vague contours, blurred on the outside, like when you are in the street on a foggy evening and the lamps have a foggy aura around them. That is how it was for human beings at that time in every respect.

If that is how things were in the daytime, how were they at night? When human beings went out of the physical body and ether body during the night, they did not become fully unconscious. It was merely a different kind of conscious awareness. At that time people would still perceive the spiritual events and spiritual entities around them, no longer as clearly as with genuine clairvoyance, but as if in a last remnant that had remained from the old clairvoyance. By day they lived in a world with blurred, nebulous boundaries. At night they lived among spiritual entities that were around them the way things are around us in the daytime today. So there was no sharp divide between day and night, and the things told in legends and myths are not popular fantasy but memories of things those human beings of old had known in the supersensible world in their state of conscious awareness. Wotan or Zeus or other supersensible divine spirits given recognition by different peoples are not popular inventions or fantasies, as learned people maintain. This can be maintained only by someone who has never come to understand the nature of popular imagination or fantasy. People would never dream of personifying things in that way. Those were experiences in earlier times. Wotan and Thor were spirits and people dealt with them the way we deal with other people today. The myths and legends are memories from times of ancient clairvoyance.

We have to be clear, however, that there was something else connected with this way of living into the spiritual, supersensible worlds. Human beings did not feel themselves to be individuals in those worlds but belonged, as it were, to higher spirits, just as our hands belong to us.

The little bit of a sense of being individual which human beings then had, would come when they went down into their physical body, being emancipated as it were for a short time from the ranks of divine spirits. That was the beginning of feeling individual. It was at a time when human beings knew very well that they had a group soul. They felt themselves to be entering into the group soul when they left their physical body and entered into supersensible awareness. Those were the old days when human beings had a tremendously strong awareness of being part of the group soul, a group I.

We now consider a second stage in human evolution, leaving aside intermediate stages. This is the stage referred to in the history of the patriarchs in the Old Testament.[65] We have already mentioned what was behind it. We mentioned the reason why the patriarchs, Adam, Noah and so on, had such a long lifetime. This was because human memory was very different from the way it is today. The memory of modern man has also become individual. A person remembers things from birth onwards, some only from a much later time. It was not like this in the old days. The experiences a father had between birth and death, the experiences of the grandfather, the great-grandfather, were in people's memory just as much as their own experiences between birth and death. Strange though it may seem to modern man, it is true that there were times when memory went beyond the individual, going back through all the blood relations. And if we ask ourselves what external signs exist that there was such a kind of memory—well, we have those names, Noah, Adam, and so on. They do not refer to individuals who were between birth and death. People with a memory limited to the time between birth and death will give a name to this one individual. In the past given names extended as far as memory went back into the generations, as far as the blood was flowing through the generations.

Adam is nothing but a name, and it went as far back as people remembered. You will not be able to understand the nature of these things unless you know how names were given in earlier times. There was a basic mediating awareness and this was completely different. Imagine the ancestor had two children, each of them also two children, the following generation two again, and so on. For all of them memory went back as far as the ancestor, and they felt at one in a memory which may be said to meet in a point up there. The people of the Old Testament brought this to expression by saying, and this applied to every individual in the Old Testament who professed this: 'I and Father Abraham are one.' The individual felt secure in conscious awareness of the group soul, in 'Father Abraham'.

The conscious awareness that was the gift which the Christ gave to humanity goes beyond this. The I is directly connected with the spiritual world in its conscious awareness, and that is reflected in the words 'Before Abraham was, the I was'[66]—or the 'I am'. There the impulse to stimulate the 'I am' enters fully into the individual.

So we see a second stage in human evolution, the group soul period, outwardly reflected in blood relationship through the generations. A nation which has specially developed this is very particularly committed to emphasizing on all occasions that as a nation they have a common group soul. This certainly held true for the peoples in the Old Testament. The conservatives in that nation objected to emphasis on the 'I am', the individual I. Reading St John's Gospel it is absolutely evident that this is the case. You only have to read the story of how Jesus talked with the Samaritan woman by the well. It is made perfectly clear there that Christ Jesus would also go to those who are not related by blood, who do not belong together by blood relationship. Read the remarkable way in which attention is drawn to this: 'for the Jews have no dealings with the Samaritans'.[67] Anyone who is gradually able to go through this in a real way, meditatively, will see how humanity advanced from the group soul to the individual soul.

History is told in a totally superficial way today. It is often considered to be a convenient tale, for it is written on the basis of documents. Consider if something had to be described on the basis of documents today, and the most important documents had been lost. A report is then made up from a jumble of documents that happen to be at hand. You do not need documents for things that have their roots in spiritual reality, for these are inscribed in the trusty, perfectly clear Akashic Record. This is difficult to read, however, because the external documents are an obstacle to reading spiritual 'writings'. We can see, however, that development from group soul to individual soul happened in times that are quite close to our own.

Taking a spiritual view of history you will have to recognize a most important period of time in early medieval times. Before that, human beings were still, even if only outwardly, part of some group or other. In early medieval times people still were given significance and value also with regard to their ability to work, by their family and in other contexts. It was a matter of course that the son would do the same as his father had done. Then came the time of great inventions and discoveries. The world made increasing demands on the abilities of the individual who would be torn away more and more from the old cohesion. We see a reflection of this in the founding of cities throughout the Middle Ages, something that happened in exactly the same way throughout Europe. To this day we can distinguish cities of this type from those based on a different model.

Another step forward from group soul to individual soul came in mid-medieval times. And looking ahead to the future we have to say to ourselves that the human being is becoming emancipated more and more from the group soul principle, growing more and more individual. If you were able to look back on earlier stages of human evolution you would see that civilizations such as the Egyptian and the Roman were all of a piece. Today there is hardly any civilization that is all of a piece. Humanity has descended to the point where not only manners and customs are individual but even opinions and professed views. There are actually people among us who consider it a great ideal for every human being to have their own religion. Some are dreaming of a time when there would be as many religions and truths as there are people.

Humanity will not evolve in that direction. They would if they were to pursue further the impulse which comes from materialism today. That would lead to disharmony, to humanity splitting apart into single individuals. However, evolution will only not take that direction if humanity accepts a spiritual movement such as spiritual science. For what is going to happen? The great truth, the great law will come into its own that the individual truths found in an inward way will also be those of greatest general validity.

I have said on a previous occasion[68] that today general agreement or congruence exists really only for mathematical truths, these being the most commonplace. No one can say that he finds the mathematical truths through outer experience; you find them in that everything is inwardly understood. To say that the three angles in a triangle add up to 180 degrees, you do this by drawing a parallel to the base line through the tip and putting the three angles together in a fan; then angle a = d, b = e, c equals itself; and together the three angles come to a straight line, 180 degrees (Fig. 8). Once you have realized this you know that it must always be so, just as you know, having realized it once, that three times three equals nine; and I do not think that you can discover this by induction.

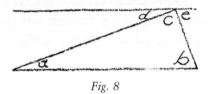

Fig. 8

The most common of all truths, those in algebra and geometry, have been inwardly found, and yet people are not in dispute over them. People are in absolute agreement here because they are at a point now where they can realize this. It is only when the pure truth is clouded by passions, by sympathy and antipathy, that there is no agreement. A time will come, though it is still far distant, when human beings will be taken hold of more and more by insight into the inward world of truth. In spite of all individuality, and although each will find his own truth in himself, there will be agreement. If the mathematical truths were not simply so evident today, passions would still create all kinds of obstacles to their acceptance. If it were a matter of cupidity, many a housewife would prefer to say that twice two makes five and not four. These things are so transparent, so simple, that they can no longer be clouded by sympathy and antipathy. Every greater area will be subject to this form of truth, and it will be possible for humanity to know more and more peace when truth is accepted in this way. Human beings have grown out of group-soul life, becoming emancipated from it more and more. If we look at the group rather than the souls we get family connections, tribal and national aspects and finally human races that go together. A group soul equals a race. All these group relations of early humanity are of a kind such that human beings grow out of them, and the more we progress the more does the concept of race lose significance.

We are in transition today, and the element of race will gradually disappear completely, with something very different taking its place. People who grasp again the spiritual truth as it has been characterized will come together of their own free will. That is the situation for a later time. Situations in earlier times were such that people were born into them. They were born into their nation, their race. Later on we will be living in situations created by human beings themselves as they form groups according to how one looks at life, where they will create communities in which they fully maintain their freedom and individual nature. It is important to realize this if we are to get the right view of such a thing as the Theosophical Society. The Theosophical Society shall be a first example of such a voluntary community, leaving aside the fact that things have not yet reached that point today. An attempt is to be made to create such a community where people come together without the difference that existed with the old group soul nature, and there will be many such associations in future. We will then no longer have to speak of racial connections but of intellectual, ethical and moral aspects when referring to the associations formed.

When people let their feelings shine together of their own free will this creates something which again goes beyond the purely emancipated human being. The emancipated human being has an individual soul; this will never be lost once it has been gained. But when people come together voluntarily they group around focal points and this gives opportunities to spirits to act like a kind of group soul but in a very different way from the group souls of old. All the earlier group souls were spirits that made human beings unfree. These new spirits, how-ever, are compatible with complete freedom, maintaining the individual nature of people. We may actually say that they manage to survive, in some respect, thanks to human unity; it will be due to human souls themselves to offer the opportunity to as many of those higher souls as possible to descend into the human realm. The more associations are formed, and the more community feeling develops in complete freedom, the more sublime spirits will come down to humanity and the faster will planet Earth be made spiritual.

We see, therefore, that to get an idea at all of future evolution people must thoroughly understand the character of group soul nature. Otherwise it may happen that emancipated on its own on Earth the individual human soul will fail to make connection and then turn into a kind of elemental spirit itself. And elementals developing from human beings would be of a truly evil kind. Elementals developed from earlier realms are most useful in our natural order, but the ones developed from human beings will not have that quality at all.

We have spoken of tied-off entities coming into existence in certain boundary regions. Such entities also arise on the boundary, at the transition from group soul nature to free groupings due to aesthetic, moral and intellectual aspects. Those group spirits will be present wherever such associations exist.

If you were able to observe certain places such as wells or springs, with rocks down below and mosses growing on them, with a kind of wall developing between plant and rock, and water seeping over it—this has to be there as well—you would see nymphs and undines as they are called to be very real indeed; this is particularly evident in such places. And where metals and other soil elements come together you get whole bundles of the spirits called gnomes. A fourth kind are the salamanders. These may be said to be the youngest in the order of all these elementals; but they are nevertheless often present. They are largely spirits that owe their existence to a tying-off process from animal group souls. Spirits like these are also looking for opportunities to find nourishment, finding it particularly where the human world enters into relationship to the animal world, relations that are sometimes not quite normal but rather abnormal. Someone who knows about these things will be aware that elemental spirits of a particularly good kind develop if there is a good relationship between a rider and his horse. Feelings, thoughts and inner impulses develop through the connection certain people have to animal groups that provide good nourishment for those salamander-like spirits. You see this especially in the way a shepherd lives with his sheep, and herders who live with their animals. Certain salamander-type elementals find nourishment in the feelings which arise when human beings and animals are thus intimate, and they will be around where such a situation exists. They are also very wise, having a wholly natural wisdom. Through these feelings, the shepherd develops abilities that allow the elementals to murmur the things they know into his ears. Many a saw or rule of life coming from that source has its origin in the situation just described. It is perfectly possible for a human being to be surrounded by subtle spiritual entities under those conditions, and they provide him with a knowledge which our clever people of today cannot even dream of. All these things have their own good reason and can certainly be observed with the methods that can be developed in occult wisdom.

In conclusion I'd like to speak of another phenomenon which may show you how certain things, for which there are only highly abstract explanations today, have in many respects sprung from a more profound wisdom. As I said earlier, when those earlier people of Atlantean times went out of their bodies during the night they lived among the spirits which we have called gods. These people were in the process of entering into physical bodily nature. But those spirits which they venerated as their gods, among them Zeus and Wotan, followed a different course of evolution. They did not go down as far as physical bodies; they did not touch the physical world. But even so there were transitions. Man has developed in that the whole of his soul and spiritual nature hardened into a physical body. In the case of humanity all the group souls went down to the physical plane, and the human physical body became a reflection of the group soul. Let us assume that a spirit such as Zeus, who was certainly real, had only lightly touched the physical plane, extending into it just a little. It would be as if you dipped a sphere in water and it got just slightly wet at the bottom. This is how certain spirits were merely touched by the physical world in Atlantean times. The physical eyes do not see the spiritual, the astral and etheric which remain. Only the small part which extends into the physical is visible. The symbolism in mythology came from such perceptions. The symbol for Zeus is the eagle and this is because his eagle nature is the small part of the sphere which touched the physical world. The bird world consists largely of the tied-off parts of spirits evolving in the supersensible world. And like with Wotan's raven or Zeus' eagle, it is the same wherever symbolism has arisen from occult facts. You will see many things more clearly if you thus consider the nature, activities and development of group souls in the various spheres.

This is what I wanted to add today to the things said on earlier occasions. It will give us a complete basis for our studies in this field.

LECTURE 12

THE aim of the studies we have been doing on several evenings in our branch is to add one thing or another to, or expand on, the themes we have been considering in the winter months. It will be understandable, therefore, that now and then a remark comes into it that seems aphoristic. For we want to add to, to round out, one thought or another, one idea or another, that has come to life in us.

On the last occasions we were mainly considering the presence of all kinds of spirits that exist between the natural worlds perceptible to the senses that we have around us. The last time we specifically saw how elementals arise where entities from different natural worlds are in contact, where a plant nestles up to a rock at a spring, for instance, where ordinary rock nestles up to the metal, as it does below ground in many cases, where communion exists as it does between bee and flower. In all these places powers develop that draw different kinds of elemental spirits into earthly existence. And in connection with these elementals we considered the fact which we called the tying-off of certain spirits from the greater context in which they were. We have seen that elementals called 'salamanders', for instance, in spiritual science, partly originate in parts tied off from animal group souls, having advanced too far, as it were, into our physical world and then been unable to find the way back and unite again with the group soul of an animal when the body of that animal dissolves. For we know that in the regular course of life the entities on this Earth, entities in the animal world, the plant world and the mineral world, have their 'I soul'—if we may call it that—and essentially have the same kind of I soul as human beings, differing from human beings only in that the I souls of those other entities are in other worlds. We know that man is the entity in our evolutionary cycle which has an individual I here on the physical plane, at least when awake during the day. We also know that the entities we call animals are in a position where, to put it roughly, animals of the same form have a group soul or a group I, and these group Is are in the 'astral world', as it is called; also that the entities we call plants have only a dreamless-sleep level of conscious awareness of the physical world here, but that they do have group Is which dwell in the lower parts of the devachanic world, and finally that the stones, the minerals, have their group souls in the upper parts of the devachanic world. A clairvoyant who moves in those worlds, the astral and devachanic worlds, is dealing with the animal souls there which are group souls, and with the plant souls and the mineral souls just as in the physical world he is dealing with human souls or human Is in his waking hours.

One thing we must clearly understand is that the human being is also in many other ways a highly complex and composite entity. We have already been considering much of the complexity on various occasions. But the human being will seem more and more complex to us the more we go into the connection with the great cosmic realities. To help us understand that this human being is not the very simple entity he may be thought to be if a naive approach is taken, we merely need to consider that the human being of the present evolutionary cycle is a very different entity during the night, from going to sleep to waking up, than he is by day. His physical body and his ether body lie in bed; the I with the astral body has been lifted out of this physical and ether body. Let us consider both, first of all the physical body and the ether body. There they lie, and leaving aside the transitional stage of dream-filled sleep, they have a level of awareness which we call empty, without perception and also dreamless. But in human beings in their present stage of evolution the I with the astral body, having left the physical and ether body, also has the dreamless level of awareness in sleep. The sleeping human being has the conscious awareness which the spreading plant cover has here in the physical world, and he has it in the parts that remain here in the physical world and also in the parts that are in the astral world during sleep. We must now give some thought to these two separate parts of the sleeping human being.

We know from other studies that this human being of the present time has evolved gradually and slowly. We know that he was given the first beginnings of a physical body in the far distant past, during the Earth's embodiment we call the Saturn state. We know that during the second embodiment of our Earth, at the Sun stage, he received the ether body or life body in addition to the physical body, that he was given the astral body during the third embodiment of Earth, the Moon stage, and that on Earth, in the present embodiment of the planet, he received the principle we call the I. That is how the human being evolved slowly and gradually. The physical body that human beings have today is indeed the oldest part of them, the part that has gone through the greatest number of transformations. It has gone through four transformations. The first beginnings of it, which the human being was given on old Saturn and which have since then gained threefold perfection (once on the Sun, the second time on the Moon and finally on the Earth), is reflected in the sense organs which human beings have today. These were very different on old Saturn; but at the time they were in their first beginnings, and the rest of the human body did not yet exist. We can look at old Saturn as a single entity with nothing but sense organs, completely covered with nothing but sense organs. The ether body was added on the Sun. The human physical body changed, and the organs we call glandular today developed. They were still most imperfect at that time, but their first beginnings did appear. The sense organs grew more perfect. Then, on the Moon, the organs were added which today, with the physical body transformed a third time under the imprint of the astral body, we call the neural organs. And finally the present-day blood system was added on Earth; it reflects the I just as the nervous system reflects the astral body, the glandular system the ether body, and the system of senses physically reflects the physical body itself.

So far we have seen in the lectures that in our Earth evolution the blood system really appeared first. We look at the physical body today and ask ourselves why today blood flows in the blood channels in its present-day form. What does it tell us? The answer is that the blood reflects the I. At this point let us deal with a possible misconception, which is that people really misunderstand the physical human body of today. This present-day physical human body has, as it were, merely the form which the physical human body can have. It existed on the Moon, on the Sun, on Saturn, but always in a different form. On the Moon, for instance, the natural world we call the mineral world on Earth did not yet exist; there was no plant world as we know it on the Sun and no animal world on Saturn, only the human being in its first physical beginnings. If we consider this we have to be clear that the human body of today really is not only physical body, but physical and mineral body, that in addition to the laws of the physical world—which make it 'physical' body—it has acquired the laws and substances of the mineral world which are present throughout it. On the Moon this physical human body had not yet made the laws of the mineral world its own; no mineral ash would have been left if it had been cremated there. For minerals in the present-day Earth sense did not yet exist then.

Let us consider, therefore. Being physical and being mineral are two completely different things. The human physical body is physical because it is governed by exactly the same laws as stones are; the human physical body is at the same time also mineral because it is impregnated with mineral substances. On Saturn the first beginnings of the physical body existed, though there were no solid bodies, no water nor gases. All there was on Saturn was heat, this state of heat. Modern physicists do not know this state of heat for they believe that heat can only develop if there are gases, water or solid bodies. That is erroneous, however. This physical human body which today has acquired the mineral world was a composition of physical laws on Saturn. These were physical laws acting in lines, in forms, laws you get to know in physics. On Saturn this physical human body was outwardly apparent only as an entity that lived in heat. We must carefully distinguish between mineral and the principle in the human body which is actually physical. These are the physical laws that govern the physical body. It is a physical principle, for instance, that our ears and our eyes are shaped so that they take in sound, or light, in a particular way. The substances impregnated with physical laws in this scaffolding structure belong to the mineral aspect of the ear and the eye.

Having got this clear, and specifically noted how the sense organs, glands, nerves and blood reflect the fourfold human being, let us turn back again to contemplation of the sleeping human being. When human beings are asleep, the physical body and the ether body are lying in the bed, and the astral body and the I are outside. But we now consider that the astral body is the principle of the nervous system and the I the principle of the blood system. During the night the astral body has therefore left the element of which it may be said to be the cause, that is, the nervous system. For it was only possible for the nervous system to arise when the astral body became part of the human being on the Moon. The astral body is thus meanly abandoning something which belongs to it, which it really is supposed to provide for in the human being. In the same way the I is abandoning something which it has brought into existence. The principles of the blood system and nervous system are outside the sleeping physical body and the sleeping ether body. These are now entirely on their own. However, something brought about as material, physical, cannot persist in the form that it has been given by a spiritual principle unless the principle itself is present. That is quite out of the question. A nervous system cannot live unless astral entities are working on it, and neither can a blood system live without the I entities. All of you are thus meanly abandoning your nervous system and your blood system with your I and your astral body at night, leaving them to other entities that are astral by nature. Spirits of like nature to your I then enter into your organism, as it were. The human organism truly is occupied by such spirits every night, spirits capable of maintaining it. The human physical body and astral body lying in the bed are then at the same time penetrated by these astral and I spirits which are actually *in* the physical body. We might call them intruders, but that is not always correct. We should perhaps call them guardian spirits, for they maintain the elements which the human being meanly abandons at night.

It is not such a bad thing for human beings to abandon their bodies every night. As I told you earlier, the astral body and the I are busy all night. They remove things worn out during the day, grown tired in a comprehensive sense, as we call it. The individual is refreshed and recovered in the morning because his astral body and I have during the night removed the tiredness that came in the day because of the

impressions gained in daytime life. This is a fact for clairvoyant observation, this wonderful night-long activity of the astral body to remove
the substances due to tiredness. I and astral body are working on the
physical body and ether body from outside. Human beings have not yet
reached the point, however, in the present cycle of their evolution where
they can do this wholly on their own. They can only do it under the
guidance of higher spirits. Every night human beings are thus taken to
the bosom, as it were, of higher spirits and these enable them to act on
their physical and ether bodies in the right way. Those are at the same
time the spirits—which is why we must not call them intruders—which
take the right kind of spiritual care of the human being's blood and
nervous system during the night.

For as long as there are no abnormalities, the spirits are able to work
together for the human being during the night. But irregularities may
well occur, and this brings us to a chapter in spiritual science that is
extraordinarily important for the inner life of man in a practical way.
One would wish that many more people learned of this not only
theoretically but to provide the most wide-ranging basis for certain
activities in man's inner life. People do not usually think that the facts of
the inner life have far, far-reaching effects. On particular occasions I
have said that the facts of the inner life are properly explained only if we
consider them in the terms of spiritual science. We all know the profound meaning of the words: 'From the spiritual-scientific point of view,
a lie is a kind of murder.' And I told you that there actually is a kind of
explosion in the astral world when someone tells a lie—to some extent
even if he just thinks it. Something happens in the spiritual world when
someone tells a lie that is much more disastrous for the spiritual world
than some kind of mishap in the physical world. But things like this,
which one also mentioned at a certain level of spiritual-scientific study,
characterizing them as far as is possible at that level, become progressively more evident and well-founded as we progress in gaining
spiritual-scientific insight.

Today we'll get to know another effect of telling lies, of slander. The
terms 'lies' and 'slander' are not at all meant in the horrible way that
they usually are in a cruder sense. But even if we colour the truth just a
little, in a more subtle way, for convention's sake perhaps, for all kinds

of social or partisan reasons, it always is a lie in the spiritual-scientific sense. In many ways the whole of human life is saturated if not with lies then certainly with manifestations tinged with untruthfulness. The enlightened materialist will at best realize that it left an impression on his physical body when someone hit his skull with an axe. He will at best also realize that it has an effect on his physical body when a train runs over him, severing his head, or if he develops an ulcer on some part of his body, and also if germs enter. In such a case the enlightened individual will accept that things do affect his body. But people do not usually consider that the human being, made to be spiritual, is a single whole, and that things which happen in the higher aspects of his bodily existence, in astral body and I, must be regarded as having actions that extend down into the physical part of it. They do not consider, for instance, that telling lies and untruthful things, and indeed untruthfulness in the conditions under which the human physical body lives, have definite effects. Clairvoyant experience may be as follows. When someone has told a lie during the day, the effect of this lie remains in the physical body and is evident to clairvoyant perception when the individual is asleep. Let us now assume the individual is altogether a liar, telling many lies. He will then have many such effects in his physical body. All this hardens in a particular way during the night, and then something highly significant happens. These inclusions, these indurations in the physical body do not agree well with the spirits that must take possession of the physical body during the night, spirits that, as we have seen, will during the night perform the functions on the physical body that astral body and I perform in the daytime. The result is that in the course of life parts of those spirits are tied off by such a lie-infested body when they are in it during the night. There we have the tying-off processes again. The consequence is that when such a person dies, his physical body will not entirely follow the route it would follow in the regular course of events, for certain entities will remain which have been produced in the physical body due to the effects of lying and slander, as it were. They have been tied off from the spiritual world. These entities or spirits, tied off by this roundabout route, flit around in our world. They belong to the class of spirits that we call 'phantoms'. This includes a group of elementals that are related to our physical body, initially invisible to physical eyes, and growing in number with lies and slander. Lies and slander are actually populating our globe with such phantoms. So here we get to know a new class of elemental spirits.

It is not only lies and slander present in the human soul but also other things in the inner life which have an effect on the living human body. The effect of lies and slander on the physical body is to make it into one that ties off phantoms. Other things act in a similar way on the ether body. Do not be surprised at such phenomena in the inner life; in spiritual life we must be able to take in things quietly and calmly. Facts like this that have a bad effect on the ether body are bad laws, for instance, or bad social institutions in some community or other. Everything that leads to discord, for instance, altogether affecting human relationships due to bad institutions, creates a mood in the life people share which is such that the effect continues on into the ether body. And everything that comes together in the ether body under the influence of such facts in the soul will in turn cause parts of the spirits acting into human beings to be tied off, and these are then also in our surroundings. They are called 'spectres', or also 'ghosts'. We see these spirits which exist in the ether world, the life world, grow out of human lives. So there are people going about among us and for someone who is able to perceive these things in the spirit their physical bodies are interlarded with phantoms, their ether bodies with spectres or ghosts. All this will as a rule spread out, populating the world on a person's death or soon after.

We see, therefore, how well spiritual, that is, non-physical events in our lives such as lies, slander, bad social institutions continue on, depositing their non-physical creations among us here around the globe. But now you are also able to understand that when physical body, ether body, astral body and I belong together in normal daytime life, and the physical body and the ether body actually have to let other spirits invade them or let things be done with them, the astral body and the I are also outside the state normal for the present cycle. They are, however, in a somewhat different position than the physical body and the ether body. Physical body and ether body have the same level of conscious awareness in sleep as plants have. But the plants do have their I up in the Devachan. This is why the physical body and ether body of sleeping human beings also have to be provided for by spirits that unfold their conscious awareness from the Devachan. The human astral body and I are one world higher up, but human beings also have dreamless sleep, like the plants. The fact that plants have only physical body and ether body and human beings have also astral body and I when asleep makes no difference where plant nature is concerned. Human beings are up in the spiritual world, in the astral world; but they are not so high up with their I that there is no justification for being asleep. The consequence is that spirits have to enter into the astral body also of sleeping human beings. And that is how it is. Influences from the devachanic world are constantly entering into the human astral body. These influences need not be at all abnormal; they can be influences coming from the higher I or self, as we call it. For human beings are gradually living their way up into the devachanic world by moving more and more towards spiritualization; and today they are already influenced in their sleep by the element that is in preparation there.

There are also other influences. Ideally people would perfectly understand one another when it comes to respect and appreciation of the freedom belonging to the soul of another. At present humanity is still far from achieving this. Just consider the way in which one soul seeks as much as possible to overcome the soul of another, unable to bear it if the other thinks and loves something different, and one soul wants to overcome and influence the other. In everything to do with soul-to-soul influences in our world, ranging from unjustifiable advice given to others to all the means people use to overcome souls, in everything which does not allow souls to face one another in freedom but uses methods of conviction, coercion, persuasion even to the smallest degree, powers act from soul to soul that influence these souls to such effect that this is reflected in the astral body during the night. The astral body then has inclusions and this causes entities to be tied off from other worlds and these flit around in our world as elementals. These spirits belong to the 'demon' class. They exist in our world solely because all kinds of intolerance of thought, rape of thought has been practised in it. The hordes of these demons have entered into our world in that way.

So today we have got to know spirits that exist just as things we perceive with our physical senses exist, spirits that certainly bring their influence to bear in human life. Humanity would have progressed in a very different way, for instance, if people did not create these demons with their intolerance, demons that are present throughout our world and constantly exert their influence on human beings. They are at the same time the spirits of prejudice. And we understand the subtleties of life if we get to know the way the spiritual world in the higher sense and our world are entangled. All these spirits exist, as I said, and flit through the world in which we live.

We now recall something else, which has also been said before. We pointed out[69] that in the last third of the Atlantean age, before the flood on Atlantis, the relationship of the human ether body to the physical body was completely different from what it had been before. Today the situation with the human head is that the physical and the ether parts of the head are essentially congruent. It was different in ancient Atlantis. Then the ether part of the head projected far out, especially in the region of the forehead. The central point in the ether body of the head and in the physical body of the head is approximately between the eyebrows. In the last third of the Atlantean age the two points came to coincide, and they are congruent today. This has made human beings capable of saying 'I' to themselves and be sentient of themselves as independent human beings. This, then, is how the ether body of the head and the physical body of the head came together. It happened so that human beings might become the sensible entities which they are within our physical world and enrich their inner life with the things taken in through impressions on the physical senses, through smell, taste, sight and so on. All this is made part of our inner life so that we will have it and be able to use it for the further development of the whole cosmos. This acquisition could not be made in any other way. And this is why we have always said that we must not see spiritual science in ascetic terms, not as the need to flee the physical world. Instead we take with us from the physical world everything that happens here, and it would be lost to the spiritual world if we did not gather it here.

Humanity is, however, moving more and more towards a new condition. We have gone through various periods of civilization in post-Atlantean times—old Indian, ancient Persian, then the one we called the Babylonian, Assyrian, Chaldean and Egyptian period, followed by the Graeco-Latin period, and we are now in the fifth period of post-Atlantean civilization. This will be replaced by a sixth and then a seventh period. In all the time right up to our own age the structure of ether body and physical body has gained in firmness, growing inwardly more solid and bonded. In future times humanity will move towards a period when the ether body gradually loosens again, growing independent. The direction will thus be reversed. Some people already have much looser ether bodies than others. This loosening of the ether body is right only for someone who has taken up so much in different incarnations and periods of civilization that on going out again the ether body takes real fruits with it from the earthly world perceived through physical senses, fruits suitable for incorporation in an ether body that is growing more and more independent. The more spiritual the ideas are which we find here in the physical world, the more will we take with us in the ether body. All ideas of usefulness, mechanical, industrial elements that serve only external needs, external life, are not suitable for incorporation in the ether body. But everything taken in by way of ideas that are artistic, beautiful and religious—and everything can be immersed in the sphere of wisdom, art and religion—will lend the ether body the ability and opportunity to be organized in an independent way. This is what we may expect, and that is why it has often been stressed here that the spiritual-scientific view of life must extend its actions and impulses to practical life, and that spiritual science must never remain a subject to entertain around the tea table or a mental occupation that lies outside ordinary life. No, it must have an influence on the whole of our cultural life. When people come to understand the thoughts of spiritual science they will also understand how everything that goes on in our time must be filled with spiritual principles. Some minds, Richard Wagner among them, have had premonitions in certain areas of thus bringing in spiritual principles. One day people will know how to build a railway station that lets wisdom shine out just as a temple does; it just has to give true expression to whatever lives in it. Much still needs to be done in this respect. That is where these impulses must take effect, and they will do so if the spiritual-scientific thought is more and more understood.

I well remember how about 25 years ago a well-known architect[70] gave an address as vice-chancellor about architectural styles. He said the wonderful words that architectural styles are not invented but grow out of the cultural life. He also showed why our age, if it allows styles to come to life at all, lets only old styles do so, being unable to find a new architectural style because the way it is it does not yet have an inner spiritual life. When the world produces spiritual life again, all things will be possible. We shall then see that the human soul shines out to us in everything that presents itself to us, just as in a medieval city the spirit came to expression in every door lock and every key. Theosophy will only be understood when it presents itself everywhere in this way, as if crystallized in its form. Then every human being will also live with another as spirit does with spirit. Human beings will more and more prepare things for them to take with them when they move up into the spiritual world again, their ether bodies growing independent. That is how people must enter wholly into the spiritual world if evolution is to continue in the right way.

Nothing symbolizes the spirit entering into the Is more beautifully than the story of Pentecost. It seems prophetic, if you think about it, how it shows the world being filled with spiritual life as 'cloven tongues like as of fire'.[71] Everything needs to be given spiritual life again. The abstract, conceptual relationship human beings have to the festival we are about to celebrate must be real, alive, again. Let us try to have a thought like the one which may arise from today's study occupy our souls exactly at the time we call Pentecost. A festival instituted out of spiritual causes will come alive again for human beings when their ether body is ripe for being active in the spirit. But if people do not take up the spirit of Pentecost the ether body will leave the physical body and not be strong enough to overcome those worlds of spectres, phantoms and demons created in earlier times, worlds that the world has created as its secondary phenomena. The subject of our next meeting will be how evolution is encouraged by the spirit, and what we are able to foresee with regard to this.

LECTURE 13

At the most recent meetings of our branch we have spoken of various points of view, all of which show how human beings mysteriously interact with spiritual worlds, spiritual entities that are really always present around us and not merely around us but in a particular respect also passing through us all the time. We always live with these spirits. We should not think, however, that a relationship develops between human beings and spiritual entities only in the relatively crude form, we might say, to which we have been referring in those last meetings. A relationship between human beings and the spiritual world also arises through the many different things people do that are more connected with the human way of thinking.

On the two last occasions we had to speak of spirits that in some respect are subordinate. But we know from earlier lectures that we are also dealing with spirits that are above man, and that connections and relationships exist also between man and more sublime spirits. We mentioned that there are sublime spirits that do not consist of physical body, ether body, astral body and beyond, as human beings do, but have the ether body as their lowest principle, and that these dwell around us, as it were. They are not visible to the ordinary eye because their bodies are subtly etheric, so that human eyes see right through them. Then we come to yet higher spiritual entities that have the astral body as their lowest principle so that the body they present to man is even less dense.

All these spirits do nevertheless have some relationship to human beings and, what is more, human beings can certainly do something to develop quite specific relationships to such spirits during their life here on Earth. Depending on whether people here on Earth do one thing or another with regard to their conditions of life, they will always establish connections with higher worlds. This may seem rather unlikely to people in our present age, said to be enlightened, though in fact it is not at all enlightened with regard to many profound truths in life.

Let us first of all take spirits which have an etheric body as their lowest principle; they are around us, live around us with this subtle ether body and send their influences and revelations down to us. Let us have them before our mind's eye and ask ourselves, 'Can human beings do anything here on this planet Earth, or rather, have human beings always done something to provide a bridge by which these spirits can connect and act more intensely on the whole human being?' Yes, human beings have always done something for this. To get a clear idea of this bridge we must enter deeply into many of the sensations and ideas we have been able to take in at our last meetings.

So we think of these spirits living out of the spiritual worlds, as it were, extending their ether bodies from there. They do not need physical bodies such as human beings have. But there is a physical body through which they can, as it were, connect their ether body with our earthly sphere, an earthly body which we can set up on our earth, as it were, and which is then a link of attraction, so that these spirits come down to this physical body with their ether bodies and make occasion to be among human beings. Such occasions for spirits to be among human beings are provided by Greek temples, for example, or Gothic cathedrals. If we set up such forms of physical reality in our earthly sphere, the way their lines and forces relate provides an occasion for the etheric bodies of those spirits to nestle close on and in them on all sides, according to the system of forces in these works of art we have set up. Art makes a true and real link between human beings and spiritual worlds. All the way up to the arts that occupy three-dimensional space we have physical bodies on Earth to which spirits with etheric bodies descend.

Spirits that have the astral body as their lowest principle do, however, need something else here on Earth for a bond between spiritual world and our Earth, and this is provided by the musical and phonetic arts. A space filled with the sound of music provides an opportunity where the very mobile astral bodies of higher spirits, defined within themselves, come into their own. There the arts, and the meaning they have for human beings, gain absolutely real significance. They are like magnets attracting spiritual entities that have the mission or task of having and wanting to do something with human beings. Our feelings for human creativity in art and human feeling for art grow deeper when we look at things in this way. What is more, our feelings may grow deeper when we take in the human well-spring of artistic work and with it also our enjoyment of it, doing so from the point of view of spiritual science. If this is our wish we must consider the different forms of human conscious awareness in greater detail.

We have for different purposes drawn attention to the fact that when human beings are awake in the daytime we have before us the physical body, the ether body, the astral body and the I, and when they are asleep we have the physical body and the ether body lying in bed, with the I and astral body outside the physical and the ether body. It will be good for present purposes to take a closer look at these two alternating states of conscious awareness over a 24-hour period. We have first of all the human physical body and then the ether or life body, then the astral body, as we call it in the most general sense—the soul body which is part of the astral body but connected with the ether body. It is the part of the human being which animals also have in physical life down on the physical plane. Then, however, we know that the principle which in its totality we call the I is connected with these three aspects of essential human nature—you can read this up in my *Theosophy*. The I really has three elements—sentient soul, rational or mind soul, and spiritual soul, and we know that the spiritual soul on its part is connected with the principle we call the Spirit Self or Manas.

Looking at this detailed analysis of the human being we are able to say the following. The principle we call 'sentient soul' which otherwise is certainly part of the astral body and is also astral by nature comes free when human beings go to sleep at night, but part of the soul body nevertheless stays with the ether body which continues to lie in bed. Essentially it is sentient soul, rational soul and spiritual soul which emerge. When people are awake in the day all this is interconnected, and because of this all of it is then also active in the human being. Changes in the physical body have an effect on the whole of inwardness, on sentient and rational soul and also the spiritual soul. All the chaotic, confused impressions human beings gain from ordinary life—just think of the many impressions we gain from morning till night, think of moving through the noise and uproar of a large city—continue on into all the elements that in daytime conscious awareness are connected with the physical body and ether body. During the night our inwardness— sentient soul, rational soul and spiritual soul—is in the astral body. There it gathers the powers, the harmonies which are lost to it due to the chaotic impressions of the day. There the human I soul, as we call it in more general terms, finds itself in a world that is more ordered, more spiritual than the one we know when awake during the day. In the morning this inwardness of soul leaves that spirituality and enters into the threefold bodily nature of physical body, ether body and the part of the astral body that is really connected with the ether body and also stays connected with the ether body during the night.

If people were never to sleep, that is, never to gather new strength from the spiritual world, everything that lives in their physical body, filling their physical body with powers, would ultimately deteriorate more and more, and be progressively undermined. But because a strong inwardness enters into the powers of the physical body every morning, new order always comes to that body—powers are reborn into the physical body, we might say. In this way the human soul quality brings something with it from the spiritual world for the elements of the human body, something that takes effect when the inwardness of soul which is outside during the night and the external physical instrument are together.

If a person is open to taking in harmonies of the spiritual world, the consequences of interaction between inwardness of soul and the actual physical instrument can fill the powers, not the material, of the physical body with capacities which we might call capacities of space. Human beings are, however, so alienated from the spiritual world in our present civilization that those very capacities of space do not make much of an impact on them. At the point where the inwardness of soul comes in contact with the densest element, the physical body, the powers brought down into it must be really strong if they are to come into their own in the robust physical body. During periods of civilization when finer feelings prevailed, the inwardnesses of soul would bring the soul impulses with them and penetrate the physical body more easily with them. People were sentient then of the forces that always pass through physical space in all directions, so that this physical space definitely was not an indifferent void but had forces move through it in all directions. One can have a feeling for the distribution of forces in space; it is created by the conditions I have just been describing. An example will give you an idea of this.

Think of one of the painters who lived in times of great art when people still had a real feeling for the forces active in space. You can see how one of them painted a group of three angels in space. You stand before the painting and immediately feel: These three angels cannot fall, it is natural for them to hover, for they hold each other up thanks to the forces in space, just as the cosmic globes keep their places in space. People who develop these inner dynamics through interaction between physical body and inwardness of soul know the feeling: It has to be like this, the three angels remain in space. You will see this particularly in the works of some of the earlier painters, probably less so in those of more recent painters. However much you appreciate Boecklin,[72] the figure hovering above his *Pietà* makes everyone feel that it may come down with a bump at any moment; it does not maintain itself in space.

All these forces moving in all directions in space—forces that a human being really feels in space—are realities, and this feeling for space gives rise to all architecture. True, genuine architecture arises from nothing else but that one places the stones or bricks in lines that must already be there in space, so that all one does is to make visible what is already present spiritually as idea. One is pushing solid matter into it. Greek architects had this feeling for space in the purest sense, all forms in their temples giving expression to the forces that lived in space, that could be felt in space The simple relationship where a column supports either horizontal or angled linear bodies speaks of spiritual forces present in space. And the whole Greek temple is nothing but a filling in with matter of whatever lives in space. Because of this the Greek temple is the purest architectural thought, crystallized space. It may seem strange to modern people, but being the physical embodiment of thoughts, the Greek temple is an opportunity for the figures which the Greeks knew as their gods truly to touch the lines in space that were familiar to them and dwell within them. It is not just an empty phrase to say that the Greek temple is the dwelling place of the god. For people who have a real feeling for such things, the Greek temple is unique in that they can envisage it with no one being around to look at it from the outside, nor anyone being present inside. The Greek temples have no need of people to look at them or enter them. Think of the Greek temple as standing on its own, with no one around anywhere near or far. It is then what it is most intensely meant to be. It is then the shelter for the god who is meant to dwell in it, the forms being such that the god can dwell there. It is only in this way that we really understand Greek architecture, the purest form of architecture in the world.

Egyptian architecture, the pyramids, for instance, is something completely different. We can only touch on this briefly. There the spatial proportions, the lines in space, are arranged in such a way that proportions and forms show the ascending soul the way to the spiritual worlds. The forms we see in the pyramids derive from the paths the soul takes into the spiritual world. Every kind of architecture thus reveals a thought that can only be grasped spiritually.

In Romanesque architecture, with the round arch, church buildings are arranged in such a way, for example, that we have a nave and side aisles, and then also the transept and apse. The whole is in the form of a cross, therefore, with a dome above There the concept of space has evolved from the tomb. You cannot think the Romanesque style in the same way as the Greek temple style. The Greek temple is the dwelling place of the god. The Romanesque building cannot be seen in any other way but that it represents a tomb. The crypt is part of it; it is not that people who are in life are not also standing in it, but it is true that it is a place where all feelings come together that relate to the preservation and protection of the dead.

The Gothic style is something else again. Not a single soul may be seen anywhere near or in a Greek temple, but it is nevertheless populated, being the dwelling place of a god. Equally truly a Gothic cathedral, with its pointed arches, is unthinkable without the faithful crowded in it. It is not complete in itself. Standing alone it is incomplete. The people inside it are part of it with hands put together in prayer echoing the pointed arch. The cathedral will only be a whole when its spaces are filled with the feelings of the devout. These are the forces that take effect in us, of which we are sentient in the physical body as we feel our way into the space. A true artist senses the space and gives it architectural form.

If we now move up to the ether body we again have the element that inwardness of soul gains in the spiritual world during the night and brings back with it on returning to the ether body. The true sculptor is sentient of this element coming to expression in the ether body and imprints it in the living forms. Now it is not the thought of space but the tendency to show and configure more than has been given by nature in the living form. The Greek artist knew more, for instance in the case of Zeus, and this 'more' was something he had brought with him from the spiritual world, something that comes alive and is open to sentience when it interrelates with the ether body.

Such interaction also exists with the principle we call the soul body. When inwardness of soul comes together with the soul body, a feeling arises for the drawing of lines, for the first elements of painting. As the sentient soul unites with the soul body and penetrates it in the morning a feeling arises for harmony of colour. These, then are the three art forms that work with external media, taking their material from the outside world.

Something else comes about because the rational or mind soul escapes to the astral world every night. When we use the term 'rational soul' in spiritual science we must not think of the sober, dry rationality we think of when we speak of the rational mind in everyday life. In spiritual science, 'rationality' is a feeling for harmony that cannot be embodied in external matter, a feeling for harmony that lives in us. This is also why we say 'rational or mind soul'. When the rational or mind soul enters every night into the harmonies of the astral world and gains awareness of them again in the astral body in the mornings—the very same astral body which does return but in modern people is not aware of its inwardness during the night—the following happens. During the night the rational or mind soul lives in the element we have always called the harmonies of the spheres, the inner laws of the spiritual world, the harmonies referred to in the School of Pythagoras as something which those who are able to extend their perceptions to the spiritual world perceive as the relationships in the great spiritual world. Goethe also referred to this when at the beginning of his *Faust* he places us in the heavens, characterizing this by saying

> The sun proclaims its old devotion
> In rival song with brother spheres,
> And still completes in thunderous motion
> The circuits of its destined years.[73]

And he stayed with the same image in Part 2, where Faust is taken up into the spiritual world:

> Hear the tempest of the Hours!
> For to spirit-ears like ours
> Day makes music at its birth.
> Hear it! Gates of rock are sundering
> And the sun-god's wheels are thundering:
> See, with noise light shakes the earth!
> Hear it blare, its trumpets calling,
> Dazzling eyes and ears appalling,
> Speechless sound unheard for dread![74]

It means that the soul lives in these harmonies of the spheres during the night, and these are ignited when the astral body gains awareness of itself. The process we see in the creative musician is none other but that the perceptions of night-time consciousness win through in daytime consciousness and become memory, memories of the astral experiences or in particular those of the rational or mind soul. All music known to man is reflection, development of unconscious experiences in the harmonies of the spheres. To be gifted in music means simply that one has an astral body which in its daytime condition is receptive to the things that have whirred through it all night. Not to be musical is to have this astral body in a condition where such recall is not possible. In music, the individual experiences the sounds coming from the spiritual world. And since music brings into our physical world something that can only be ignited in the astral, I am saying that it brings the human being together with the spirits that have the astral body as their lowest principle. Human beings live among those spirits during the night; they experience their deeds in the harmony of the spheres and reflect this in their earthly music here on earth. As this, the element of these spiritual entities, enters into this earthly sphere, floating through it and alive in it, those spiritual entities have opportunity to let their astral bodies enter again into the billowing ocean of musical influences. The art creates a bridge between these spirits and human beings in that the rational soul gains living experience of their deeds during the night and brings sentience of impressions gained with it into the physical world. So we see how the art of music, as we call it, arises at such a level.

What does the spiritual soul hear when it enters into the spiritual world during the night, though in the present cycle of human evolution this does not come to conscious awareness? It hears the words of the spiritual world. Communications are murmured which it can receive only from the spiritual world. Words are murmured and when these words are taken through into daytime consciousness they turn out to be the fundamental powers of poetry. Poetry thus is the shadow image of things which the spiritual soul experiences in the spiritual world during the night. We have occasion here truly to think about how human beings bring about shadow images, revelations of spiritual reality here on our globe thanks to their connection with higher worlds—to this alone—in the five arts of architecture, sculpture, painting, music and poetry. This is only so, however, if the art truly rises above seeing things with our physical senses. Naturalism, roughly speaking, where people only imitate things seen in the outside world, has nothing in it that human beings bring with them from the spiritual world. The fact that we now have such a purely superficial art in many areas, merely seeking to imitate what exists out there, proves that the people of our age have lost their connection with the spiritual and divine world. Someone whose interest is wholly focused on the physical world outside, only on the things the physical senses will allow to exist, is so powerfully influencing his astral body because of interest being limited to the physical world outside that it grows deaf and blind when it is in the spiritual worlds during the night. Magnificent spherical harmonies may sound, sublime spiritual worlds murmur to the soul, but it brings nothing with it into daytime life. People are derisory about the idealistic, spiritualist art, saying that art exists only to photograph external reality, for this is the only way in which it would have something real, something solid, to stand on.

This is how people speak whose feelings and sentience are materialistic, and they do not have the realities in the spiritual world. A true artist will say something different. He will say something like 'When I hear the sounds of the orchestra it is as if I was hearing the sounds of an archetypal music speak, music that was there when no human ear existed to hear it.'[75] Or he may say: 'The music of a symphony reflects insight into spiritual worlds, something more sublime and significant than anything that can be logically proved and established by drawing conclusions.'[76]

Those were the words of Richard Wagner[77] who wanted people to have a real feeling that at the point where true art comes in one must at the same time also rise above the superficial and sensual. When it is said from the spiritual-scientific point of view that something lives in human beings that transcends human nature, something superhuman in modern man that must show itself to be more and more perfect in future incarnations, Richard Wagner's feeling is 'I do not want figures that are there before me and walk across the stage like everyday people in the earthly sphere.' He wants people who are above the common round. He therefore takes mythological figures of a more all-embracing content than ordinary people. He is looking for the superhuman in the human. He wants to present the whole human being with all the spiritual worlds that shine in on the human being of the physical world on Earth. Relatively early in his life he had two images before him: Shakespeare[78] and Beethoven. His artistic genius saw Shakespeare to be such that he said to himself: 'If I take everything that Shakespeare has given to humanity, I see figures on stage who take action.' Actions—and in this context words are also actions—arise when the soul has felt things that cannot show themselves outwardly in space, things are already behind it. The soul has felt the whole range from pain and suffering to pleasure and happiness, and been aware of how one action or another arises from one nuance or another. In a Shakespeare play, Richard Wagner feels, everything appears merely in the form of a result, gaining configuration in space and so turning into action in the external world. It is the only form of drama where the inner can be presented in outward form and at best one can get an inkling of what lives in the soul, what is going on as the action proceeds.

The other image that came to him was of the composer of symphonies. For him, a symphony reflected everything that lived in the soul, the whole range of feelings—pain and suffering, pleasure and happiness in every nuance. It comes into its own in the symphony, he said to himself, but it does not turn into action, it does not go out into the surrounding world. An image came to him which suggested, as it were, that on one occasion this inner aspect of creative work shattered, was flowing out. Beethoven stayed within the musical frame in his creative work, but on one occasion he did go outside it, in the Ninth Symphony,[79] where feelings reached such a pitch that they broke out in words.

These inner images of the two artists gave rise to a vision in his soul: Beethoven and Shakespeare in one![80] It would need a long exposition to show how Richard Wagner sought to create a harmony between Shakespeare and Beethoven in the particular way in which he handled the orchestra, so that the inner element came into its own in music, flowing into action at the same time. Profane language was not enough for him, it serves to speak of events on the physical plane. For him, the language which can only be given in the sounds of song became the means of expressing something that goes beyond physical human nature and is superhuman.

Theosophy must not only be spoken in words or felt in thoughts. Theosophy is life. It lives in the world process, and when one says that it is meant to bring the different, separate streams in human souls together in one great river we see this feeling as it lives in the artist who sought to bring together the individual means of expression so that together, as one, they reflect what lives in the totality. Richard Wagner does not wish to be a musician, nor a dramatist, nor a poet. For him, everything we have seen trickling down from spiritual worlds is the means for uniting with something higher in the physical world. He has some idea as to what human beings will experience when they enter more and more in a living way into the period of evolution into which, well, humanity has to enter in that way, where the Spirit Self or Manas unites with the things that human beings have brought with them from earlier times. And with Richard Wagner, some idea of the great impulse of humanity to bring together the things that arose in times of separation lies in the coming together of individual forms of artistic expression. In other words, some idea lives in him as to what human civilization will become when everything that lives in the soul is imbued with the Spirit Self principle or Manas, when the soul in its fullness has immersed itself in the spiritual worlds. In terms of spiritual history it is of profound significance that the first dawn for humanity has appeared in art for living towards the future that lies before them, when everything which human beings have gained in the different fields will come together in an all-culture, a total culture In a sense the arts are definitely the precursors of spirituality coming to revelation in the sense-perceptible world. And much more important than individual sayings in Richard Wagner's prose works is the basic trend in all of them, a religious, hallowed approach full of wisdom, which is present in all of them and given the most beautiful expression in his brilliant essay on Beethoven.[81] You have to read more between the lines to feel the breath of air that heralds the dawn.

We see how by taking the spiritual-scientific point of view we can deepen human activities that come to fulfilment in human actions. Today we have seen this in the sphere of the arts. There human beings do something, achieve something which makes it possible for the gods to dwell with them, if we may put it like this. They are giving the gods opportunity to dwell in the earthly sphere. If the aim is for spiritual science to make people aware that that spiritual world interacts with physical life, art has certainly done this in physical life. Art, being spiritual, will always be part of our culture if human beings enter at all into spirituality with their souls. Looking at anything like this broadens things which otherwise are told as mere theory, mere philosophy of life into impulses that fill our life and can tell us what is to be and has to be. With Richard Wagner, musician and poet, the new star has risen, the star which sends the light of spiritual life to the Earth. The vital impulse he has given must broaden out more and more and the whole of external life will once again be the mirror image of the soul.

Everything we have in the world around us can become a mirror image of the soul. Do not take this to be something superficial but see it as something we can gain from the science of the spirit. It will be the way it was centuries ago, when every lock, every key we came across was the image of something which people had felt, of which they had been sentient. Profane buildings are profane only for as long as human beings are unable to impress the spirit into them. The spirit can be impressed everywhere. The image of the railway station may come to mind that will be artistically conceived again. We do not have this today. But when people come to feel what forms should be again, they will feel that the railway engine may be configured architecturally, and that the station might be something that relates to the engine as the sheltered housing for something given expression in the architectural form of the engine. Only then will they be like two things that belong together if considered architecturally. Then, however, it will not be immaterial what we take to be left or right in the form.

When human beings will learn how the inner comes to expression in the outer there will yet again be a civilization. Truly, there have been times when there was as yet no Romanesque architecture, no Gothic, only the people who bore in their souls a new civilization that was to come as they gathered down in the catacombs of the ancient Roman city. But something that lived in them, something which could only be engraved in sparse forms in the ancient earth caves, something you see on the sarcophagi of the dead, was beginning to dawn there. It is something we see in the Romanesque arches, columns, apse. The thought was taken out into the world. If the early Christians had not borne the thought in their souls it would not be there for us to see in what has become world culture. A theosophist only feels himself to be a theosophist when he bears a future civilization in his soul. Others may well ask: 'What have you actually achieved?' And he will then say to himself: 'Well, consider what the Christians in the catacombs did achieve, and what has become of it!'

Let us try and in our minds broaden out the limited sentient impulse that lives in our soul when we sit together, more or less as the thoughts of the Christians were able to broaden out as far as the marvellous round arches in the cathedrals of a later time. Think of our sentience in hours when we are together gradually broadening out and spreading out in the world. We then have the impulses in us which we should have if we are aware that theosophy is not meant to be a leisure pursuit for a few people who meet for it but something that must be taken out into the world. When the souls sitting here in their bodies reincarnate they will find that some of the things that live in them today have been brought to realization. These are the thoughts we take with us as we meet for the last time in this season and work through the winter's spiritual-scientific thoughts. Let us apply the spiritual-scientific thoughts in such a way that they shall act as cultural impulses. Let us endeavour to saturate our souls with sentience and feelings in this way, and let this live towards the summer sunshine which shows us the cosmic power at work, doing so from outside, in the physical sphere. Our soul will then more and more gain the mood and the ability to take into the outside world the things it experiences in the spiritual worlds. This is part of the theosophist's development. And we'll take further steps forward when we take those feelings and that sentience with us, and with them take in the strength that summer can give.

Notebook pages relating to the lecture given on 16 May 1908 (Archive No. NB 352)

16th May 1908 Lodge Berlin

Being too much tied up with / one's race takes the soul into the [. . .] / for clinging to the race. / Then however return to / group soul.
Gnomes avoid fertile soil
Undines conduct a kind of war against / all aquatic animals.

Elemental spirits. Body, soul
Spiritual soul can only be adequately / developed by entering fully / into the phys. body.

If the opportunity is not adequately / made use of, the spiritual soul stays infantile.

It will then not be able in future / to have the strength so that on its part / it will be able to develop / the phys. body. It continues to be active / as nature spirit.

Why apes do not / achieve perfection?

NOTES

Text sources: Apart from the lecture given on 13 May 1908, the transcripts in this volume are derived from shorthand records made by Walter Vegelahn. He had taken down many lectures given by Rudolf Steiner before and during the First World War. The lecture of 13 May 1908 was taken down by Clara Michels and Magdalena von Spaun. Transcripts by Johanna Muecke, Franz Seiler, Agnes Friedlaender and Katharine Schallert are also available for some of the lectures. These were consulted, so that minor additions and corrections were possible for the 2nd and 3rd editions.

No changes were made in the text for the 4th edition of 2001. It was reviewed once more by Anna Maria Balastèr and Ulla Trapp, notes have been extended, and entries from Rudolf Steiner's notebook added for the lecture on 16 May 1908.

The German title of the book goes back to the editor of the first German edition.

The *drawings* in the text were made by Hedwig Frey, based on sketches by the stenographers. Original blackboard drawings have not survived.

1. Lectures given at the Besant Branch in October and November 1908 published in English are *Occult Signs and Symbols*; *Christmas*.
2. E.g. in the lecture given in Berlin on 4 November 1905, in *Foundations of Esotericism*.
3. Berlin, 28 January 1907, in *Original Impulses for the Science of the Spirit*.
4. Vladan Đorđević, *Das Ende der Obrenovitsch* (Death of Draga Obrenović, formerly Mašin, Queen of Serbia, assassinated together with King Alexander I of Serbia on 11 June 1903 in Belgrade), published in Leipzig in 1905.
5. Richard Wagner (1813–83). His 'music dramas' included *Tristan and Isolde*, *Tannhäuser*, *Ring of the Nibelungs* and *Parsifal*.
6. In the first lecture in this volume. See also notes 1 and 2.
7. See notes 1 and 2.
8. Goethe's *Faust*, lines 449 and 450. Translation by David Luke, OUP.
9. Revelation 4:6–8.
10. The term 'pushed through' is given in all four records.
11. Revelation 5:6 ff.
12. Combining the views of Immanuel Kant (1724–1804) and Pierre Simon de Laplace (1749–1827, French mathematician and astronomer) on the origins of our planetary system.
13. It has not been possible so far to establish which journal or which author.
14. E.g. on 26 December 1907 (not translated into English).
15. See the essay (in German) on chlorophyll and Chlorosan by Prof. Emil Buergi (Bern), in which he writes about the investigations he conducted, together

with other scientists, for several years. *Das Chlorophyll als Pharmakon*, pub. by Georg Thieme, Leipzig 1932.

Rudolf Steiner was able to refer to those investigations in 1908 because he knew the Buergi family personally. Mrs Buergi was a member of the Theosophical, later Anthroposophical Society and ran the Johannes Branch in Bern.

16. Buergi states in his book (pp. 9 ff.) that there is a connection and stresses that the difference exists. Blood forms a similar compound with iron as chlorophyll does with magnesium. To quote (p. 10): 'In it (chlorophyll), and in chlorophyll and its derivatives altogether, magnesium is bound in a way similar to that in which iron is bound to the blood substances.'

17. See lecture of 2 June 1907, in *Theosophy of the Rosicrucian / Rosicrucian Wisdom*.

18. Reference to Wagner's words in Goethe's *Faust*, Part I, line 573.

19. One record of the lecture differs here: 'Their lowest principle is Spirit Self or Manas. This now forms a mantle around the whole Earth, being the spirit of which it is said "For in him we live, and move, and have our being." ' (Acts 17:28)

20. *Cosmic Memory* or *Submerged Continents*.

21. See Preface to *Cosmic Memory* or *Submerged Continents*.

22. Also in a lecture given on 17 March 1908, not translated into English.

23. Discovered by Ernst Chladni, German physicist (1756–1827).

24. See the lecture of 24 March 1908 in this volume.

25. See the lecture of 24 March 1908 in this volume (towards the end).

26. E.g. in a lecture given on 2 June 1907, in *Theosophy of the Rosicrucian / Rosicrucian Wisdom*.

27. Germanic tribes in the western part of Germany in the Migration Period .

28. Romans 4:16, 'Abraham, who is the father of us all'.

29. Genesis 5.

30. Baruch de Spinoza, philosopher (1632–1677). See his main work *Ethics*.

31. See the lecture of 29 February 1908 in this volume.

32. See in C.G. Harrison's *The Transcendental Universe*, 6th lecture: 'But the principalities of Light, perfect and blessed emanations of the Divine Wisdom, recognised in the Divine Love a purpose above and beyond anything that the highest wisdom could attain to. It was no less than the redemption of the body by sacrifice, and, before this mystery, they cast their crowns of wisdom at the feet of the Mystic Lamb, and veiled their faces in adoration.' Rev. 4:10–11: 'The four and twenty elders fall down before him that sat on the throne, and worship him that lives for ever and ever, and cast their crowns before the throne, saying, You are worthy, O Lord, to receive glory and honour and power, for you have created all things, and for your pleasure they are and were created.'

33. John 6:39–40.

34. Luke 14:26 and 18:29–30; Matthew 10:37.

35. Hammurabi (1793–1750 BC), king of Babylon, had Babylonian law codified.

36. Paul, Romans 4:16.

37. John 10:30.

38. In the beginning God created the heaven and the earth. . . . And God said, Let there be light. Genesis 1:3.

39. 'I am all that has been, and is, and shall be . . .' after Plutarch (on Isis and Osiris). Inscription on Isis temple at Sais, Egypt.

40. In March and April 1908 Rudolf Steiner gave lectures in Lund, Malmö, Stockholm, Uppsala, Kristiania (Oslo), Gothenburg and Copenhagen.

41. The Codex Argenteus, Silver Bible, was the Gothic bishop Wulfila's (Ulfila's) translation of the Bible into Gothic, made in the fourth century AD. It was written in gold and silver ink on vellum stained a royal purple. Only parts of the manuscript still exist. They were found at the Benedictine abbey of Werden on the Ruhr [river in Germany] in the sixteenth century, taken to Prague and then to Sweden, from there taken to the Netherlands, where they were bound in silver (hence the name). Today in the library at Uppsala University.

42. Public lecture given in Stockholm on 1 April 1908. (No notes or script available.)

43. 'On Good Friday (1857, in the place of rest [Asyl] by the green hill, small cottage in the grounds of the Wesendonck Villa in Zurich) I woke to bright sunshine, birds singing, and was at last able to sit on the merlon and enjoy the much longed for silence, so full of promise. Full of this I suddenly realized that it was Good Friday and remembered how significant this warning had been for me once before in Wolfram's *Parsifal*.' (Richard Wagner, *My Life*, II).

44. Completed in the summer of 1882.

45. *Signs and Symbols of the Christmas Festival*, lecture given on 17 December 1906.

46. 1) 'The World Ash Yggdrasil', *Golden Blade* 1957, 2) 'Myths and Symbols' typescripts Z329, 256 and 306, Rudolf Steiner House Library, London.

47. Mainly Democritus and Epicurus. See Rudolf Steiner's *The Riddles of Philosophy*.

48. Hermann Ebbinghaus (1850–1909), *Outline of Psychology* (Leipzig 1908). The passage in question is in the chapter on interaction and parallelism. There Ebbinghaus contradicted the view that the brain was an instrument of the soul, and—referring to the principle of conservation of energy and the experiments done by Rubner and Atwater—decided on psycho-physical parallelism.

49. Matthew 28:5, 6 and others.

50. Concerning the contrast between and the coming together of the Christmas and Easter thought, see among others the lecture given on 27 March 1921, *Thoughts on Easter / Easter / The Festivals and their Meaning*.

51. See lecture given in Leipzig on 1 July 1906. Typescript NSL 336–345 (Popular Occultism), Rudolf Steiner House Library, London.

52. The archangels are listed in the 20th chapter of the Book of Enoch: Uriel, Raphael, Raguel, Michael, Sariel, Gabriel, Remiel; four archangels are given in chapter 40: Michael, Raphael, Gabriel and Phanuel.

53. In the Book of Enoch it is said of Phanuel that he is set over the repentance unto hope of those who inherit eternal life (1 Enoch 40:9).

54. Sariel (Saraqael) said to be set over the spirits that sin in the spirit.

55. Giordano Bruno (1548–1600), Italian philosopher. His theories of the infinite nature of the universe and the multiplicity of worlds brought him in conflict with Church dogma. He was condemned by the Inquisition and burned at the stake. His principal work was *De l'infinto universo*.

56. See above all Rudolf Steiner's *Occult Science*, chapter 13, 'World Evolution and the Human Being'.
57. Matthew 3, Mark 4, Luke 1.
58. See lectures of 15 February and 24 March in this volume.
59. 'That which was from the beginning ... which we have seen with our eyes ... and our hands have handled ...', Epistle of John 1:1, also John 20:25–9.
60. See introductory words of lectures given on 6 January and 15 February 1908, in this volume.
61. We'd draw attention here to Paracelsus' *Liber de Nymphis, Sylphis, Pygmaeus et Salamandres*.
62. John 8:32.
63. See note 61. The term 'lemurs' for sylphs could not be substantiated. Perhaps the stenographer misheard?
64. Rudolf Steiner was probably alluding here to people like Bruno Wille (1860–1928) and his novel *Offenbarungen des Wacholderbaumes* [Revelations of the juniper tree], and to the writer Wilhelm Boelsche (1861–1939). See *Course of my Life / Story of my Life*.
65. Genesis 5.
66. John 8:58.
67. John 4:9.
68. Lecture given in Berlin on 27 November 1903. Not available in English. German collected works GA 52.
69. In the lecture given on 13 April 1908, in this volume.
70. Freiherr [baron] Heinrich von Ferstel (1828–83). Built the Votive Church in Vienna, for example.
71. Acts 2:3.
72. Arnold Boecklin (1827–1901), Swiss painter. His *Pietà* is in the Basle Art Museum.
73. Goethe, *Faust*, Part I, Prologue in Heaven, lines 243 ff.
74. Goethe, *Faust*, Part II, lines 4667–4674.
75. Quoted from Richard Wagner's *A Pilgrimage to Beethoven*, Collected works vol. 7: 'The instruments represent the rudimentary organs of Creation and Nature; what they express can never be clearly defined or put into words, for they reproduce the primitive feelings themselves, those feelings which issued from the chaos of the first Creation, when maybe there was not as yet one human being to take them up into his heart.' [Translation by William Ashton Ellis.]
76. It has not so far been possible to trace this quotation, but the thought expressed in it is fully represented in the *Beethoven* text Wagner wrote in Tribschen on the occasion of Beethoven's hundredth birthday.
77. Both statements are to be found in Wagner's collected works.
78. William Shakespeare (1564–1616). Ludwig van Beethoven (1770–1827), see *Beethoven* in Wagner's collected works.
79. See Wagner's *Beethoven*.
80. See Richard Wagner, *My Life*, 1: 'Soon I developed an inner image of a most sublime, celestial originality (of Beethoven who had just died), something

beyond all compare. This image merged with that of Shakespeare in my mind. In ecstatic dreams I met both of them, saw them, talked with them, and was in floods of tears on awakening.' Wagner was 14 years old at the time.

81. See notes 75 and 76.

RUDOLF STEINER'S COLLECTED WORKS

The German Edition of Rudolf Steiner's Collected Works (the *Gesamtausgabe* [GA] published by Rudolf Steiner Verlag, Dornach, Switzerland) presently runs to 354 titles, organized either by type of work (written or spoken), chronology, audience (public or other), or subject (education, art, etc.). For ease of comparison, the Collected Works in English [CW] follows the German organization exactly. A complete listing of the CWs follows with literal translations of the German titles. Other than in the case of the books published in his lifetime, titles were rarely given by Rudolf Steiner himself, and were often provided by the editors of the German editions. The titles in English are not necessarily the same as the German; and, indeed, over the past seventy-five years have frequently been different, with the same book sometimes appearing under different titles.

For ease of identification and to avoid confusion, we suggest that readers looking for a title should do so by CW number. Because the work of creating the Collected Works of Rudolf Steiner is an ongoing process, with new titles being published every year, we have not indicated in this listing which books are presently available. To find out what titles in the Collected Works are currently in print, please check our website at www.rudolfsteinerpress.com (or www.steinerbooks.org for US readers).

Written Work

Public Lectures

Lectures to the Members of the Anthroposophical Society

SIGNIFICANT EVENTS IN THE LIFE OF RUDOLF STEINER

1829: June 23: birth of Johann Steiner (1829–1910)—Rudolf Steiner's father—in Geras, Lower Austria.

1834: May 8: birth of Franciska Blie (1834–1918)—Rudolf Steiner's mother—in Horn, Lower Austria. 'My father and mother were both children of the glorious Lower Austrian forest district north of the Danube.'

1860: May 16: marriage of Johann Steiner and Franciska Blie.

1861: February 25: birth of *Rudolf Joseph Lorenz Steiner* in Kraljevec, Croatia, near the border with Hungary, where Johann Steiner works as a telegrapher for the South Austria Railroad. Rudolf Steiner is baptized two days later, February 27, the date usually given as his birthday.

1862: Summer: the family moves to Mödling, Lower Austria.

1863: The family moves to Pottschach, Lower Austria, near the Styrian border, where Johann Steiner becomes stationmaster. 'The view stretched to the mountains ... majestic peaks in the distance and the sweet charm of nature in the immediate surroundings.'

1864: November 15: birth of Rudolf Steiner's sister, Leopoldine (d. November 1, 1927). She will become a seamstress and live with her parents for the rest of her life.

1866: July 28: birth of Rudolf Steiner's deaf-mute brother, Gustav (d. May 1, 1941).

1867: Rudolf Steiner enters the village school. Following a disagreement between his father and the schoolmaster, whose wife falsely accused the boy of causing a commotion, Rudolf Steiner is taken out of school and taught at home.

1868: A critical experience. Unknown to the family, an aunt dies in a distant town. Sitting in the station waiting room, Rudolf Steiner sees her 'form,' which speaks to him, asking for help. 'Beginning with this experience, a new soul life began in the boy, one in which not only the outer trees and mountains spoke to him, but also the worlds that lay behind them. From this moment on, the boy began to live with the spirits of nature ...'

1869: The family moves to the peaceful, rural village of Neudörfl, near Wiener-Neustadt in present-day Austria. Rudolf Steiner attends the village school. Because of the 'unorthodoxy' of his writing and spelling, he has to do 'extra lessons.'

1870: Through a book lent to him by his tutor, he discovers geometry: 'To grasp something purely in the spirit brought me inner happiness. I know that I first learned happiness through geometry.' The same tutor allows him to draw, while other students still struggle with their reading and writing. 'An artistic element' thus enters his education.

1871: Though his parents are not religious, Rudolf Steiner becomes a 'church child,' a favourite of the priest, who was 'an exceptional character.' 'Up to the age of ten or eleven, among those I came to know, he was far and away the most significant.' Among other things, he introduces Steiner to Copernican, heliocentric cosmology. As an altar boy, Rudolf Steiner serves at Masses, funerals, and Corpus Christi processions. At year's end, after an incident in which he escapes a thrashing, his father forbids him to go to church.

1872: Rudolf Steiner transfers to grammar school in Wiener-Neustadt, a five-mile walk from home, which must be done in all weathers.

1873–75: Through his teachers and on his own, Rudolf Steiner has many wonderful experiences with science and mathematics. Outside school, he teaches himself analytic geometry, trigonometry, differential equations, and calculus.

1876: Rudolf Steiner begins tutoring other students. He learns bookbinding from his father. He also teaches himself stenography.

1877: Rudolf Steiner discovers Kant's *Critique of Pure Reason*, which he reads and rereads. He also discovers and reads von Rotteck's *World History*.

1878: He studies extensively in contemporary psychology and philosophy.

1879: Rudolf Steiner graduates from high school with honours. His father is transferred to Inzersdorf, near Vienna. He uses his first visit to Vienna 'to purchase a great number of philosophy books'—Kant, Fichte, Schelling, and Hegel, as well as numerous histories of philosophy. His aim: to find a path from the 'I' to nature.

October 1879–1883: Rudolf Steiner attends the Technical College in Vienna—to study mathematics, chemistry, physics, mineralogy, botany, zoology, biology, geology, and mechanics—with a scholarship. He also attends lectures in history and literature, while avidly reading philosophy on his own. His two favourite professors are Karl Julius Schröer (German language and literature) and Edmund Reitlinger (physics). He also audits lectures by Robert Zimmerman on aesthetics and Franz Brentano on philosophy. During this year he begins his friendship with Moritz Zitter (1861–1921), who will help support him financially when he is in Berlin.

1880: Rudolf Steiner attends lectures on Schiller and Goethe by Karl Julius Schröer, who becomes his mentor. Also 'through a remarkable combination of circumstances,' he meets Felix Koguzki, a 'herb gatherer' and healer, who could 'see deeply into the secrets of nature.' Rudolf Steiner will meet and study with this 'emissary of the Master' throughout his time in Vienna.

1881: January: '... I didn't sleep a wink. I was busy with philosophical problems until about 12:30 a.m. Then, finally, I threw myself down on my couch. All my striving during the previous year had been to research whether the following statement by Schelling was true or not: *Within everyone dwells a secret, marvelous capacity to draw back from the stream of time—out of the self clothed in all that comes to us from outside—into our innermost being and there, in the immutable form of the Eternal, to look into ourselves.* I believe, and I am still quite certain of it, that I discovered this capacity in myself; I had long had an inkling of it. Now the whole of idealist philosophy stood before me in modified form. What's a sleepless night compared to that!'

Rudolf Steiner begins communicating with leading thinkers of the day, who send him books in return, which he reads eagerly.

July: 'I am not one of those who dives into the day like an animal in human form. I pursue a quite specific goal, an idealistic aim—knowledge of the truth! This cannot be done offhandedly. It requires the greatest striving in the world, free of all egotism, and equally of all resignation.'

August: Steiner puts down on paper for the first time thoughts for a 'Philosophy of Freedom.' 'The striving for the absolute: this human yearning is freedom.' He also seeks to outline a 'peasant philosophy,' describing what the worldview of a 'peasant'—one who lives close to the earth and the old ways—really is.

1881–1882: Felix Koguzki, the herb gatherer, reveals himself to be the envoy of another, higher initiatory personality, who instructs Rudolf Steiner to penetrate Fichte's philosophy and to master modern scientific thinking as a preparation for right entry into the spirit. This 'Master' also teaches him the double (evolutionary and involutionary) nature of time.

1882: Through the offices of Karl Julius Schröer, Rudolf Steiner is asked by Joseph Kurschner to edit Goethe's scientific works for the *Deutschen National-Literatur* edition. He writes 'A Possible Critique of Atomistic Concepts' and sends it to Friedrich Theodore Vischer.

1883: Rudolf Steiner completes his college studies and begins work on the Goethe project.

1884: First volume of Goethe's *Scientific Writings* (CW 1) appears (March). He lectures on Goethe and Lessing, and Goethe's approach to science. In July, he enters the household of Ladislaus and Pauline Specht as tutor to the four Specht boys. He will live there until 1890. At this time, he meets Josef Breuer (1842–1925), the co-author with Sigmund Freud of *Studies in Hysteria*, who is the Specht family doctor.

1885: While continuing to edit Goethe's writings, Rudolf Steiner reads deeply in contemporary philosophy (Edouard von Hartmann, Johannes Volkelt, and Richard Wahle, among others).

1886: May: Rudolf Steiner sends Kurschner the manuscript of *Outlines of Goethe's Theory of Knowledge* (CW 2), which appears in October, and which he sends out widely. He also meets the poet Marie Eugenie Delle Grazie and writes 'Nature and Our Ideals' for her. He attends her salon, where he meets many priests, theologians, and philosophers, who will become his friends. Meanwhile, the director of the Goethe Archive in Weimar requests his collaboration with the *Sophien* edition of Goethe's works, particularly the writings on colour.

1887: At the beginning of the year, Rudolf Steiner is very sick. As the year progresses and his health improves, he becomes increasingly 'a man of letters,' lecturing, writing essays, and taking part in Austrian cultural life. In August–September, the second volume of Goethe's *Scientific Writings* appears.

1888: January–July: Rudolf Steiner assumes editorship of the 'German Weekly' (*Deutsche Wochenschrift*). He begins lecturing more intensively, giving, for example, a lecture titled 'Goethe as Father of a New Aesthetics.' He meets and becomes soul friends with Friedrich Eckstein (1861–1939), a vegetarian, philosopher of symbolism, alchemist, and musician, who will introduce him to various spiritual currents (including Theosophy) and with whom he will meditate and interpret esoteric and alchemical texts.

1889: Rudolf Steiner first reads Nietzsche (*Beyond Good and Evil*). He encounters Theosophy again and learns of Madame Blavatsky in the Theosophical circle around Marie Lang (1858–1934). Here he also meets well-known figures of Austrian life, as well as esoteric figures like the occultist Franz Hartmann and Karl Leinigen-Billigen (translator of C.G. Harrison's *The Transcendental Universe*). During this period, Steiner first reads A.P. Sinnett's *Esoteric Buddhism* and Mabel Collins's *Light on the Path*. He also begins travelling, visiting Budapest, Weimar, and Berlin (where he meets philosopher Edouard von Hartmann).

1890: Rudolf Steiner finishes volume 3 of Goethe's scientific writings. He begins his doctoral dissertation, which will become *Truth and Science* (CW 3). He also meets the poet and feminist Rosa Mayreder (1858–1938), with whom he can exchange his most intimate thoughts. In September, Rudolf Steiner moves to Weimar to work in the Goethe-Schiller Archive.

1891: Volume 3 of the Kurschner edition of Goethe appears. Meanwhile, Rudolf Steiner edits Goethe's studies in mineralogy and scientific writings for the *Sophien* edition. He meets Ludwig Laistner of the Cotta Publishing Company, who asks for a book on the basic question of metaphysics. From this will result, ultimately, *The Philosophy of Freedom* (CW 4), which will be published not by Cotta but by Emil Felber. In October, Rudolf Steiner takes the oral exam for a doctorate in philosophy, mathematics, and mechanics at Rostock University, receiving his doctorate on the twenty-sixth. In November, he gives his first lecture on Goethe's 'Fairy Tale' in Vienna.

1892: Rudolf Steiner continues work at the Goethe-Schiller Archive and on his *Philosophy of Freedom*. *Truth and Science*, his doctoral dissertation, is published. Steiner undertakes to write introductions to books on Schopenhauer and Jean Paul for Cotta. At year's end, he finds lodging with Anna Eunike, née Schulz (1853–1911), a widow with four daughters and a son. He also develops a friendship with Otto Erich Hartleben (1864–1905) with whom he shares literary interests.

1893: Rudolf Steiner begins his habit of producing many reviews and articles. In March, he gives a lecture titled 'Hypnotism, with Reference to Spiritism.' In September, volume 4 of the Kurschner edition is completed. In November, *The Philosophy of Freedom* appears. This year, too, he meets John Henry Mackay (1864–1933), the anarchist, and Max Stirner, a scholar and biographer.

1894: Rudolf Steiner meets Elisabeth Förster Nietzsche, the philosopher's sister, and begins to read Nietzsche in earnest, beginning with the as yet unpublished *Antichrist*. He also meets Ernst Haeckel (1834–1919). In the fall, he begins to write *Nietzsche, A Fighter against His Time* (CW 5).

1895: May, *Nietzsche, A Fighter against His Time* appears.

1896: January 22: Rudolf Steiner sees Friedrich Nietzsche for the first and only time. Moves between the Nietzsche and the Goethe-Schiller Archives, where he completes his work before year's end. He falls out with Elisabeth Förster Nietzsche, thus ending his association with the Nietzsche Archive.

1897: Rudolf Steiner finishes the manuscript of *Goethe's Worldview* (CW 6). He moves to Berlin with Anna Eunike and begins editorship of the *Magazin fur Literatur*. From now on, Steiner will write countless reviews, literary and philosophical articles, and so on. He begins lecturing at the 'Free Literary Society.' In September, he attends the Zionist Congress in Basel. He sides with Dreyfus in the Dreyfus affair.

1898: Rudolf Steiner is very active as an editor in the political, artistic, and theatrical life of Berlin. He becomes friendly with John Henry Mackay and poet Ludwig Jacobowski (1868–1900). He joins Jacobowski's circle of writers, artists, and scientists—'The Coming Ones' (*Die Kommenden*)— and contributes lectures to the group until 1903. He also lectures at the 'League for College Pedagogy.' He writes an article for Goethe's sesquicentennial, 'Goethe's Secret Revelation,' on the 'Fairy Tale of the Green Snake and the Beautiful Lily.'

1898–99: 'This was a trying time for my soul as I looked at Christianity. . . . I was able to progress only by contemplating, by means of spiritual perception, the evolution of Christianity. . . . Conscious knowledge of real Christianity began to dawn in me around the turn of the century. This seed continued to develop. My soul trial occurred shortly before the beginning of the twentieth century. It was decisive for my soul's development that I stood spiritually before the Mystery of Golgotha in a deep and solemn celebration of knowledge.'

1899: Rudolf Steiner begins teaching and giving lectures and lecture cycles at the Workers' College, founded by Wilhelm Liebknecht (1826–1900). He will continue to do so until 1904. Writes: *Literature and Spiritual Life in the Nineteenth Century; Individualism in Philosophy; Haeckel and His Opponents; Poetry in the Present;* and begins what will become (fifteen years later) *The Riddles of Philosophy* (CW 18). He also meets many artists and writers, including Käthe Kollwitz, Stefan Zweig, and Rainer Maria Rilke. On October 31, he marries Anna Eunike.

1900: 'I thought that the turn of the century must bring humanity a new light. It seemed to me that the separation of human thinking and willing from the spirit had peaked. A turn or reversal of direction in human evolution seemed to me a necessity.' Rudolf Steiner finishes *World and Life Views in the Nineteenth Century* (the second part of what will become *The Riddles of Philosophy*) and dedicates it to Ernst Haeckel. It is published in March. He continues lecturing at *Die Kommenden*, whose leadership he assumes after the death of Jacobowski. Also, he gives the Gutenberg Jubilee lecture before 7,000 typesetters and printers. In September, Rudolf Steiner is invited by Count and Countess Brockdorff to lecture in the Theosophical Library. His first lecture is on Nietzsche. His second lecture is titled 'Goethe's Secret Revelation.' October 6, he begins a lecture cycle on the mystics that will become *Mystics after Modernism* (CW 7). November–December: 'Marie von Sivers appears in the audience....' Also in November, Steiner gives his first lecture at the Giordano Bruno Bund (where he will continue to lecture until May, 1905). He speaks on Bruno and modern Rome, focusing on the importance of the philosophy of Thomas Aquinas as monism.

1901:   In continual financial straits, Rudolf Steiner's early friends Moritz Zitter and Rosa Mayreder help support him. In October, he begins the lecture cycle *Christianity as Mystical Fact* (CW 8) at the Theosophical Library. In November, he gives his first 'Theosophical lecture' on Goethe's 'Fairy Tale' in Hamburg at the invitation of Wilhelm Hubbe-Schleiden. He also attends a gathering to celebrate the founding of the Theosophical Society at Count and Countess Brockdorff's. He gives a lecture cycle, 'From Buddha to Christ,' for the circle of the *Kommenden*. November 17, Marie von Sivers asks Rudolf Steiner if Theosophy needs a Western-Christian spiritual movement (to complement Theosophy's Eastern emphasis). 'The question was posed. Now, following spiritual laws, I could begin to give an answer....' In December, Rudolf Steiner writes his first article for a Theosophical publication. At year's end, the Brockdorffs and possibly Wilhelm Hubbe-Schleiden ask Rudolf Steiner to join the Theosophical Society and undertake the leadership of the German section. Rudolf Steiner agrees, on the condition that Marie von Sivers (then in Italy) work with him.

1902:   Beginning in January, Rudolf Steiner attends the opening of the Workers' School in Spandau with Rosa Luxemburg (1870–1919). January 17, Rudolf Steiner joins the Theosophical Society. In April, he is asked to become general secretary of the German Section of the Theosophical Society, and works on preparations for its founding. In July, he visits London for a Theosophical congress. He meets Bertram Keightly, G.R.S. Mead, A.P. Sinnett, and Annie Besant, among others. In September, *Christianity as Mystical Fact* appears. In October, Rudolf Steiner gives his first public lecture on Theosophy ('Monism and Theosophy') to about three hundred people at the Giordano Bruno Bund. On October 19–21, the German Section of the Theosophical Society has its first meeting; Rudolf Steiner is the general secretary, and Annie Besant attends. Steiner lectures on practical karma studies. On October 23, Annie Besant inducts Rudolf Steiner into the Esoteric School of the Theosophical Society. On October 25, Steiner begins a weekly series of lectures: 'The Field of Theosophy.' During this year, Rudolf Steiner also first meets Ita Wegman (1876–1943), who will become his close collaborator in his final years.

1903:   Rudolf Steiner holds about 300 lectures and seminars. In May, the first issue of the periodical *Luzifer* appears. In June, Rudolf Steiner visits

London for the first meeting of the Federation of the European Sections of the Theosophical Society, where he meets Colonel Olcott. He begins to write *Theosophy* (CW 9).

1904: Rudolf Steiner continues lecturing at the Workers' College and elsewhere (about 90 lectures), while lecturing intensively all over Germany among Theosophists (about 140 lectures). In February, he meets Carl Unger (1878–1929), who will become a member of the board of the Anthroposophical Society (1913). In March, he meets Michael Bauer (1871–1929), a Christian mystic, who will also be on the board. In May, *Theosophy* appears, with the dedication: 'To the spirit of Giordano Bruno.' Rudolf Steiner and Marie von Sivers visit London for meetings with Annie Besant. June: Rudolf Steiner and Marie von Sivers attend the meeting of the Federation of European Sections of the Theosophical Society in Amsterdam. In July, Steiner begins the articles in *Luzifer-Gnosis* that will become *How to Know Higher Worlds* (CW 10) and *Cosmic Memory* (CW 11). In September, Annie Besant visits Germany. In December, Steiner lectures on Freemasonry. He mentions the High Grade Masonry derived from John Yarker and represented by Theodore Reuss and Karl Kellner as a blank slate 'into which a good image could be placed.'

1905: This year, Steiner ends his non-Theosophical lecturing activity. Supported by Marie von Sivers, his Theosophical lecturing—both in public and in the Theosophical Society—increases significantly: 'The German Theosophical Movement is of exceptional importance.' Steiner recommends reading, among others, Fichte, Jacob Boehme, and Angelus Silesius. He begins to introduce Christian themes into Theosophy. He also begins to work with doctors (Felix Peipers and Ludwig Noll). In July, he is in London for the Federation of European Sections, where he attends a lecture by Annie Besant: 'I have seldom seen Mrs. Besant speak in so inward and heartfelt a manner. . . .' 'Through Mrs. Besant I have found the way to H.P. Blavatsky.' September to October, he gives a course of thirty-one lectures for a small group of esoteric students. In October, the annual meeting of the German Section of the Theosophical Society, which still remains very small, takes place. Rudolf Steiner reports membership has risen from 121 to 377 members. In November, seeking to establish esoteric 'continuity,' Rudolf Steiner and Marie von Sivers participate in a 'Memphis-Misraim' Masonic ceremony. They pay forty-five marks for membership. 'Yesterday, you saw how little remains of former esoteric institutions.' 'We are dealing only with a "framework". . . for the present, nothing lies behind it. The occult powers have completely withdrawn.'

1906: Expansion of Theosophical work. Rudolf Steiner gives about 245 lectures, only 44 of which take place in Berlin. Cycles are given in Paris, Leipzig, Stuttgart, and Munich. Esoteric work also intensifies. Rudolf Steiner begins writing *An Outline of Esoteric Science* (CW 13). In January, Rudolf Steiner receives permission (a patent) from the Great Orient of the Scottish A & A Thirty-Three Degree Rite of the Order of the Ancient

Freemasons of the Memphis-Misraim Rite to direct a chapter under the name 'Mystica Aeterna.' This will become the 'Cognitive-Ritual Section' (also called 'Misraim Service') of the Esoteric School. (See: *Freemasonry and Ritual Work: The Misraim Service*, CW 265). During this time, Steiner also meets Albert Schweitzer. In May, he is in Paris, where he visits Edouard Schuré. Many Russians attend his lectures (including Konstantin Balmont, Dimitri Mereszkovski, Zinaida Hippius, and Maximilian Woloshin). He attends the General Meeting of the European Federation of the Theosophical Society, at which Col. Olcott is present for the last time. He spends the year's end in Venice and Rome, where he writes and works on his translation of H.P. Blavatsky's *Key to Theosophy*.

1907: Further expansion of the German Theosophical Movement according to the Rosicrucian directive to 'introduce spirit into the world'—in education, in social questions, in art, and in science. In February, Col. Olcott dies in Adyar. Before he dies, Olcott indicates that 'the Masters' wish Annie Besant to succeed him: much politicking ensues. Rudolf Steiner supports Besant's candidacy. April-May: preparations for the Congress of the Federation of European Sections of the Theosophical Society—the great, watershed Whitsun 'Munich Congress,' attended by Annie Besant and others. Steiner decides to separate Eastern and Western (Christian-Rosicrucian) esoteric schools. He takes his esoteric school out of the Theosophical Society (Besant and Rudolf Steiner are 'in harmony' on this). Steiner makes his first lecture tours to Austria and Hungary. That summer, he is in Italy. In September, he visits Edouard Schuré, who will write the introduction to the French edition of *Christianity as Mystical Fact* in Barr, Alsace. Rudolf Steiner writes the autobiographical statement known as the 'Barr Document.' In *Luzifer-Gnosis*, 'The Education of the Child' appears.

1908: The movement grows (membership: 1,150). Lecturing expands. Steiner makes his first extended lecture tour to Holland and Scandinavia, as well as visits to Naples and Sicily. Themes: St. John's Gospel, the Apocalypse, Egypt, science, philosophy, and logic. *Luzifer-Gnosis* ceases publication. In Berlin, Marie von Sivers (with Johanna Mücke (1864–1949) forms the *Philosophisch-Theosophisch* (after 1915 *Philosophisch-Anthroposophisch*) *Verlag* to publish Steiner's work. Steiner gives lecture cycles titled *The Gospel of St. John* (CW 103) and *The Apocalypse* (104).

1909: *An Outline of Esoteric Science* appears. Lecturing and travel continues. Rudolf Steiner's spiritual research expands to include the polarity of Lucifer and Ahriman; the work of great individualities in history; the Maitreya Buddha and the Bodhisattvas; spiritual economy (CW 109); the work of the spiritual hierarchies in heaven and on earth (CW 110). He also deepens and intensifies his research into the Gospels, giving lectures on the Gospel of St. Luke (CW 114) with the first mention of two Jesus children. Meets and becomes friends with Christian Morgenstern (1871–1914). In April, he lays the foundation stone for the Malsch model—the building that will lead to the first Goetheanum. In May, the International Congress of the Federation of European Sections of the

Theosophical Society takes place in Budapest. Rudolf Steiner receives the Subba Row medal for *How to Know Higher Worlds*. During this time, Charles W. Leadbeater discovers Jiddu Krishnamurti (1895–1986) and proclaims him the future 'world teacher,' the bearer of the Maitreya Buddha and the 'reappearing Christ.' In October, Steiner delivers seminal lectures on 'anthroposophy,' which he will try, unsuccessfully, to rework over the next years into the unfinished work, *Anthroposophy (A Fragment)* (CW 45).

1910:   New themes: *The Reappearance of Christ in the Etheric* (CW 118); *The Fifth Gospel; The Mission of Folk Souls* (CW 121); *Occult History* (CW 126); the evolving development of etheric cognitive capacities. Rudolf Steiner continues his Gospel research with *The Gospel of St. Matthew* (CW 123). In January, his father dies. In April, he takes a month-long trip to Italy, including Rome, Monte Cassino, and Sicily. He also visits Scandinavia again. July–August, he writes the first mystery drama, *The Portal of Initiation* (CW 14). In November, he gives 'psychosophy' lectures. In December, he submits 'On the Psychological Foundations and Epistemological Framework of Theosophy' to the International Philosophical Congress in Bologna.

1911:   The crisis in the Theosophical Society deepens. In January, 'The Order of the Rising Sun,' which will soon become 'The Order of the Star in the East,' is founded for the coming world teacher, Krishnamurti. At the same time, Marie von Sivers, Rudolf Steiner's co-worker, falls ill. Fewer lectures are given, but important new ground is broken. In Prague, in March, Steiner meets Franz Kafka (1883–1924) and Hugo Bergmann (1883-1975). In April, he delivers his paper to the Philosophical Congress. He writes the second mystery drama, *The Soul's Probation* (CW 14). Also, while Marie von Sivers is convalescing, Rudolf Steiner begins work on *Calendar 1912/1913*, which will contain the 'Calendar of the Soul' meditations. On March 19, Anna (Eunike) Steiner dies. In September, Rudolf Steiner visits Einsiedeln, birthplace of Paracelsus. In December, Friedrich Rittelmeyer, future founder of the Christian Community, meets Rudolf Steiner. The *Johannes-Bauverein*, the 'building committee,' which would lead to the first Goetheanum (first planned for Munich), is also founded, and a preliminary committee for the founding of an independent association is created that, in the following year, will become the Anthroposophical Society. Important lecture cycles include *Occult Physiology* (CW 128); *Wonders of the World* (CW 129); *From Jesus to Christ* (CW 131). Other themes: esoteric Christianity; Christian Rosenkreutz; the spiritual guidance of humanity; the sense world and the world of the spirit.

1912:   Despite the ongoing, now increasing crisis in the Theosophical Society, much is accomplished: *Calendar 1912/1913* is published; eurythmy is created; both the third mystery drama, *The Guardian of the Threshold* (CW 14) and *A Way of Self-Knowledge* (CW 16) are written. New (or renewed) themes included life between death and rebirth and karma and reincarnation. Other lecture cycles: *Spiritual Beings in the Heavenly Bodies and in the Kingdoms of Nature* (CW 136); *The Human Being in the Light of Occultism, Theosophy, and Philosophy* (CW 137); *The Gospel of St. Mark* (CW 139); and *The Bhagavad Gita and the Epistles of Paul* (CW 142). On May 8, Rudolf Steiner celebrates White Lotus Day, H.P. Blavatsky's death day, which he had faithfully observed for the past decade, for the last time. In August, Rudolf Steiner suggests the 'independent association' be called the 'Anthroposophical Society.' In September, the first eurythmy course takes place. In October, Rudolf Steiner declines recognition of a Theosophical Society lodge dedicated to the Star of the East and decides to expel all Theosophical Society members belonging to the order. Also, with Marie von Sivers, he first visits Dornach, near Basel, Switzerland, and they stand on the hill where the Goetheanum will be built. In November, a Theosophical Society lodge is opened by direct mandate from Adyar (Annie Besant). In December, a meeting of the German section occurs at which it is decided that belonging to the Order of the Star of the East is incompatible with membership in the Theosophical Society. December 28: informal founding of the Anthroposophical Society in Berlin.

1913: Expulsion of the German section from the Theosophical Society. February 2–3: Foundation meeting of the Anthroposophical Society. Board members include: Marie von Sivers, Michael Bauer, and Carl Unger. September 20: Laying of the foundation stone for the *Johannes Bau* (Goetheanum) in Dornach. Building begins immediately. The third mystery drama, *The Soul's Awakening* (CW 14), is completed. Also: *The Threshold of the Spiritual World* (CW 147). Lecture cycles include: *The Bhagavad Gita and the Epistles of Paul* and *The Esoteric Meaning of the Bhagavad Gita* (CW 146), which the Russian philosopher Nikolai Berdyaev attends; *The Mysteries of the East and of Christianity* (CW 144); *The Effects of Esoteric Development* (CW 145); and *The Fifth Gospel* (CW 148). In May, Rudolf Steiner is in London and Paris, where anthroposophical work continues.

1914: Building continues on the *Johannes Bau* (Goetheanum) in Dornach, with artists and co-workers from seventeen nations. The general assembly of the Anthroposophical Society takes place. In May, Rudolf Steiner visits Paris, as well as Chartres Cathedral. June 28: assassination in Sarajevo ('Now the catastrophe has happened!'). August 1: War is declared. Rudolf Steiner returns to Germany from Dornach—he will travel back and forth. He writes the last chapter of *The Riddles of Philosophy*. Lecture cycles include: *Human and Cosmic Thought* (CW 151); *Inner Being of Humanity between Death and a New Birth* (CW 153); *Occult Reading and Occult Hearing* (CW 156). December 24: marriage of Rudolf Steiner and Marie von Sivers.

1915: Building continues. Life after death becomes a major theme, also art. Writes: *Thoughts during a Time of War* (CW 24). Lectures include: *The Secret of Death* (CW 159); *The Uniting of Humanity through the Christ Impulse* (CW 165).

1916: Rudolf Steiner begins work with Edith Maryon (1872–1924) on the sculpture 'The Representative of Humanity' ('The Group'—Christ, Lucifer, and Ahriman). He also works with the alchemist Alexander von Bernus on the quarterly *Das Reich*. He writes *The Riddle of Humanity* (CW 20). Lectures include: *Necessity and Freedom in World History and Human Action* (CW 166); *Past and Present in the Human Spirit* (CW 167); *The Karma of Vocation* (CW 172); *The Karma of Untruthfulness* (CW 173).

1917: Russian Revolution. The U.S. enters the war. Building continues. Rudolf Steiner delineates the idea of the 'threefold nature of the human being' (in a public lecture March 15) and the 'threefold nature of the social organism' (hammered out in May-June with the help of Otto von Lerchenfeld and Ludwig Polzer-Hoditz in the form of two documents titled *Memoranda*, which were distributed in high places). August–September: Rudolf Steiner writes *The Riddles of the Soul* (CW 20). Also: commentary on 'The Chymical Wedding of Christian Rosenkreutz' for Alexander Bernus (*Das Reich*). Lectures include: *The Karma of Materialism* (CW 176); *The Spiritual Background of the Outer World: The Fall of the Spirits of Darkness* (CW 177).

1918: March 18: peace treaty of Brest-Litovsk—'Now everything will truly enter chaos! What is needed is cultural renewal.' June: Rudolf Steiner visits Karlstein (Grail) Castle outside Prague. Lecture cycle: *From Symptom to Reality in Modern History* (CW 185). In mid-November, Emil Molt, of the Waldorf-Astoria Cigarette Company, has the idea of founding a school for his workers' children.

1919: Focus on the threefold social organism: tireless travel, countless lectures, meetings, and publications. At the same time, a new public stage of Anthroposophy emerges as cultural renewal begins. The coming years will see initiatives in pedagogy, medicine, pharmacology, and agriculture. January 27: threefold meeting: ' We must first of all, with the money we have, found free schools that can bring people what they need.' February: first public eurythmy performance in Zurich. Also: 'Appeal to the German People' (CW 24), circulated March 6 as a newspaper insert. In April, *Towards Social Renewal* (CW 23) appears— 'perhaps the most widely read of all books on politics appearing since the war.' Rudolf Steiner is asked to undertake the 'direction and leadership' of the school founded by the Waldorf-Astoria Company. Rudolf Steiner begins to talk about the 'renewal' of education. May 30: a building is selected and purchased for the future Waldorf School. August–September, Rudolf Steiner gives a lecture course for Waldorf teachers, *The Foundations of Human Experience (Study of Man)* (CW 293). September 7: Opening of the first Waldorf School. December (into January): first science course, the *Light Course* (CW 320).

1920: The Waldorf School flourishes. New threefold initiatives. Founding of limited companies *Der Kommende Tag* and *Futurum A.G.* to infuse spiritual values into the economic realm. Rudolf Steiner also focuses on the sciences. Lectures: *Introducing Anthroposophical Medicine* (CW 312); *The Warmth Course* (CW 321); *The Boundaries of Natural Science* (CW 322); *The Redemption of Thinking* (CW 74). February: Johannes Werner

Klein—later a co-founder of the Christian Community—asks Rudolf Steiner about the possibility of a 'religious renewal,' a 'Johannine church.' In March, Rudolf Steiner gives the first course for doctors and medical students. In April, a divinity student asks Rudolf Steiner a second time about the possibility of religious renewal. September 27–October 16: anthroposophical 'university course.' December: lectures titled *The Search for the New Isis* (CW 202).

1921:   Rudolf Steiner continues his intensive work on cultural renewal, including the uphill battle for the threefold social order. 'University' arts, scientific, theological, and medical courses include: *The Astronomy Course* (CW 323); *Observation, Mathematics, and Scientific Experiment* (CW 324); the *Second Medical Course* (CW 313); *Colour*. In June and September–October, Rudolf Steiner also gives the first two 'priests' courses' (CW 342 and 343). The 'youth movement' gains momentum. Magazines are founded: *Die Drei* (January), and—under the editorship of Albert Steffen (1884–1963)—the weekly, *Das Goetheanum* (August). In February–March, Rudolf Steiner takes his first trip outside Germany since the war (Holland). On April 7, Steiner receives a letter regarding 'religious renewal,' and May 22–23, he agrees to address the question in a practical way. In June, the Klinical-Therapeutic Institute opens in Arlesheim under the direction of Dr. Ita Wegman. In August, the Chemical-Pharmaceutical Laboratory opens in Arlesheim (Oskar Schmiedel and Ita Wegman are directors). The Clinical Therapeutic Institute is inaugurated in Stuttgart (Dr. Ludwig Noll is director); also the Research Laboratory in Dornach (Ehrenfried Pfeiffer and Gunther Wachsmuth are directors). In November–December, Rudolf Steiner visits Norway.

1922:   The first half of the year involves very active public lecturing (thousands attend); in the second half, Rudolf Steiner begins to withdraw and turn toward the Society—'The Society is asleep.' It is 'too weak' to do what is asked of it. The businesses—*Der Kommende Tag* and *Futurum A.G.*—fail. In January, with the help of an agent, Steiner undertakes a twelve-city German lecture tour, accompanied by eurythmy performances. In two weeks he speaks to more than 2,000 people. In April, he gives a 'university course' in The Hague. He also visits England. In June, he is in Vienna for the East–West Congress. In August–September, he is back in England for the Oxford Conference on Education. Returning to Dornach, he gives the lectures *Philosophy, Cosmology, and Religion* (CW 215), and gives the third priests' course (CW 344). On September 16, The Christian Community is founded. In October–November, Steiner is in Holland and England. He also speaks to the youth: *The Youth Course* (CW 217). In December, Steiner gives lectures titled *The Origins of Natural Science* (CW 326), and *Humanity and the World of Stars: The Spiritual Communion of Humanity* (CW 219). December 31: Fire at the Goetheanum, which is destroyed.

1923:   Despite the fire, Rudolf Steiner continues his work unabated. A very hard year. Internal dispersion, dissension, and apathy abound. There is conflict—between old and new visions—within the Society. A wake-up call is needed, and Rudolf Steiner responds with renewed lecturing vitality. His focus: the spiritual context of human life; initiation science; the course of the year; and community building. As a foundation for an artistic school, he creates a series of pastel sketches. Lecture cycles: *The Anthroposophical Movement; Initiation Science* (CW 227) (in England at the Penmaenmawr Summer School); *The Four Seasons and the Archangels* (CW 229); *Harmony of the Creative Word* (CW 230); *The Supersensible Human* (CW 231), given in Holland for the founding of the Dutch society. On November 10, in response to the failed Hitler-Ludendorff putsch in Munich, Steiner closes his Berlin residence and moves the *Philosophisch-Anthroposophisch Verlag* (Press) to Dornach. On December 9, Steiner begins the serialization of his *Autobiography: The Course of My Life* (CW 28) in *Das Goetheanum*. It will continue to appear weekly, without a break, until his death. Late December–early January: Rudolf Steiner re-founds the Anthroposophical Society (about 12,000 members internationally) and takes over its leadership. The new board members are: Marie Steiner, Ita Wegman, Albert Steffen, Elizabeth Vreede, and Guenther Wachsmuth. (See *The Christmas Meeting for the Founding of the General Anthroposophical Society*, CW 260). Accompanying lectures: *Mystery Knowledge and Mystery Centres* (CW 232); *World History in the Light of Anthroposophy* (CW 233). December 25: the Foundation Stone is laid (in the hearts of members) in the form of the 'Foundation Stone Meditation.'

1924:   January 1: having founded the Anthroposophical Society and taken over its leadership, Rudolf Steiner has the task of 'reforming' it. The process begins with a weekly newssheet ('What's Happening in the Anthroposophical Society') in which Rudolf Steiner's 'Letters to Members' and 'Anthroposophical Leading Thoughts' appear (CW 26). The next step is the creation of a new esoteric class, the 'first class' of the 'University of Spiritual Science' (which was to have been followed, had Rudolf Steiner lived longer, by two more advanced classes). Then comes a new language for Anthroposophy—practical, phenomenological, and direct; and Rudolf Steiner creates the model for the second Goetheanum. He begins the series of extensive 'karma' lectures (CW 235–40); and finally, responding to needs, he creates two new initiatives: biodynamic agriculture and curative education. After the middle of the year, rumours begin to circulate regarding Steiner's health. Lectures: January–February, *Anthroposophy* (CW 234); February: *Tone Eurythmy* (CW 278); June: *The Agriculture Course* (CW 327); June–July: *Speech Eurythmy* (CW 279); *Curative Education* (CW 317); August: (England, 'Second International Summer School'), *Initiation Consciousness: True and False Paths in Spiritual Investigation* (CW 243); September: *Pastoral Medicine* (CW 318). On September 26, for the first time, Rudolf Steiner cancels a lecture. On September 28, he gives his last lecture. On September 29, he withdraws to his studio in the carpenter's shop; now he is definitively ill. Cared for by Ita Wegman, he continues working, however, and writing the weekly installments of his *Autobiography* and *Letters to the Members/Leading Thoughts* (CW 26).

1925: Rudolf Steiner, while continuing to work, continues to weaken. He finishes *Extending Practical Medicine* (CW 27) with Ita Wegman. On March 30, around ten in the morning, Rudolf Steiner dies.

INDEX